£10

First edition
plw 2020
29/10

DEAR MAURICE

Frontispiece: Maurice Lindsay, after receiving his degree of D.Litt. (*honoris causa*) from the University of Glasgow in 1982.

DEAR MAURICE

*Culture and Identity
in late 20th-Century Scotland*

*A Tribute to Maurice Lindsay
on his 80th Birthday*

Edited by Lester Borley

TUCKWELL PRESS

First published in Great Britain in 1998 by
Tuckwell Press Ltd
The Mill House
Phantassie
East Linton
East Lothian EH40 3DG
Scotland

ISBN 1 86232 041 1

British Library Cataloguing-in-Publication Data
A catalogue record for this book is available
from the British Library

Typeset in Sabon by Carnegie Publishing Ltd, Lancaster
Printed and bound by Bookcraft (Bath) Ltd, Midsomer Norton, Wiltshire

Contents

Contents

PART THREE: SECURING THE HERITAGE

Foreword

An eightieth birthday is always a matter for congratulation. This book, however, is a celebration – a celebration prepared by a few of Maurice Lindsay's countless friends to mark the range and significance of his activities during the first eighty years of his life. Activities which are still being pursued with such zest as to make one hope that this birthday is but a staging post leading to more and still greater achievements in the years to come. His unique contribution to the culture of Scotland has been his active involvement in so many parts of it. He has never been diffident in voicing trenchant but well-grounded opinions about anything that comes to his notice, but he regularly produces his own work for public inspection and criticism. Music, poetry, prose, broadcasting, architecture, painting, civic design, garden history have all benefited from his incisive contributions, and the encouragement given by him to young practitioners of these arts will ensure that the hard-won lessons of his experience will survive.

It is a testimony to the admiration and affection in which he is held that so many of his distinguished friends have agreed to contribute to this appreciation – for them, to be included in this role of honour was reward enough, but they deserve the thanks of all of us for their contributions which have established the intellectual calibre of the publication. My thanks must also go to the four sponsors, the Bank of Scotland, the Barcapel Trust, the Leventis Foundation and Shell UK, whose generous undertaking to back the venture ensured that it got off the ground. They can congratulate themselves on their enterprise in fostering a work which will be a source book for future historians of post-war Scotland.

The idea for the book came from its editor, Lester Borley, who alone has persuaded the contributors to conform to his overall concept, to deliver their pieces on time and in the correct format and has tactfully persuaded them to adjust their text when necessary. The Scottish Civic Trust, of which Maurice was the founder Director, has done much of the re-typing and the publishers, John and Val Tuckwell, have been continuously helpful throughout, producing an elegant volume which has surpassed all our expectations.

This Foreword, however, would be incomplete without recording my own gratitude to Maurice and Joyce Lindsay for all the pleasure and interest which I have derived from their friendship over the last thirty years and for the unflagging support which they have given to the many ventures in which we have been jointly involved. In case he should now be thinking of taking life rather more easily, I will remind him of Queen Mary's comment on Queen Wilhelmina's abdication – 'Eighty is no age to be giving up anything'.

James Dunbar-Nasmith

Dr Maurice Lindsay CBE D.Litt TD

BORN 18 July 1918, the son of Matthew and Eileen Lindsay. Raised in the West of Scotland, he was educated at Glasgow Academy and the Scottish National Academy of Music (now the RSAMD). He met his wife Joyce Gordon during the war, and they were married in 1946; they produced one son and three daughters.

His war service was in military intelligence in London, as a Captain in the Cameronians. He was continuously active in his spare time publishing collections of his own and other Scottish poetry, and through his love and knowledge of music began to develop a flair for sound broadcasting.

In 1946 Maurice became the drama critic of the *Scottish Daily Mail*, and became music critic for the *Bulletin*, now defunct. His career continued with the BBC, especially in news presentation, and he then became the first programme controller for Border TV in 1961, going on to become its Production Controller, Features Executive and Chief Interviewer.

A switch in his career occurred in 1967 when he became the first Director of the Scottish Civic Trust. This enabled him to deploy his considerable skills as a communicator to increase public awareness of the need for conservation. He was involved in many causes and campaigns to secure the future for the architectural heritage and the social environment of Scotland. Whilst this work was all-absorbing, he also became involved in several Europe-wide conservation campaigns and was Secretary General of Europa Nostra between 1983 and 1991, at the same time being a Member of the Historic Buildings Council for Scotland and a Trustee of the National Heritage Memorial Fund.

Throughout his life he has been a poet, editor, anthologist and a prolific writer on many subjects which took his fancy, often in collaboration with his wife Joyce.

Another, and perhaps more significant, reason for my comparative literary isolation has been the fact that I have always done more than one thing. With my mother's artistic ancestry and my father's background of hard-headed business practicality, I embody a kind of personal dichotomy to satisfy which I have needed both the leisure necessary for creative effort yet also, though less urgent, from time to time the responsibilities of administration. Consequently, having been poet, music critic, radio and television news reporter, programme controller of a television station and, latterly, environmentalist, in the eyes of many I come automatically under the strong suspicion of being a jack of all trades. 'Do more than one thing tolerably well in Scotland and they hate you', I once exaggeratedly remarked to the colourful Nicholas Fairbairn, Scotland's first Solicitor General in Mrs Thatcher's government.

'My dear Maurice', he drawled, 'do *one* thing tolerably well in Scotland and they hate you!' In a country where, football apart, unassuming mediocrity is now regarded as a major social virtue, perhaps he had a point.

(*Thank You for Having Me*, page 174)

Introduction

Lester Borley

MAURICE LINDSAY is known to a greater number of people in Scotland than he will ever know himself. His mastery of the written and spoken word coupled with his energy and imagination has produced a non-stop, effervescent torrent of comment and criticism about the nation's culture and identity.

It was never the intention to produce a biography, as such, to celebrate his eightieth birthday. His own memoir, *Thank You for Having Me*, meets that need in part. The purpose, therefore, of this Festschrift was to focus on the times in which Maurice came to maturity and developed his own contribution to the life of Scotland. There are, as you might imagine, many strands to this, and my task has been to weave the individual contributions of so many friends and colleagues with appropriate knowledge of the many facets of his life and times into a fitting tribute.

The contributions have been grouped in three parts. The first deals with his early development and the period in which he tested his sense of identity as a Scot, and gradually evolved his personal style as a poet, writer and broadcaster.

The second section is concerned with the fabric of the nation's culture and identity and the many aspects of its landscape, literature, language and artistic achievement which inform and shape the attitudes and opinions of those who live in Scotland, or share its culture though scattered through many parts of the world.

The third section is concerned with that period of Maurice Lindsay's life in which he was involved closely with others in shaping and developing a public awareness of the need to conserve the rich heritage of the manmade and natural environment of Scotland, and to set this within the broader context of Scotland's place within Europe.

The collection of essays has been assembled at a significant moment in the history of Scotland, when its people have opted for Devolution. As the end of our century coincides with that of the

Millennium, it is a good time for reflection on the nature of Scotland's culture and identity.

Bill Leggat Smith has produced a vignette of Maurice as a soldier, having been a contemporary at Glasgow Academy. Whilst he had doubts about Maurice's efficiency as a soldier, he thought him much better employed in the War Office, adding 'while he might not have been greatly exercised by military matters, even I could see that he had a breadth of vision combined with an ability to concentrate'.

It was at this time that Maurice Lindsay began to be influenced by the English poets whose work he admired. As a schoolboy I myself came upon the work of the Apocalyptic poets, particularly Henry Treece, but I had thought no further about them until reading George Bruce's essay on Maurice Lindsay's poetry. I now realise why I enjoy his work. Because of a long friendship and professional association, George Bruce has been uniquely placed to observe Maurice Lindsay's development as a poet, and his essay is therefore one of the few biographical contributions which we invited.

Throughout his life, Maurice has been a poet first and whatever else second. He was much influenced by the poetry of Hugh MacDiarmid. As Paul Scott points out, Maurice himself has written that he was 'totally obsessed by a desire to return to Scotland to play some part in reshaping it along, as I thought, the brave lines of MacDiarmid's vision of independence'. His writing reflects Glasgow's 'virile bustle of change', and observes the 'sharp thrust of Glasgow's debased Scots speech, jabbing through elisions and buttressed with sexual oaths'. It was a rich vein which he would explore in the poetry which flowed from his pen. As he developed as a writer and critic, he set his face against the 'tradition of pretence' and, when he became the Music Critic of *The Bulletin*, found himself in conflict with outworn traditions and 'the complete acceptance of the third-rate', which he clearly discarded.

To augment the contributions from George Bruce and Bill Leggat Smith, other aspects of the man's character are revealed in contributions from Mary Marquis, a colleague from Border Television, and Harry Smith, his collaborator in the great success of New Lanark.

However, for the most part, the following essays are aimed more at the broad picture of a changing Scotland in the last half of the twentieth century. As well as Hugh MacDiarmid and Compton Mackenzie, other well-kent folk who walk across our pages include Tom Johnston, possibly the most far-sighted Secretary of State, Sir

Robert Matthew who returned from London to his roots in Edinburgh, Sir Robert Grieve, whose vision of a New Jerusalem may not have materialised in the way that he wished, and that subtle charmer, Jack Muirshiel, who was such an effective chairman of the Scottish Civic Trust at its inception.

There are some notable essays in this collection on the literature and language of Scotland. Paul Scott claims that 'our literature is our recorded experience, our collective memory. Without it you are a stranger in your own land'. Cairns Craig suggests that the rise of literary criticism goes hand-in-hand with the reinvention of nationalities across Europe in the aftermath of the First World War. In his view, 'the task of literary criticism is to establish a national identity through literature that would be a bulwark both to the internal threats to western societies from the alienated masses of the industrial cities, while at the same time justifying the nation's sense of its own historic significance in the increasingly competitive world of capitalism in the first half of the twentieth century'.

He stresses that 'in the world of multinational media and of multinational popular culture, Scotland's relations with England seemed, from the 1950s onwards, less and less significant in comparison with its relations with America ... An American spirit rises through the revitalisation of Glasgow to reveal an alternative relationship of language to reality, one that passes not through the Scottish dictionary or the English tradition but through the living voice of this particular place'.

In his sweeping survey of the historical background to Scottish Studies, Sandy Fenton shows how these have led us to a sense of national consciousness, clarifying social groupings and regional variations. These are echoed in John Foster's survey of the post-war movement to protect the manmade and natural landscapes of Scotland. The concept of the cultural landscape is slowly gaining acceptance among those who seek to distinguish the culture and identity of nations. It therefore seems appropriate for the essays on the creative and visual arts of Scotland to be associated with those which explore the landscape, language and social customs of the Scottish people.

Sir William Kerr Fraser, in his essay on the political context and change, poses Maurice Lindsay's own question 'What do you mean when you speak of Scotland?' The answer Maurice suggested is that Scotland is an attitude of mind. As Permanent Under Secretary at the Scottish Office, Kerr Fraser was in a unique position to observe Scotland fighting its corner in the post-war industrial decline: 'It remained the business of the Scottish Office to be Scottish and different; and as Mrs Thatcher looked around her great Departments of State, somehow the Scottish Office did not behave like 'one of us'. It was not of course consciously defiant. It was just one of those periods when, to those running the Union, Scotland was a quietly awkward squad'.

With the prospect now of a Scottish Parliament, Kenneth Roy, in his survey of journalism in the post-war period, points out that 'the opportunities for print journalism in Scotland are more alluring than at any time since the Act of Union. Whatever else the Parliament may do, it will make Edinburgh an interesting city and Scotland a nation worth reporting'.

Whilst it is perfectly proper to be Scottish and to be different, there are occasions when it is sensible to collaborate with others sharing the same ideals, such as conserving the environment. Michael Middleton, the former Director of the Civic Trust, points out: 'forty years ago the word environment was not in wide usage. Of course the same period has seen many shifts in public attitudes as old frameworks, old certainties, have been replaced by new challenges, new alignments'. The Scottish Civic Trust's response to these questions was of course instinctive but gained immeasurably from collaboration with others dealing with similar problems.

The need to create a climate of public opinion was tackled with energy. John Gerrard describes the achievements of the Scottish Civic Trust through partnerships with local authorities and amenity societies in Scotland. This is illustrated in two short case-studies by Brian Lambie about Biggar and Harry Smith on New Lanark. Maurice Lindsay was of course the indefatigable director of the Scottish Civic Trust, whose achievement was coincident with the expansion of the assistance provided by the Historic Buildings Council for Scotland, which is well covered in the contribution of David Walker to this collection of essays.

Other notable campaigns and causes have been described by Sir Alan Hume, on the remarkable collaborative exercise in the Edinburgh New Town, and by James Stevens Curl on the ambitious programme of the European Architectural Heritage Year. James Stevens Curl points out that all these successes were achieved against the backdrop of the three-day week, and the economic crisis which beset the United Kingdom halfway through the campaign.

Our survey ends with two tableaux set on a broader stage. That contributed by Brian Lang, formerly director of the National Heritage Memorial Fund, explains the significance of the national heritage in Scotland, set within the United Kingdom remit of his organisation. The fact that it had a Scottish chairman as well as a Scottish director was probably no bad thing for those of us who were engaged in trying to save the best of Scotland's cultural heritage.

The Scottish Civic Trust, together with the National Trust for Scotland and with many other Scottish members, have sustained their commitment to the cause of Europa Nostra, the pan-European federation of voluntary amenity organisations once led by Duncan Sandys. Maurice Lindsay became its Secretary General in 1983 at a time when the whole future of Europa Nostra was in very grave doubt. 'That it flourishes today is in no small measure due to his canny native perseverance and, when necessary, powerful directness of mind', as John Gerrard puts it so succinctly. The final contribution is appropriately by Dr Tim O'Driscoll of Dublin who, describing the achievements of Europa Nostra, reminds us of Scotland's historic role within Europe.

This is necessarily only a brief survey of the rich contents of this Festschrift prepared in honour of Maurice Lindsay. Mary Marquis, a fellow pioneer of Border Television, recalls that 'When he left his home on Loch Lomondside for Carlisle all those years ago, Maurice Lindsay wrote pensively that "the exuberance of youth had sunk beyond a lost horizon". Not so, even allowing for poetic licence. It was exactly that ever-youthful zest which made him such a positive force in Border's beginnings, and which certainly enriched the quality of life for the young people who worked with him. As the essayist, Walter Pater, once famously observed of art and artists, "To burn always with this hard, gem-like flame, to maintain this ecstasy, is success in life" '.

Maurice always had something perceptive or amusing to say about a good deal of the life of Scotland – and beyond. Therefore, to give a flavour of the man himself, and to sustain a running reference to him as the book unfolds, we have inserted quotations from two of his works, *Thank You for Having Me: A Personal Memoir* (1973) and *Selected Poems 1942–1972* (1983) between the contributions. We are most grateful to Mr John Hale, of Robert Hale Ltd, the publishers, for so kindly granting us permission to do so.

PART ONE:
THE FORMATIVE YEARS

An engraving by Joseph Swan, from the painting by John Fleming,
of 'Dumbarton Castle & Town'.
Reproduced by permission of the Mitchell Library, Glasgow.

One of my close colleagues at the War Office was the author James Pope-Hennessey, by then already the winner of the 1934 Hawthornden Prize with his book *London Pride*. James, an Intelligence expert, possessed a kind of Byronesque beauty. He was a sophisticated and entertaining companion on the long regular stints of duty when together we formed one of several teams that took it in turn to prepare overnight situation reports on the Far Eastern theatre of the war. Our reports had a distinguished readership, which included the King, the Chief of the Imperial General Staff, Sir Alan Brooke – always testy over hesitant morning explanations – and, the most exacting reader of them all, the Prime Minister, Winston Churchill.

Once, in a thoughtless midnight moment, I referred to the Burmese town of Myitkyina as 'a city'. Returning from breakfast I found myself summoned to the august presence to defend my choice of word. 'Are you the officer who described Myitkyina as a city?' he inquired through a cloud of cigar smoke. I confessed that I was. 'Justify yourself', he commanded.

Naturally, I was not so foolish as to appear before the most important person in Britain without having thought out some kind of riposte. I therefore proceeded to reel off an impressive list of statistics; population figures, the number of pagodas and temples the place possessed; even the name of Myitkyina's cinema. None of this frantic attempt to secure major urban status for Myitkyina was of the slightest avail. 'But has it a *cathedral*?' the famous voice thundered, characteristically emphasising the middle syllable. I admitted that it had not. 'Then in future call it a township', he pronounced, dismissing me with a wave of his cigar.

As I left the presence, General Sir Ian Jacob, then in charge of Churchill's military officers, said, 'Don't worry. He does this every day to a Junior and a Senior staff officer, just to keep them on their toes. You should hear how he treats the seniors!'

(*Thank You for Having Me*, pages 81–2)

CHAPTER ONE

Soldiering

William Leggat Smith

MAURICE and I were contemporaries at The Glasgow Academy in the years immediately before 1939 but our paths did not cross. He was a year below me in class, which in schoolboy terms is an age, but I think I was aware of this odd chap who managed to avoid the football pitches – not easily done in those days – and who was the first Academy boy in history to take Higher Music as a Leaving Certificate subject. In fact we had some things in common. Both of our fathers had been in the 1914–1918 War and as a result, although I do not think they ever met, were strong supporters of the League of Nations. That had the effect that their sons were of a pacifist persuasion and not enthusiastic members of the OTC, quite the reverse in fact. But the rise of Hitler and the German expansions of 1937 and 1938 and the failure of Britain and France to offer any resistance made it clear that war was coming.

I had gone to Oxford in 1936 and, having come down in the summer of 1939, I went along to the empty warehouse on the South side of Glasgow where a second line battalion of the Cameronians (Scottish Rifles) was forming. This was the 9th Battalion, the second line of the 7th which was a Territorial battalion with a long and honourable history.

I was welcomed and was, I must admit, slightly surprised to find Maurice already there, he having enlisted in 1938. The battalion had very few other ranks but almost a full complement of officers – a somewhat motley assortment of elderly first war veterans and young men in their early twenties who had been in the OTC sections of the Glasgow schools which had such a body. All of us were well aware of the history of 1914–18 and we did not expect that many of us would survive this war but all had felt it was our public duty to enrol and serve.

Although there were two or three other Glasgow Academicals in the mess, Maurice and I very quickly recognised a kindred spirit in the other and established a friendship which has lasted all our lives;

the sort of friendship which although we may not meet for ten years
just takes up where we left off ...

I have to say that Maurice was not a very enthusiastic infantry
soldier, but neither was I. He was conscientious and diligent and
entirely reliable but his strong sense of the ridiculous kept getting in
the way. We were part of the 15th (Scottish) Division, and for all
the years from 1939 till the end of 1942 the role of the battalion was
coastal defence and latterly a source of reinforcements for Africa and
the Far East. This could have been demoralising but Maurice found
plenty of interests to occupy his mind. Somewhere I think he says
that he started writing poetry at the end of the war, but I know that
he was active in that field certainly by 1941, for my wife and I
treasure an epithalamium which he dedicated to us on our marriage
that year. Also at that time he was beginning to write articles for
various rather specialised – and perhaps rather precious – periodicals.
On one occasion he enlisted the help of my wife and me so that he
could write a paper on Boccherini. She translated an Italian essay on
the composer, and the translation of a French one was my contribution. Maurice very honourably shared the small cheque with his
collaborators!

Meantime of course the war was going on, and he had progressed
from platoon commander to battalion Intelligence Officer, a post
which gave him plenty of time for pursuits not strictly military. One
of these was chamber music. We were stationed just south of
Newcastle-on-Tyne. Maurice had his violin with him and he con-
trived to find two gentlemen instrumentalists on a violin and a viola.
These middle-aged verging on elderly gentlemen came out to the villa
on the outskirts of South Shields, which he and I occupied. There
was no furniture except folding chairs, purloined I am pretty sure
from a nearby church, and the sky was visible through the ceiling
of the staircase. For a week or two this group met in our bedroom
and played, I think, mostly Mozart and Haydn. I was the audience
and had the duty of turning the sheet for Maurice. Since I cannot
read music and do not have much of an ear, it is remarkable that
our friendship was unimpaired. This cultural exercise came to a
sudden end when the two professionals – for that is what they turned
out to be – presented an account for their services.

Not long after this episode I left the battalion to become an
instructor in the School of Infantry and did not get back until shortly
before the Normandy landings. I was not the least sorry to find that

Maurice had been found unfit for overseas service because of a damaged arm. I am sure he would have acquitted himself admirably, but might have come to harm because he had left his steel helmet in his billet or forgotten to load his revolver. He was much better employed in the War Office and what is more, he was able, in London, to meet and make his mark with a great many of the people with whom he was to work in the remarkably full and useful life which he has made.

I do not know what Maurice thought about his time in the army – whether it was just wasted or if he used it to assemble his thoughts and ideas. I favour the latter, for in the time I spent with him, while he may not have been greatly exercised by military matters, even I could see that he had a breadth of vision combined with an ability to concentrate. These attributes, which in my experience are not often found together, are I think shown by, and are surely responsible for, the unique contribution, in so many fields, which he has made to the cultural life of Scotland and beyond.

Captain Maurice Lindsay of the Cameronians
(Scottish Rifles), which he joined as a Territorial
before the 1939–45 War.

Glasgow. A virile bustle of change, sheer with life: a fricative edge of social difference; ocean-going ships, nosed high in docks or moored to quays almost at the grey heart of the city; cranes towering like flattened questionmarks over the Clyde and the depressed streets of the thirties; horse-drawn lorries labouring up hilly West Nile Street; tramcars squealing as they took the corner of Renfield Street and Sauchiehall Street; the stale smell of booze at pub corners; the staler waste of men in dirty white cravats, hanging about the flapping doors of their empty days; the sharp thrust of Glasgow's debased Scots speech, jabbing through elisions and buttressed with sexual oaths.

(*Thank You for Having Me*, pages 15–16)

CHAPTER TWO

Scotland: Context and Change

William Kerr Fraser

I LEFT SCHOOL in 1946 and 'went up to the Yoonie' at Glasgow. Most of those beside me in the lecture rooms were men (and a few women) matured in war and dressed in blazers protected from the moths during the absence of their owners – or demob suits recently acquired from a grateful country. The food in the University refectories was at best simple and at worst inedible: gastronomically there was still a war on. We danced at the Union on Saturday nights, deciphered our lecture notes in the evenings and had our eyes on two horizons – the next exams and beyond that a job, both of them as certain as the rising of the sun.

Life was not grim, as it had been just two short years before when the Home Service brought news of conflict and the sound of death from Northern France and places much more distant – not grim but certainly earnest, a sort of bleak normality compared with the remembered excitement of air raids and news of victories won.

But in the late '40s there was a different sort of excitement in which some of us were caught up. A Labour Government committed to change was installed in Westminster and Whitehall. It wisely avoided renewing the failed promise of a land fit for heroes, but there was an almost universal conviction that things would get better. How in all conscience could it be otherwise after six years of war? In fact it could well have been otherwise, but that is another story.

Superimposed on this British excitement was another, Scottish and strongly pervasive, among the students at Gilmorehill. Rumbling away throughout the War Scottish national feeling had been fed from various sources. Tom Johnston, though not by then a nationalist, was a distinctively *Scottish* Secretary of State for Scotland. There were battle honours won by Scottish regiments with their kilts and pipes and strong local links in dfferent parts of Scotland. A third tributary was the SNP which, unlike other parties, fought by-elections (and among themselves) throughout the War – and lost, until in 1945 Dr Robert McIntyre became for a short period their first MP.

Beside the Thames the legislators were hard at work changing the industrial scenery. We were told we were the owners of the coal mines throughout Britain and of the railways as well. What was decided in London affected us all. Seen from Whitehall, the Scots were British for almost all practical purposes. But some differences were accepted. Thanks to Tom Johnston there was the North of Scotland Hydro Board; and when the rest of the electricity industry was nationalised in 1947, the new organisation was distinctively Scottish.

And of course there was the Scottish Office, settled in its new headquarters on Calton Hill. The distinctiveness of Scotland was its *raison d'être*. It had absorbed the old Boards and its Secretary of State sat at the Cabinet table. Parliament recognised the distinctiveness of Scotland by establishing new procedures. But the minutiae of Parliamentary procedures and the development of administrative structures do not set the heather – or indeed anything else – on fire. In the late 1940s that was the role of John McCormick and the Scottish Covenant which we signed in our hundreds of thousands, solemnly pledging ourselves 'in all loyalty to the Crown and within the framework of the United Kingdom, to do everything in our power to secure for Scotland a Parliament with adequate legislative authority in Scottish affairs'.

What we got was a Royal Commission and the third son of the Earl of Moray as Secretary of State. It was not this combination which doused the fire in the heather but more likely a failure of nerve, a feeling that there were more important things to engage our interests. 'The Covenant Movement', says Andrew Marr, 'carried on but had nowhere to go.'

This seems a good point to pause and ask Maurice Lindsay's question, 'What do you mean when you speak of Scotland?' The answer he suggested was that Scotland is an attitude of mind. Fuelled by grievances, real and imagined, grounded on the marshy soil of half-remembered history lessons, and fostered on the terraces of Hampden Park and Murrayfield, what do we mean when we speak of Scotland? It is an area defined on a map, a place for living for a population whose roots lie mainly within its boundaries. But it is also home to tens of thousands who are passing through or whose settling there has not erased their nostalgic links with England or Ireland or more distant lands.

I put 'British' on my visa applications but when I reach my destination and am asked to explain myself I am Scottish first and British second. I do not know whether this is properly described as patriotism or nationalism: I regard myself as a patriot but not a nationalist. I suppose this approach – 'Scottish' first and 'British' second – is a product of my attitude of mind, and I know that it is not shared by friends whose claim to Scottish roots is possibly stronger than I can make. I regard my position as in the middle: perhaps I am the sort of Scot whom Alastair Dunnett had in mind when he suggested that only the Scots are trying to make the British idea work because 'no Englishman in his right mind ever refers to Britain when the word England will do'.

There are, of course, different kinds of roots. Geography plays a part as well as genes. When Parliament was considering in the 1970s the legislation which was intended to give Scotland the sort of Parliament which the Covenant envisaged thirty years before, the Shetlanders and the Orcadians expressed a strong preference for government from Whitehall rather than from Edinburgh. So it is not just one attitude of mind but many, and this has probably never been so clearly demonstated as in the second half of the twentieth century.

The Covenant had not been the only reason for the heady political atmosphere at the beginning of 1951. It was particularly intoxicating at that time at Glasgow University where large men in soft hats, suspected (correctly) to be from the Metropolitan Police, were to be seen moving around the Students' Union hoping to confirm their justifiable suspicions about the perpetrators of the break-in at Westminster Abbey on Christmas Eve. There was some expectation that the Stone of Destiny, which had been removed that night, might appear in the St Andrew's Halls where John McCormick was installed as Rector of the University before a roused and rousing and packed audience which was goaded into ever more riotous behaviour by photographers from *Life* magazine whose presence was itself proof of an expectation that changes of great moment were imminent.

At that time Glasgow was a special case. Things looked rather different on the other side of Scotland when in the next year the doucer students of Edinburgh University elected as their Rector Sir Alexander Fleming, expatriate Scot, Nobel Laureate and world figure. It was an interesting, perhaps symbolic, contrast – McCormick, the Glasgow lawyer, failed Parliamentary candidate, powerful speaker, committed to change, seen, if at all, from furth of Scotland as parochial and insular ... and Fleming, speaking in the same distinctively Scottish tones, shy, acknowledging his Scottish roots and the value of his Scottish education but having made his career outside Scotland, playing the part of the 'lad o' pairts' to an international audience. We were proud of Fleming as a fellow Scot. He was not disturbing as McCormick sought to be disturbing in his call to action. But in the 1950s there seemed to be a diminishing number of Scots who wanted to be disturbed.

Life was improving – for most. The children of those who, in the '20s and '30s, went by rail to St Andrews or Scarborough for their honeymoons, began their married lives in bumpy planes heading for Italy or Spain. There they may have taken a dim view of the toilet facilities, but their gastronomic horizons were greatly enlarged. Partly as a result of this there was greater variety in the shops at home, rationing finally ended, and 'eating out' was no longer restricted to weddings, birthdays and funerals. Foreign travel may have made us more sophisticated – perhaps even critical about the way things were done at home – but paradoxically it made us more appreciative of coming home, home being for this purpose not so much Scotland but Britain where the people all spoke our language and drove on the left.

Those who sought to persuade the Scots that they were *as Scots* hard done by were having little success at that time. They got no help from the main political parties. It is, of course, the stock-in-trade of politicians when in opposition to seek to generate dissatisfaction with whoever is in power, and the polls in the '50s and '60s suggested that the Labour Party had considerable success in doing so. Its success, however, had nothing to do with building representative democratic machinery into the substantial degree of administrative autonomy represented by the Scottish Office. Indeed Hugh Gaitskell said that the Labour Party was against home rule for Scotland and its Scottish Conference repudiated devolution at the end of the '50s.

From time to time the issue surfaced when EIIR pillar boxes exploded or the serious press gave space to commentators on Lord Cooper's assertion that the doctrine of Parliamentary sovereignty did not apply in Scotland. Only a small minority were interested in philosophical issues like that. What made an impact on the majority was the sight of New Towns and new houses and the rising towers of the Forth Road Bridge. More of us had cars to use on the new roads which made it easier for us to see more of Scotland, where the National Trust for Scotland and other bodies and individuals were encouraging us to take a pride in our country and our heritage in an entirely non-political way. It would have been rather out of tune with the Scottish character (whatever that is) if we had all assented to Harold Macmillan's assertion that in Britain 'we had never had it so good'; but at that time the soil of Scotland was not well suited for the planting of revolution.

The developing estates of the National Trust *for Scotland* (it laid great emphasis on the last two words) and the new Highlands and Islands Development Board were representative of one kind of Scotland, but it was not the Scotland in the forefront of the minds of those who were concerned with ideas of Scottish sovereignty and what, some years later, came to be called the 'democratic deficit'. The first was the Scotland of the mountain and the flood and the clan reunions for which Americans and Canadians bought kilts and shared the uncertainty of the resident Scots about the words (and meaning) of Auld Lang Syne. It was a mixture of scenery and sentiment encouraged by visiting politicians and actresses and industrialists who came across the Border or the seas and prefaced their speeches and interviews when in Scotland with references to their crofting great-grandfathers, or more recent ancestors who had punched rivets into ships in Clyde yards. They spoke with feeling and with pride and sometimes a little condescension; and if we in the local audience sometimes found the schmalz a little hard to take, our sense of Scottishness was certainly strengthened by this evident desire to be one of us.

It was all of a piece with remembered songs and verses about bleeding with Wallace and being led by Bruce. The blood stirs (mine certainly does) at 'breathes there a man with soul so dead who never to himself has said this is my own, my native land'. It is diluted at Burns Suppers at the end of January and bubbles in August at the Edinburgh Festival which is both Scottish and international and affords an opportunity for an annual sport of complaining that the Festival is not Scottish enough. Not surprisingly, that sport engages the interest of few of those who attend the official Festival from abroad (for this purpose including England). More significantly, there is no great outburst of sympathy for it from the resident Scots who sit beside them at the Usher Hall or the Festival Theatre.

Between all these manifestations of Scottish sentiment on the one hand and political Scottishness on the other there is and was a substantial gap: certainly until 1967 political nationalism was a minority sport marked by stridency and lost deposits. But after the Hamilton by-election things were never quite the same again.

True, the SNP winner of Hamilton in 1967 was the loser of Hamilton in 1970. But since Winnie Ewing's victory the SNP has never been unrepresented in Parliament. It is a simple fact that in the year following the by-election the Leader of the Conservative Opposition promised a Scottish Assembly and the Labour Government set about the establishment of a Royal Commission on the Constitution whose lengthy deliberations were dominated by Scottish issues.

These were exercises in containment. In the event they led nowhere. If Scotland is an attitude of mind, there must somewhere be a mind. The trouble was – and is – that it never seems possible to make it up. In the 1966 General Election Labour won nearly half the votes in Scotland – a total, one might think, sufficient to provide a basis for the necessary self-assurance to enable the Party to play a dominant role in the political expression of Scottishness. But for the next thirty years its main unifying stimulus in Scotland seems to have been its attitude to the Nationalists – which varied from strong distaste to unconcealed hatred. These feelings – which were reciprocated – had to find their expression at Westminster, in the Scottish local authorities and in the Scottish press. There was no focus for it in Scotland itself, except now and again in the annual General Assemblies of the Church of Scotland.

The political map changed in 1974, a year in which there were two General Elections. In the first the SNP won seven seats: in the second this went up to eleven, with 30% of the vote. Most of the distinctively Scottish media became even more distinctively Scottish. The English watched in disbelief – if they watched at all – as devolution dominated the Parliamentary timetable for three sessions. And all for nothing, as matters turned out. Maurice Lindsay again:

> An Assembly! we shout,
> then vote the thing out
> and get back to the business of girning.

My recollection of the 1980s – looking out on Scotland, as it were, from the Scottish Office – is of polls which showed that there was a strong continuing desire for devolution but no clear idea of what that meant. The 1978 Act had been repealed (with relish, on the motion of Mr Rifkind), and anyway there was a feeling that it would not have worked. There were attempts to suggest that somehow the very small majority for the implementation of the Act would have been greater if Parliament had not imposed a minimum voting percentage. We Scots are great ones for the excuses.

A much more significant message from the polls was that devolution, whatever that meant, was well down the priority list. People felt much more strongly about education and housing and health and the rates and jobs. It was no consolation that as the unemployment rate rose, it rose more slowly than in other parts of Britain. Oil from the North Sea was a boon to the GDP and the SNP, and exciting variations on the microchip theme provided lots of new jobs in pleasant surroundings. But around the country were bleak reminders of job-creating dreams which had somehow gone sour – Invergordon, Linwood and Bathgate, for instance; and the bell was tolling for Ravenscraig and Rosyth.

Within the Scottish Office there was a sort of understanding that the word 'devolution' would not be used in our dealing with Ministers. Nevertheless it remained the business of the Scottish Office to be Scottish and different; and as Mrs Thatcher looked around her great departments of state, somehow the Scottish Office did not behave like 'one of us'. It was not, of course, consciously defiant. It was just one of those periods when, to those running the Union, Scotland was a quietly 'awkward squad'.

Scotland – context and change? How is it to be pinned down for examination when there are so many different Scotlands? It is at different times a place, a people, a chain of historical events. It is proud roots and stifling convention, according to taste. It is a nation without a nationality, a state within a state. It is a set of balances, and of these the balance between head and heart may in the end turn out to be the most important. Easy to say, of course, but not easy to distinguish whether head or heart ruled when, amid a welter of mixed motives, clear answers were given in 1997 to two questions posed by the Westminster Parliament. Those who wanted a third question – about independence – were voted down, but there is no reason to think that it will go away.

Extraordinarily widely read, the spare and wiry George Bruce preserved his wellspring of enthusiasm into his seventies, perhaps because originally he trained to become a professional footballer. From the fifties until this day, I have shown him the final draft of virtually everything I have written in verse. His detailed criticism has been of the utmost value. He had never let himself be influenced by prejudices of any kind, and although his own style differs fundamentally from my own, he has always been able to put his finger unerringly upon a weakness or a fault. Nor was he very short of praise when he felt it to be due.

(*Thank You for Having Me*, pages 92–3)

CHAPTER THREE

Man and Poet

George Bruce

HIS FIRST LOVE was music, and but for the accident of a broken wrist, the effects of which were prolonged, he might have been a violinist. By the mid-30s he had enjoyed a wide range of musical experience, but he also read poetry. Auden and MacNeice were favourite poets, and he was soon producing 'imitative verses'. Initially the voices that caught his ear were English, and these through which his poetic sensibility developed were the late, very late, romantic poets, 'the Georgian poets', and the more urbane Auden, MacNeice, Spender and C Day Lewis. He was born too late to feel the dramatic force of Eliot's *The Waste Land*, which changed the course of English poetry, nor was his ear caught by the astringent rhythms and economic language of Pound's *Mauberly*, which was important to my generation in giving temper to our verses. Pound was the first poet I discussed with Norman MacCaig and Iain Crichton Smith. Not that MacCaig found his direction in poetry readily. Like others he fell for the Apocalyptics' non-rational mode current before his clarity and wit prevailed. The sense of a debate with the self rarely, if ever, troubled Maurice – though he took a look at the Apocalyptics, but his interest in the competent, smooth flow of the non-Scottish poets of the late '30s gave him a technical basis, and allowed him to develop a style which, particularly when applied to Scottish scenes and situation, resulted in his personal voice.

Because he published much – he had four collections by the time he was 25 – many poems were flawed. He had also by 1943 published a notable anthology, the first *Poetry Scotland*. There were extra-literary reasons for his confidence – his ability to manage whatever post he held to the benefit of his aesthetic interests. Admittedly his first job in a colour printing firm, involving writing Christmas jingles, did not call for great literary skills, but it increased his recognition of the course he most wanted to pursue. Before war broke out he joined a Territorial battalion of the Cameronians, and after six months in the ranks was commissioned. During the crisis of Dunkirk

Captain Maurice Lindsay, 9th Battalion, Cameronians, posted to Essex, to resist the expected German invasion, had one main concern on his mind – 'I worried dreadfully over the possibility that my natural ineptitude in the practicalities of military business might be responsible for the death of some of those I was leading'. He need not have worried, for as the result of a further accident, also involving his wrist, he was 'medically down-graded'. Thereafter various army administrative jobs claimed him, one of which caused him to go to Perth, where he called at 27 Wilson Street, in the hope of meeting the poet William Soutar, but after more than eleven years in bed Willie was too ill to meet Maurice. Whatever his occupation his final vocation, that of poet, drew Maurice Lindsay into that activity, and activities associated with it. He was still, however, with the battalion, and I shall never forget the invitation from Captain Maurice Lindsay, written in green ink, to contribute to *Poetry Scotland* number one.

Then it was evident he knew the contemporary literary scene in Scotland, and indeed throughout the United Kingdom. Wherever Maurice went he found opportunities to practise his literary and musical interests. In Keighley in Yorkshire he played his violin; at Diss, having left the battalion to become a trainee Staff Officer, he organised a weekend Recorded Music Club, which led to his broadcasting in Forces Music Magazine, and more significantly to a friendship with Alec Robertson. As a result Maurice Lindsay made broadcasts on music and poetry – his first on Boccherini, on whom he became an authority. Then Alec Robertson invited him to prepare a programme on contemporary Scottish poetry, for which he became an ambassador in England. The circumstance of his being made at home by distinguished musicians and musicologists, and aware of contemporary English styles which suited his own verse making, might have drawn him away from the rough-edged, though virile, Scots. The opposite was the case. In his autobiography, *Thank You for Having Me*, he wrote:

'In the prevailing wartime climate of English-dominated Britishness, it irked me that much of the fine Scottish poetry produced in the twenties and thirties had attracted little attention in England; and the same was true of good new work then being written. Especially unworthy of such neglect, it seemed to me, were the breathtaking early lyrics of 'Hugh MacDiarmid' (C. M. Grieve), whose work had recently temporarily ousted that of A. E. Housman from my affections.

During one of my time-wasting training courses, I met in London the editor of the then influential magazine *Poetry London*, a lavish publication modelled on the pre-war literary periodical *Poetry Chicago*. *Poetry London*'s typography was clean and imaginative, and it had richly-coloured lithograph covers designed by some of the most highly-regarded artists of the day. It was run by a charming Sinhalese, Meary J Tambimuttu.

At our first meeting 'Tambi', as his friends called him, told me of his ambition to inspire similar publications in other countries to proclaim the 'new poetry': 'an honest poetry about anything and everything, and not afraid of emotion.' 'Why not *Poetry Scotland*', I suggested'.

So *Poetry Scotland* came into being. It was published by William MacLellan, at 240 Hope Street, Glasgow. It was mid-war, but the young poet and the young publisher were full of hope. Surprisingly the anthology included sections of poetry from Wales, England and Ireland, for which Lindsay was severely taken to task in the Introduction by Compton Mackenzie. Rightly or wrongly it indicated his wide range of knowledge of new poetry within the United Kingdom.

What mattered, however, was how conversant Lindsay was with the Scottish achievement, which involved three languages, and how responsive he was to the varied character of the achievement. This his *Editorial Letter* reveals in its opening paragraphs:

> Scotland, as seen by some literary critics, still suffers from a Burns hangover. One of the main purposes of POETRY-SCOTLAND is to show Scotland herself, and the outside world, that she can produce poetry today, which is as strong and moving as the poetry of England, Ireland, Wales or America.
>
> Poetry must take an interest in the controversial fields of religion and politics. But poetry is first and foremost a way of living; or at least an attitude to life. Therefore POETRY-SCOTLAND can have no axe to grind and no creed to further − except the creed of artistic strength for Scotland. Accordingly, the Scottish section of this collection contains poems written in English, in Gaelic, and in Lallans. Writing in Lallans, Douglas Young and Sydney Smith follow the earlier example of Hugh MacDiarmid and William Soutar. Both of them are completely conscious socially, and their writing relates to, and comments upon, the events of these unhappy times. In Gaelic, Sorley MacLean and George Hay have brought new breath to the forms and fancies of that language. Their English translations are in themselves moving. In English, there are perhaps two camps − the older poets, with Edwin Muir as their leader, and the Scottish writers of the New Apocalypse. Mr Muir is represented in this collection, and so are some of the leading Scottish Apocalyptics − sparsely, alas, because they are nearly

all in the Forces and serving overseas. And there are a few individualists, like Adam Drinan, who do not belong to any school. So, in the Scottish section of this first POETRY-SCOTLAND, most of the leading Scottish poets alive to-day are presented side by side.'

Well may Maurice Lindsay deserve the small self-congratulation he gave himself forty years after the first number of *Poetry Scotland* in 1943, in his Autobiography of 1983 where he writes:

'That issue of *Poetry Scotland* included the first publication of MacDiarmid's 'Two Memories' and 'A Glass of Pure Water', Sydney Goodsir Smith's 'Largo', George Bruce's 'Inheritance', and Edwin Muir's 'A Birthday', all poems that have since become known through inclusion in later anthologies'.

He was 25. Three years later he produced *Modern Scottish Poetry*, an *Anthology of the Scottish Renaissance, 1920–1945*, published by Faber. It occurred when what has been called 'the second wave of the Scottish Renaissance' was underway, into which Maurice plunged with the impetuosity of youth – an impetuosity which continued to manifest itself from time to time, sometimes to his disadvantage over the years, particularly in print. But there was no fluctuation in his general view as to what was good in poetry, as well might be, for the stature of the major figures in the movement, Hugh MacDiarmid, Sorley Maclean, and Edwin Muir, had been confirmed by poets and critics. Of the first edition of *Modern Scottish Poetry* Duncan Glen wrote: 'An important landmark in twentieth-century poetry'. The blurb on the second edition, published in 1966, comments on the 1943 edition:

'By selecting only the best and by bringing together the various strands in English, Scots and Gaelic which have made up the twentieth century revival of poetry in Scotland, this book not only increased the general awareness of what was happening in its field, but played no small part in encouraging the further development of the revival movement ...'

The book had the effect which its editor desired. It spread the knowledge that there existed in Scotland a corpus of confident, distinctive writing. The second edition added new names. The Gaelic contribution, still small, was strengthened by the inclusion of Derick Thomson, and with Scots given new authority by the presence of Alexander Scott, the pressure diminished to follow the leadership of MacDiarmid, in all but his example of Lallans. A diversity of character in English writing was evident in writers born in the '20s and after, such as Edwin Morgan, George Mackay Brown, Iain Crichton Smith, and Stewart Conn. It was not a case of including 'early work' by these writers, who are now centre-stage and known to all interested in the continuity of Scottish poetry. To the contrary, poems such as Edwin Morgan's *King Billy*, George Mackay Brown's *Stromness Market*, Iain Crichton Smith's *Old Woman* and Stewart Conn's *Todd*, still strike home.

By the 1950s the reach of the poetic imagination in Scotland had extended on the great originals of the Scottish literary revival. Extended, because without MacDiarmid it is doubtful if we would have the brilliant eccentricities of Sydney Goodsir Smith. It is doubtful we would have George Mackay Brown, different as is his poetry, without Edwin Muir – I refer specifically to the religious theme, for which, it must be admitted, Maurice Lindsay has no partiality.

Gaelic is quite another matter. The strength of its tradition may have saved it from the excesses of the 'Kailyard' school, though the mould of the past had to be broken as it was by Sorley Maclean, and the course of the new given a different turn by Derick Thomson and others. Iain Crichton Smith had the advantage of working in Gaelic and English. In this totality of expression some of those who found their distinctive voices without the sense of excluding English traditional modes may be considered. One thinks immediately of the forthright wit of Norman MacCaig, and there are G. S. Fraser and Maurice Lindsay himself – the former who spent almost his entire professional life in England, who became alive when he dealt with Scottish subject, and the latter, who at one stage was influenced by MacDiarmid for the worse, but whose beginning at least was given an early poise by the English writers whom he named as favourites.

Like probably the majority of young poets, Maurice Lindsay's early writings included a number of love poems, but unlike them they had merit and they got published. He shared the common experience of youth, the awakening to the wonder of loving another person. Such a condition generally leads to loose expressions of professions of adulation. No so in Lindsay's case. He is already in his early twenties working a disciplined verse to his purpose and in a mode which he has practised throughout his writing of poetry. It can accommodate intelligence and emotion. The point at which a true love poem is made, as distinct from a communication of affection between two people, has been referred to by T. S. Eliot, though in a different context, as 'depersonalisation'. It is very unexpected that this could be achieved by the youthful poet separated from his beloved. Yet this is the essential nature of the achievement of *The Sudden Picture*. There he places himself as a figure in a context. In it he is the subject and the observer of the subject. It is the time of war, 'Now all the roads of Europe lead to horror', and therefore of separation.

He recollects his girl:

> I remember you, leaning against a wind of Tay.

The natural conversational tone is caught, and continues:

> I might have told you just the usual stories.

These simple statements, which in their ordinariness bring the reader into the presence of a person, suggest both the precariousness of the individual and set a value on the individual. The young man posits the intensity of his love against the massive, impersonal tragedies of war:

> But I said nothing, for the sudden picture
> you made against a light blown from the sea
> mocked war's unnatural, accidental virtue
> and meant far more than Stalingrad to me.

'During my final months at the War Office I had fallen in love, proposed and been accepted.' Maurice Lindsay writes in his Auto-biography: 'It was therefore crucial that I should find some sort of career offering financial prospects'. There was 'the prospect of a Music Talks producer's job with the BBC in London' but 'I was totally obsessed, however, by a desire to return to Scotland and play some part in reshaping it along, as I thought, the brave lines of MacDiarmid's vision of independence'. On 3rd August 1946 Maurice Lindsay was married to Joyce Gordon in Westbourne Church, Glasgow. As a freelance dealing with the Arts he was a great success. For fourteen years he was music critic of *The Bulletin*, though broadcasting was his main source of income.

In 1949 he suggested to Andrew Stewart, then Director of the Scottish Home Service, a series of broadcasts of new poetry. The project was submitted to me, then a producer in Aberdeen. I thought the scope should be widened. So 'Scottish Life and Letters' came about, jointly edited by Maurice and myself. As indicated by the title, the scope was wide. Novelists, poets including the Irish poet James Stephens, and the Welsh poet, Dylan Thomas, composers,

Francis George Scott, Vaughan Williams, Thea Musgrave, with appropriate musical illustration, painters, Robin Philipson, Anne Redpath, Sir William MacTaggart, and more directly useful members of society, fishermen, for instance, were interviewed, and, of course, new poetry.

We held a poetry competition, in which there were over three hundred submissions, the judges being the two editors and Aidan Thompson, the Assistant Head of Scottish Programmes. Despite our different approaches to the subject, Maurice and I finished up with a leet of six poets in the same order, barring the first two, Norman MacCaig and Sydney Goodsir Smith, and this without previous consultation. Maurice explained to me he simply had 'a gut feeling'. I did not go into the matter, but considered that that feeling must be predetermined by the company one kept in one's reading. In a letter to Robert Bridges the Jesuit poet, Gerard Manley Hopkins, referred to this matter as very important in defining one's taste.

At any rate absence of good sense, it seemed to me, prolonged a literary dispute about 'Lallans', into which Maurice entered with his customary zeal. Since, in my view, it held up his progress to his central achievement in poetry, and since he published a book entirely in Lallans, with an Introduction by Hugh MacDiarmid, the matter requires some attention. *Hurlygush*, published in 1946, was dedicated 'For My Wife, and my friends, Francis George Scott, C. M. Grieve (one notes the preference for the personal name), Robert Kemp and Douglas Young'. The list reads a little like a rallying call against the enemy, who was at the time Sir James Fergusson of Kilkerran. He led the attack in *The Glasgow Herald* (of which Lindsay gives a fair account in *Thank You for Having Me*), against those who wrote 'synthetic Scots' or, as Douglas Young put it, 'plastic Scots'. The implication was that MacDiarmid and his followers wrote in a constructed language, and others in the dialect of their native place, as did Sir Alexander Gray.

How then – I put the question rhetorically – could MacDiarmid's lyrics, such as *The Watergaw, The Eemis Stane, Empty Vessel*, be so beautiful and so true if they were constructions? Of course they were not. Brought up in the Borders, Scots speakers, we wrote with a Scots idiom as our basis. In that circumstance any additional vocabulary could be absorbed into the given texture of his speech. For generations words and phrases outwith the locality of the writer's home had been accepted as required. Even Charlee Murray from

Alford, Aberdeenshire, with its markedly eccentric speech from classic Scots ('steen' for 'stane', 'beets' for 'buits'), when he required a strong line, would substitute the 'wh' sound for 'fa'. Robert Louis Stevenson, in his collection of poems in Scots, *Underwoods*, wrote: '... I wrote my Scots as well as I was able, not caring if it hailed from Lauderdale or Angus, from the Mearns or Galloway; if I had ever heard a good word, I used it without shame'.

It was noticeable, however, that those of 'the second wave' of the Literary Revival, who had a home background of Scots, wrote with a sense of security and authority the others did not possess. I think particularly of Alexander Scott from Aberdeen, and Alastair Mackie, also from Aberdeen. But there is more to poetry than the above terms of reference. While many of the short lyrics, by Sydney Goodsir Smith, published in the Saltire Society's selections of 1947, give the impression of being thought of in English, Scots words being substituted for English, the brilliance of his *Under The Eildon Tree* is indisputable. It can stand in the company of *A Drunk Man looks at the Thistle* – MacDiarmid's masterpiece according to David Daiches – and not be found wanting. In his Autobiography, Maurice Lindsay is more apologetic about *Hurlygush* than need be. He wrote:

> The fact of the matter was that with the exception of about half-a-dozen poems and a series of bairn-rhymes I wrote for my two eldest children my Scots verse was very much contrived under the stimulus of nationalism.

The absence of Scots speech in his home could not exclude its resonances, as spoken in town and country, from reaching the attentive ear of the poet, and this is nowhere more evident than in the title poem, 'Hurlygush'. It begins with the rugged robustness of:

> The hurlygush and hallyoch o the watter.

In the last verse the sensation of the power of the burn is summed up in:

> as if a volley o the soun had brocht me
> doun tae the pool whaur timeless things begin.

There is a racy vitality in this which could not be achieved in modern English, as it is in 'Whaup i the Raip'. It begins:

> There's a whaup i the raip, the fairmer cried

and well he might, for he has discovered his 'dochter ... hauf naked', her bird having left in haste. Lindsay was not to pursue the folk tradition, but in the book following *Hurlygush*, *At the Wood's Edge* (1950), he discovers a mode of Scots which allows him to paint a picture with delicacy. 'On Seeing a Picture of Johann Christian Fischer in the National Gallery, Edinburgh' begins:

> Johann Christian Fischer? Mm – the face is kindly,
> the wig weil-snod, the features firmly set,
> as leanan on a harpsichord by Kirkman
> wi quill in haun you scrieve a menuet.

The balance of Scots and English could well have been characteristic of the speech of the professional people of the period of the Enlightenment. One thinks of that urbane society, confident of itself, requiring no raw-edged protesting voice to make itself known. In this poem I could imagine there was almost a directive to Maurice. Certainly I find this element increasingly present in his poetry, finding fulfilment in charitable, warm poems about a range of people, frequently country people, the poems all in English, culminating in work published in the 1960s.

From 1950 there was such a proliferation of works through the medium of radio and, later, television, and of writings, generally associated with the arts but not always, that only a small selection can be mentioned here. Within the wide range of Maurice Lindsay's interests there were unifying factors. In the early 1950s the American-born Mrs Farquharson of Invercauld, perceiving the success of the Festival at Haddo House organised by June Gordon, the Marchioness of Aberdeen and Temair, an accomplished musician, decided that there should be an annual festival at Braemar. She approached Maurice Lindsay. The financial resources were restricted, as was the space on the stage of the former United Free Church. She was immediately captivated with the idea of doing 'something about Burns'. The outcome was a production of Burns's *The Jolly Beggars*. This 'cantata' – as Burns called it – was left by Burns, according to Maurice, in an unperformable state. He explained the position to the composer, Cedric Thorpe Davie, who set it for four voices and an instrumental quartet. The result was stunning. On 25th January 1954 Maurice Lindsay introduced the first full-scale television production from Scotland for the BBC. In 1959 for the occasion of the bicentenary of Burns's birth, *The Jolly Beggars* was part of the official programme of the Edinburgh International Festival. By 1954 he had published *Robert Burns: The Man, his Work, the Legend*. He admitted there were several inaccuracies in it, and was pleased to have the opportunity of correcting them in the second edition in 1968. Little wonder there were mistakes. In 1953 he had published *The Lowlands of Scotland*, a survey taking in topography, history and literature. The first volume dealt with Glasgow and the North, the second volume with Edinburgh and the South. In his *Thank You for Having Me*, he noted it had been in print for more than thirty years. Nor was this the end of his publishing interests.

The Exiled Heart, Poems 1941–1956, revealed the developing talent and its maturity; I wrote an Introduction, commenting on the poem on the musician Johann Christian Fischer: 'The accent ... is on firmness and discernment rather than on sentiment ...' I also drew attention, in the main section of the book, to 'the absence of the protesting voice and the presence of a reflective voice ...' This tone is caught again in a different context in *Cantata for a Summer's Day*, an early collaboration with the composer Thea Musgrave. The work was developed from an idea which I had proposed.

I had had for many years a strong affection for Alexander Hume's poem *Of the Day Estivall*, in which the poet (*c.* 1556–1609) takes the reader through a summer day, contemplating its sights and sounds. I thought that its narrative of the day's progress could be treated as a recitative, and that its phases could provide the opportunity for inserting lyrics, which I would draw from contemporary or near-contemporary poets of the late sixteenth century, but I could not find sufficient to match the requirements. It would provide, I thought, a fifteen-minute item for 'Scottish Life and Letters'. It lasted 40 minutes. I now realised one voice was required and it must be that of my co-editor, Maurice Lindsay, and in any case I would require his agreement to the idea and his proposal of a composer. He proposed Thea Musgrave. This was the first collaboration between Maurice Lindsay and Thea Musgrave. Encouraged by Robin Richardson who at this time was producing musical features for BBC television and radio, a 45-minute opera was written. *The Abbot of Drymock* did not find its way to the television screen, Robin Richardson having been replaced by a producer who showed no understanding of the opera's witty score and words. However, it got its first production at Morley College, London, with Benjamin Luxon, then relatively unknown, in the title role. On 30th March 1967, *The Decision*, by Thea Musgrave with libretto by Maurice Lindsay, was premiered by the New Opera Company in the Sadlers Wells Theatre. This was a major undertaking. It was translated into

German, but the size of the forces required was daunting and no production was undertaken there. At least it was another demonstration of the range of Maurice Lindsay's talents. And all this is done while keeping the wolf from the door.

Fate, however, stepped in when one day Maurice met the Scottish News Editor in Broadcasting House. James Kemp said to him (I quote from the Autobiography):

'Why are you too high and mighty to do news and current affairs broadcasting?'

'I'm not,' I said.

'Then why don't you?'

'Nobody's asked me.'

'I'm asking you now.'

'Good. Then I shall.'

So he engaged on ten years of news reporting, for six of which he 'put together the Scottish news bulletins on Saturdays'. He comments: 'I loved every moment of it. News is about people, and people make up life'. In the course of these activities he found time to research, put together and publish *The Burns Encyclopaedia*. He also co-edited 'Counterpoint' with me, the first arts series of programmes to be broadcast from Scotland. It was transmitted on BBC1 from December 1958. Its run was shortened after Maurice and I were rebuked by the Controller of BBC Scotland for showing a clip from *The Thirty-nine Steps*, in which Kenneth More starred. The clip contained a sexual implication, but the rebuke was beyond our comprehension. It was, after all, taken from a 'U' film. This was a factor in Maurice determining to leave the BBC. He was to become the first Programme Controller of Border Television.

From Gartocharn, near Loch Lomond, the Lindsay family moved first to Annan and then to the Cumbrian village of Heads Nook. Here, while employed by Border Television, he produced two collections of poetry, *Snow Warning* (1962) and *One Later Day* (1964). Of *Snow Warning*, Maurice Lindsay wrote in his Autobiography, 'I found my own consistent voice for the first time', the significant word being 'consistent', for he had written poetry which called for attention, though obscured by publishing what reflection might have told him was sometimes less worthy of his ability, which he admits, when he wrote, continuing the sentence, 'though not yet a cure for my bad wartime habit of publishing too much that was insufficiently revised'. There was also a tendency to be too readily dismissive of what did not immediately appeal to him, or look beyond the flaws as in the cases of MacDiarmid's very long, admittedly amorphous poems. So MacDiarmid's *In Memoriam James Joyce* was for him 'chopped-up prose'. I believe there is a great deal more to it than that.

Literary journalism demands an immediate response and so is liable to be flawed. When a history of a literature is undertaken, clearly different conditions are required, and not only for research, but for the contemplation of judgements. These should not be difficult on writers long dead, but great care is required in the consideration of contemporaries or near-contemporaries.

In 1977 Maurice Lindsay published a *History of Scottish Literature*. It is a large volume of 496 pages; it deals with the subject comprehensively. In 1975 the first number of *The Scottish Review* was published by The Scottish Civic Trust and The Saltire Society. Of its Editorial Board, of which I was a member, it would not be unfair to say that a main burden of the work fell upon Dr Lindsay. In so far as he was Director of the Civic Trust, and a fair proportion of the subject matter belonged to the area of the Trust, it was proper that its Director should have a strong say in the Magazine.

The matter is mentioned because it was hard to believe that a book of such substance as this *History* could have been written in the conditions described. Not only that, it conveys the sensation of personal interest, and reflection on all of our greater writers, especially Sir Walter Scott.

Scott he admired above all others. He wrote of him '... the creative imagination of Sir Walter Scott is still the first literary asset Scotland possesses'. He draws attention to the 'immense variety' of characters Scott created. In that variety, even in small sketches, how strong and vividly alive are the country people. Maurice Lindsay mentioned how he himself achieved a 'consistent voice for the first time in *Snow Warning* and *One Later Day*', but in those books where he deals with country people the tone is also robust, the verse more flexible than before, and the presences of men, women and beasts, physical. Take almost any six or so lines from *Kelso Horse Show* and these words apply:

> But sold or bought, the time and the place are the horses;
> the sweet smell of their sweat, the strung hay
> they munch their breath on, the patient stable darkness
> rippling their flanks, commotions the livelong day

till it breaks away from its minute by minute grazing,
from Countified calls to bawdy Irish curses.

The characters of such places are not readily likeable, and far from
the centre of modern society, which does not mean they are treated
as curiosities. In each case Maurice Lindsay is with them at their
centre, and in so doing, the reader is both inside and outside the
persons, breathing the air they breathe, as in 'Any Night in the
Village Pub,' when:

he'd shoulder the pub door open, scrape his boots
on the edge of their chatter, order his pint and chaser,
then stand, propped there, a tree propped up by its roots.

The sense of place and person is overpowering, and so the poem
ends:

... till he banged down his angry money,
and breenged back into the darkness from which he'd come,
leaving them, oddly disturbed, a whiff of carbolic and dung.

Maurice Lindsay has made poem after poem of this order, where
without comment from him we know and feel the presence of the
person, and understand. 'Farm Woman' begins:

She left the warmth of her body tucked round her man
before first light, for the byre, where mist and the moist
hot breath of the beasts half-hid the electric veins
of the milking machines ...

When he writes about children his senses seem to become as alert to
the smells and sounds, to the complete sensation of living, as the
child himself. So in 'Picking Apples:

... Through a tussle of leaves
and laughter the apples thud down; thud on the orchard grasses
in rounded, grave finality, each one after
the other dropping; the muffled sound of them dropping
like suddenly hearing the beats of one's own heart
falling away, as if shaken by some storm
as localised as this ...

The poem does not end at this evocation of a happening in time and
place:

I experience fulfilment, suddenly aware
of some ripe, wordless answer, knowing no such
answers exist; only questions, questions, the beating years,

that dropped apples ... the kind of touch and go
that poetry makes satisfaction of;
reality, with nothing more to show
than a brush of branches, time and the apples falling,
and shrill among the leaves, children impatiently calling.

This is the recognition of an environment which nature and nurture has provided, in which a person can be a person. And out of his acknowledgement of the precariousness and transience of a moment of life Maurice Lindsay has made music, not a music which is an escape from facts, but which draws on a 'reality' – the word is in inverted commas for he uses it in the poem.

At the same time as he is producing the two books he is holding down a job. More accurately he is bringing to life Border Television. The mere listing of names may indicate the range and distinction of the persons who appeared with him for 'in depth' interview. To name a few: General Sir Brian Horrocks, The Reverend Dr George McLeod, Stirling Moss, Kingsley Amis, Dame Sybil Thorndyke, Sir Bernard Fergusson, and Sir Compton Mackenzie. As Maurice put it himself: 'Poets and politicians, scientists and pop stars, painters and academics, serious policemen and petty criminals; all of them turn up in the interviewer's guest chair'. Perhaps the most surprising to turn up was Sir Hugh Carleton Greene, then Director General of the BBC.

Of course there was music and poetry. The Cumbrian poet, Norman Nicholson, was commissioned to write a verse play for Christmas, to music by Thea Musgrave. Songs by that highly individual composer from the Borders, Francis George Scott, were quite frequently broadcast. On one occasion I had the honour to introduce a selection sung by Bill McCue. Such a gale of fresh air was blowing through two studios of Border Television that it was impossible to believe that its creator would ever find it necessary to transfer his talents elsewhere. The Scottish Civic Trust was the last to receive this benefit – and so to Glasgow, and then to a house again within sight of the Clyde.

I visited all of them. After my first visit to Maurice and Joyce's present home my mind went back to the beginning of the friendship, to the first letter in green ink, and beyond this to Joyce, whom I met before I met Maurice, when she was a student. At the end of my lecture she came forward and uttered a simple phrase with such modesty and affection that I never forgot the moment of more than fifty years before. So it found its way into these lines.

The ghosts of your homes wander through
my address books. The aches of iron trams,
juddering and squealing through Hillhead,
founder on your step at Athole Gardens.
Elegant Southpark Avenue fades in a dull evening.
At Gartocharn, dogs howl, children tumble,
horses nose your doors, the loch stays
at a distance; the broad parks of Annan –
gone. I remember a red gown, a girl
in misty St Andrews, who had, she said,
'a friend called Maurice Lindsay.'
Before the unchanging features of friendship
the irritations of the silly world vanish.

As music critic of a popular daily paper, a television presenter, literary historian, journalist and conservationist, throughout my professional life I have been an unashamed populariser. There are, of course, two kinds of popularisers, and it is important to distinguish between them. There are those who think the achieving of popularity for their product more important in itself than the integrity of what they are seeking to popularise; and those who regard the work of popularisation as a matter of packaging and presentation, insisting that the qualitative standards inherent in the material must remain inviolate. It is to this latter category that I belong.

Soon after I became music critic of *The Bulletin*, I found myself in conflict with outworn traditions and the complacent acceptance of the third rate.

(*Thank You for Having Me*, pages 122–3)

CHAPTER FOUR

Journalism in Scotland

Kenneth Roy

NOT MANY PEOPLE remember *The Bulletin*. It belonged to a breed now extinct in Britain: the tabloid newspaper of decent values which you wouldn't mind showing to your maiden aunt. In 1948, the year of his thirtieth birthday, Maurice Lindsay was already well-established as its music critic.

In the Glasgow Room of the Mitchell Library, I went looking for evidence of young Lindsay's critical abilities. The first edition of the year – January 2 – had nothing with his byline, though much else of passing interest. The eleven items on the front page included a photograph of the 'new luxurious Third Class sleeper'; news of a windfall for shareholders 'in railway, canal, and inland navigation undertakings'; and a report of crowd trouble at a Ne'er Day football match.

Post-war rationing severely restricted the size of newspapers. There was no space for the acres of lifestyle junk, vacuous 'profiles', celebrity gossip and over-written features which have come to disfigure the broadsheet as well as the downmarket press in more recent years. Within eight tightly packed pages *The Bulletin* somehow had to encompass what was happening in the world at large as well as on its own doorstep. News reporting was straightforward and necessarily fairly terse. Fact and opinion were kept apart, rather than fudged as they are today.

The paper's leading article, gracefully set out over a double column amounting to about 800 words, expressed trenchant, well-argued opinions on international and domestic issues from an essentially liberal standpoint. 'The main complaint of Scots today,' reflected one of the first leaders of 1948, 'is that more and more of their affairs are controlled by people some 400 miles away in the South who know and care very little about Scotland.'

Despite the chronic shortage of space, the paper also found room for lighter material – a place-name quiz, a cartoon strip (Lavinia Derwent's Tammy Troot), erudite historical articles by J. M. Reid, and intelligent, pithy coverage of the arts and literature. Peggy Phillips contributed a regular radio review and there were overnight notices of productions in the main Glasgow theatres.

Maurice Lindsay made his first appearance of 1948 in the edition of January 5. Unlike established names like Peggy Phillips and J. M. Reid, the music critic had to be content with initials rather than a full-blown byline. On this occasion 'M.L.' found himself hemmed in by a notice of *The Dead Slow Worm* ('Not Mr Compton Mackenzie's best book'), an article headed 'Wake Up Your Liver Bile', and an agency report from Pittsburg, USA, concerning Mrs Phillis Rocca (38), who was cured of an attack of hiccoughs after six days. (By a lumbar puncture of the spinal column with a hollow needle, should the reader ever be similarly afflicted).

The heterogeneity of the page was another characteristic of papers in those days: articles and news items of many different kinds jostled for attention in the same congested space. Indeed I had to look quite hard to find M.L. in this busy department store of a newspaper – especially as some costive sub-editor had chosen to print his review in miniscule type and to append the world's dreariest headline:

WEEK-END CONCERTS

Beethoven's Seventh Symphony was the only really substantial item on the programme of the Scottish Orchestra's concert in St. Andrew's Hall, Glasgow, on Saturday night. Under Walter Susskind they gave a virile performance, marred only by some painfully pronounced horn inadequacies.

The review continued for about 200 words – not significantly less than the space given to arts notices in the incomparably bigger newspapers of today.

A few days later, M.L. was back with a review of a Milngavie Music Club recital under the heading

UNUSUAL AND SATISFYING:

The harp is, perhaps, not to be heard at its best as a solo instrument, at any rate this side of heaven; but Miss Pielou demonstrated just how much her instrument can do on its own.

His next contribution sounded a note of exasperation:

There seems to be a sorry lack of co-ordination among concert promoters in Glasgow, for last night we had the choice of three piano recitals.

At one of these recitals, the soloist had to combat 'a squeaky pedal and a small audience'.

M.L. was fortunate: unlike the pianist with the squeaky pedal he performed in distinguished company before a large audience. *The Bulletin* was a popular paper and made no bones about it: unlike its snobbish older sister, the *Glasgow Herald*, it was not much interested in business or City news. It was more pictorial in its approach, appealed strongly to women, and more than lived up to its reputation as a 'family paper'. People felt an affection towards *The Bulletin* and for a long time it was part of the fabric of West of Scotland society.

M.L. was fortunate in another sense: he happened to be young and working as a critic at a time when popular newspapers saw it as part of their function to comment on music, drama and books. There was no false division between the arts and the rest of life: a painfully inadequate horn in the St. Andrew's Hall was just as worthy of mention as Mrs Rocca's recovery from hiccoughs. A similar newspaper today would follow a very different agenda.

In our house, we didn't take *The Bulletin*. M.L.'s paper was regarded as a bit above us. We read the traditional organ of the Scottish working-class, *The Daily Record*. Does that sound terribly low? It shouldn't. Before me is a facsimile of a *Daily Record* front page from October 1946, when I was one year old and Maurice Lindsay had just been appointed music critic of *The Bulletin*.

This tabloid-sized page is full of interest. There are ten items (about the same number as carried by the more upmarket *Bulletin*) and the headlines show the remarkable range of subject matter covered by a mass-circulation daily newspaper in the immediate post-war era:

Goering Knows His Fate Today (Nuremberg trials); A-Bomb Can't Be Outlawed (speech by an 'atom expert'); Jews Save Ship From 'Frogmen' (despatch from Jerusalem); Fight Against Smoke in City Blaze (Glasgow fire); British Quit The Lebanon; Ounce of New Poison Could Kill Millions (chemical warfare experiments in the United States); Jimmy Finds His Father (local human interest story); The Sun Recorder Told Me (sketch about weather forecasting); Ellen Back (Minister of Education returns from Prague); £109 'Snatched' (robbery in Glasgow). In addition there are three small photographs on the page, as well as several discreet display advertisements and the weather forecast.

Someone of limited education who wished to keep abreast of the news for a few minutes each day – a typical *Daily Record* buyer, in other words – would have gained a reasonable knowledge of the world just from reading that front page. Its admirable balance of heavy items and light, international news and domestic, was popular journalism at its best and most responsible – highlighting important events and issues, making them accessible to ordinary people, and presenting them without spin or bias.

Contrast *The Daily Record* of October 1, 1946, with the same newspaper's front page on the day I am writing this – October 1, 1997. There are no news items on the front page. There is no text. The page is overwhelmed by the headline 'Care For Britain and It Will Care For You' alongside a near-lifesize photograph of the Prime Minister's face. The tone is shamelessly propagandist: any pretence of impartiality has been abandoned. The reader is invited to turn to pages 2 and 3 where 'Blair's vision for the 21st century' (as outlined in a speech to the Labour Party conference) will be uncritically – indeed ecstatically – received by the paper's political editor.

However, it appears that news of the selfless credo now officially in favour has yet to reach the promotions department of *The Daily Record*. The rest of the front page panders as blatantly as ever to discredited Thatcherite values with its succession of teasers for prize games and reader offers. 'Nine Free Goes on the Lotto' is today's concession to caring for Britain.

The changes in newspapers over the span of Maurice Lindsay's long career amount to nothing less than a revolution: the wrong sort of revolution. The growth of electronic media, making news so instantly available that it comes squirting into the house like an overflowing tap, has made some of the changes inevitable. Broadsheet papers concentrate less on orthodox reporting, the faithful transmission of what someone said or did, and more on background analysis and interpretation of events. The proceedings of Parliament, for example, are not reported in any depth: Lobby briefings have usurped the old-fashioned workings of the democratic process in which newspapers played a vital role. (It will be interesting to see whether the Scottish papers adopt the same policy towards coverage of the Parliament in Edinburgh.)

But the rise of television as the public's primary source of news and information cannot wholly explain the main distinguishing feature of this revolution: the relentless progress downmarket.

Newspapers have fallen to a new brutality; and it is obvious practically everywhere you look.

In the year Maurice Lindsay joined Border Television as its programme controller, I took up a somewhat lowlier job as junior reporter of *The Falkirk Mail*. Readers mercilessly ribbed the local press, dismissing it as 'the two-minute silence', and the *Mail* was no exception. Still, I felt as a boy of seventeen that I was doing something rather useful and the *Mail* was a worthwhile part of the community it served. I was proud to have become a reporter (though I hadn't the nerve to think of myself as a journalist).

The chief reporter, an admirable man called Frank Thomson (a 'kenspeckle figure', as they used to say in Scotland), generously took me under his wing. He introduced me to the courts, the Council meetings, the agricultural shows, the junior football matches, the drama festivals and, of course, to the ceaseless rounds of calls on police and fire stations. Every event in Falkirk and district remotely worth reporting we dutifully attended. The accounts of Town Council meetings were particularly thorough: there was a general view, so tacitly understood it required no discussion, that the public had a right to know what decisions were being made in its name. Frank's immaculate shorthand note flowed over the page on these important occasions.

One of the great losses to Scotland is that Council meetings are no longer reported with the same attention to detail, accuracy and fairness. We can do without Parliamentary reports in the national press, for television and radio offer an alternative. People in the cities and towns have no such alternative. Every Council meeting which goes scantily reported, or is reported melodramatically in terms of 'rows' and 'splits', or is not reported at all, represents another blow against local democracy and makes corruption and arrogance – of the sort we witnessed last year in the West of Scotland – more likely.

The vigilant role of the local press has been quite consciously abandoned by newspaper managements. Several years ago I challenged the editorial director of a large group of weekly newspapers to defend his editorial values. He did not attempt to do so: his reply was expressed purely in marketing terms. 'If you try to get people to read your paper on the traditional virtues, you won't exist for very long,' he replied. 'That is why the puzzles and the competitions and the human interest stories are coming in, rather than the more orthodox sources of community information.'

This was a disturbing insight into the new brutality and a sign that it had contaminated one of the last bastions of journalistic integrity. I cannot now pick up a local paper (except in parts of the Highlands where vulgarity, like protestantism, has never managed to penetrate) without a sense of revulsion and shame at how the honourable traditions of the weekly press have been lowered. With its emphasis on punning headlines and snappy paragraphs, its coarse tabloid habits of language and attitude, local journalism has ceased to be the fiercely independent defender of 'caring Britain' and has become a breeding ground of illiteracy and cynicism.

From *The Falkirk Mail* I went, via *The Greenock Telegraph*, to *The Glasgow Herald*. My work there attracted the attention of Maurice Lindsay at Border; I was invited to Carlisle for an interview and an audition. Overtaken by nerves, I fluffed every line. The job went to David Rose, an able reporter who is still seen most nights on ITN. Maurice made an eminently sensible choice.

I didn't mind: television would have been fun, but I was still entranced by the idea of newspapers. The printed word seemed to me to possess a dignity and permanence that transient images on a screen would never match. Besides, there was nothing to equal the heady excitement of the night's first edition rolling off the presses.

Working for the *Herald* in the late 1960s was a privilege never to be repeated: I was barely twenty years old, ill-educated, had travelled little, experienced less. Every evening around 9.30, the gentlemen journalists who supervised the newsroom left for the pub, leaving the reporters to answer the telephone, which rarely rang, and tidy up any late copy, not the most arduous task. It left an hour between the first and second editions for fierce topical debate on anything that took our fancy – politics, arts, books, religion. The atmosphere, as I know now but only dimly perceived then, was more common room than newsroom.

The building was full of giants, men and women of intellectual authority and serious literary ability: George MacDonald Fraser, the deputy editor, who left abruptly to become a full-time novelist; Christopher Small, the finest dramatic critic outside London; William Hunter, a magician of idiomatic prose; Hugh Cochrane, the spruce and sardonic (London) *Times* correspondent who rented a desk ... I could go on.

The Herald, like *The Falkirk Mail* in a purely local context, had not shaken off the belief that meetings and events were there to be covered by reporters clutching notebooks and pens, and that the telephone was a poor substitute for eye-witness journalism, however inadequate the eye, however modest the journalism. Press releases were comparatively rare; the whole PR machine was in its infancy; even cabinet ministers could be called at home without the filtering influence of advisers and spin doctors. Barely thirty years ago, newspaper journalists operated in a completely different culture.

Today's *Herald* is a larger product in every way. There are so many pages in an average edition that the available talent is spread painfully thin. The paper has more columns than ancient Rome. Features run on and on. Meaningless supplements, the profligate use of photographs and extravagant headlines, never-ending sport ... the formula is familiar. *The Herald* is no worse, in some respects a good deal better, than some. But it has not been immune from the revolution. It too has changed, and suffered in the process.

I have not discussed this question with Maurice Lindsay, but I wonder whether M.L. would give a career in newspapers a second thought were he starting out tomorrow. My suspicion is that, as an ambitious and versatile young man, he would think first and foremost of broadcasting if he thought of a media career at all.

Yet, if only we knew it, the opportunities for print journalism in Scotland are more alluring than at any time since the Act of Union. Whatever else the Parliament will do, it will make Edinburgh an interesting city and Scotland a nation worth reporting. If the Parliament succeeds, it may lead to independence. If it flops, it may still lead to independence, but it will certainly lead to a most newsworthy chaos. Oh, to be alive in Scotland at the new millennium!

But let's not get carried away. *The Scotsman* is owned by the Barclay brothers, who also control *Scotland on Sunday* and the *Edinburgh Evening News*. *The Herald* is owned by Scottish Television, which also controls the Glasgow *Evening Times*. A major shareholder in Scottish Television is the Mirror Group, which also owns *The Daily Record*. It is hard to see how these cosy, interweaving mega-monopolies will produce the vibrant, questioning Scottish press that the referendum vote has made essential.

New technology should have encouraged the start of small, independent titles, for print is cheap and accessible in a way that it wasn't even ten years ago. For some reason, this alternative press has not emerged. It is more than ever important that it should: not only to give all the M.L.s of the late 1990s a break, but to challenge the complacency of the established Scottish media. We can hope.

———————————————•—◆—•◆•———————————————

Black-and-white television could do little enough for painting, though the advent of colour television was, in due course, to spread the public enjoyment of the visual arts in much the same way as radio widened the appreciation of music in the twenties. Emilio Coia suffered no such diminution through the absence of colour when he appeared in Counterpoint to talk about the cartoonist's art. While I interviewed him he produced a cartoon [below] of me in view of the camera, a device other less skilful cartoonists were to repeat with me in later years. All of this now perhaps seems 'old hat', but in the early fifties it was being done in Scotland for the first time. We were certainly enacting Ezra Pound's injunction to 'make it new'.

(*Thank You for Having Me*, page 143)

———————————————•—◆—•◆•———————————————

with apologies!

COIA

CHAPTER FIVE

Television Broadcasting

Robert Logan

MAURICE LINDSAY started me in television virtually on the day of the first transatlantic transmission by a new form of communication: the Telstar satellite. My summer sojourn as a researcher at Border Television was more down to earth, meant to be just a stopgap between graduation and the start of a radio training course with the BBC in London; yet that random conjunction retains a greater significance than it had for me at the time, and represents a piquant anomaly in the landscape of broadcasting thirty-five years later.

Border Television had begun broadcasting to its twin audiences, English and Scottish, the previous autumn, as the masts of Independent Television, the viewers' first alternative to BBC programmes, sprang up across the country. No development since, even the seminal creations of BBC2 and Channel 4, or the seismic change represented by direct reception from a new generation of satellites, has had the impact of the arrival of commercial television. The social and economic transformations in this period of the Macmillan government, ushered in with the end of rationing and the invention of hire purchase, meant the rapid dissemination of consumer goods such as the refrigerator, the washing machine and the television set. Acutely conscious – and envious – of the American example, the public was at once fascinated and appalled by its own appetite for consumerism. The much-celebrated Gibbs SR toothpaste advertisement which in 1955 heralded the new choice of programmes began a process of beguiling J. B. Priestley's 'admass' into acceptance of its new role, and its new purchasing power. We are all consumers now, and broadcasting has become a commodity.

Luckily, as we are appreciating anew, the crucial commodity was recognised to be programmes, and the key talent programme makers. Provoked by the irruption of the commercial rival, boldly competing both for audiences and for talent, the BBC responded remarkably promptly. Its budgets had to be drastically revised to accommodate the new fees demanded by artists; the new facility with which production staff moved employment was not so easily accommodated. Local drama warlords attracted marauding bands of warrior directors with the offer of fiercely-protected creative freedom to work with the new writing names: Hopkins, Stoppard, Prior, McGrath, Waterhouse and Hall. While theatre critics were remarking on cultural phenomena labelled 'angry young men' and 'kitchen-sink drama', more than half of the viewing population was identifying with the new, recognisable voices in 'Z-Cars' and 'Coronation Street', and deliberately adjusting its domestic timetables to make a date with 'Armchair Theatre' and 'Play of the Week' (as well as with 'Panorama' and 'Grandstand').

Marooned in an industrial estate on the edge of Carlisle, the programme makers of Border Television were remote from much of this ferment, documenting for their two demanding (often conflicting) audiences the agricultural shows, fish stocks, Common Ridings, floods and mountain rescues preoccupying an area of debatable land from Berwick-on-Tweed to the Isle of Man. Maurice, who had come from the equally parochial ambience of the Scottish arm of the BBC, presided benignly on screen over the nightly magazine 'Lookaround', and offscreen fought his Programme Executive corner with the sales department and other sceptics to include programmes about Burns and the Edinburgh Festival. For much of its existence, Border has been able to boast that its local magazine vied, in the regional Top Ten most-viewed programmes, with the national soap operas and peak-time entertainments. The regional character of ITV, enshrined in the licences awarded to each area broadcaster, curbed the relentless dependency on quantifying the audience; failed to redress the imbalance between minnows and sharks in the federation, so that showbiz barons carved up the peak hours between them; was for long an inhibition on mergers and takeovers in the industry; and helped to foster the 'independent' contribution to the least worst television in the world, paradoxically a public service provided by private contractors funded from the sale of advertising time.

One key to the unexpected longevity of this arrangement has been the nature of its regulation. Legislators have been attracted to the business of broadcasting like moths to a flame, arguing that spectrum scarcity needed their arbitration while actually anxious to keep some control over what might be said. In the event, that essential distinction between legislature and executive ensured a measurable arm's length protecting the direct supervision of broadcasting for its first thirty years. Burton Paulu, quoted in the ITA's annual *ITV 1966*, concluded, 'The British, with their genius for compromise, have devised a method which enables a regulatory body to insist on high standards of programming and advertising without interfering with the freedom of expression so essential to the life of a democratic country'. That's not to deny some element of interference: Parliament debated muzzling the broadcasters during the Suez crisis, and news has never been more managed than in time of war. Nevertheless, the sanitising of Vietnam wasn't effective enough to prevent public opinion forcing the military/political complex to pull out; the deadpan delivery of Mr. Ian Macdonald didn't quell public questions at the time of the Falklands adventure; and even the sense of riding along with the smart bombs in the Gulf didn't really fool us into thinking that this was a cleaner form of warfare. I witnessed the arrival of the Special Branch at Queen Margaret Drive, determined to burrow into all our archives to find something, anything, with which to hang an awkward investigator. Politics has seen the rise of the spin doctor into a relatively public form of influence, perhaps so visible as to lose its full effect; but the most direct effect politicians have is when they're dispensing new licences to broadcast.

The creation of ITV was due as much to the government's *laissez-faire* attitude as to the determination of its progenitors, men like Norman Collins. Meanwhile the BBC, under men like Hugh Carleton Greene, was being edged into modernisation. Its approach to news, stung by the iconoclastic approach of ITN, became less cautious and drab, and with the arrival of 'Tonight', a new breed of current affairs programme-makers was given its opportunity by the redoubtable Grace Wyndam Goldie. Their arrival and swift rise to controlling positions changed forever the relationships between reporters and politicians, between BBC Governors and managers, and most significantly between the BBC and the public. The sharper, more human scripts for performers like Hancock and Braden, and the connections between the new programme controllers and their Oxbridge Revue contemporaries, moved the medium away from variety and the stage towards the satire of TW3 and inventive use of the drama studio. I first encountered Bryan Izzard directing a Fringe double-bill of Ionesco and Adamov; next when he was seconded to Border, directing Robin Hall and Jimmie McGregor on a steamroller and sticking Maurice halfway up the studio wall kicking his heels ... Radio faced the twin threats of television and the pirates, until the government obliged the BBC to legitimise pop music with its own network, and the other 'streamed' channels 2, 3 and 4 were created – in anticipation of today's continuous themed niche channels on cable and satellite. Auntie still seemed slightly stilted, and it required the formation of the shoestring local radio stations to take the Corporation down to grass roots. This structure was only tentatively extended to Scotland; and management had reason to be wary of the independent cast of stations like Radio Highland, broadcasting much of its output in Gaelic, and Radio Shetland, whose audience ignored the existence of the BBC and used it as a very local noticeboard (school and scout parties, hopping islands for annual camp, would call in with a message of reassurance to be broadcast to anxious parents).

There were other signs of democratic change. Maurice's days with the BBC Scottish Home Service had been part of a confident, dominant medium in close dialogue with a traditional culture, sure of its distinctive place within the United Kingdom, but mediating firmly an output which understated the radical nature of the Scots. The challenges of the '60s, coinciding with large-scale structural change in Scotland's traditional heavy industries, created much uncertainty and scepticism at the same time as sending shipyard workers into car factories and fishermen on to oilrigs. Growing globalisation in transport and communications, new markets in Europe, and the discovery of offshore oil in commercial quantities, led to reassessments of individual opportunities which found expression in a remodelled nationalist movement whose successes in by-elections and municipal government caused the Heath and Douglas-Home administrations to give serious consideration to home rule. Broadcasting had gained new concessions to cover the hustings in full, and the reports and debates reached increasingly discriminating audiences. The Scottish Office won a burgeoning autonomy, with the Barnett formula recalculating the original Goschen arrangement to maintain a positive fiscal discrimination in Scotland's favour. Public agencies such as the Highlands and Islands Development Board and the Scottish Development Agency began taking belated steps to regenerate Scotland's economic fabric, and Silicon Glen was one outcome.

Especially under the controllership of Alasdair Milne, who brought useful London connections, BBC Scotland gained advanced technical facilities, including a drama studio capable of supplying classic serials for BBC2 before that channel could be received in Scotland. It hosted the latter years of 'Doctor Finlay's Casebook' before progressing through 'This Man Craig', 'The Borderers' and 'Sutherland's Law' to 'The Vital Spark'. Milne also inaugurated a significant, if technically cumbersome, format in 'Nationwide', which allowed for both national and local content and as good as 'united' the country. It is remembered more for the lady who harried Mrs. Thatcher about the Belgrano, and often mocked for its post-'Tonight' fascination with performing pets; but it brought regional newsrooms into reluctant cooperation and obliged the BBC to re-assess its national duties. Meanwhile the Broadcasting Council for Scotland pushed for more autonomy, and enjoyed it for a spell with an independent-minded Controller, Alastair Hetherington, until cen-tralist tendencies prevailed and the 1979 referendum ended in tears. The Nationalists, in a desperate throw, provoked the demise of the Lib–Lab pact and gave Thatcherism its chance.

This was to make possible Channel 4 and the emergence of the independent producers, characterised by John Harvey Jones at the Edinburgh Television Festival as being in a lifestyle rather than a business as long as they accepted commissions without profit. They were in the minority in the acquisitive '80s. Coincidentally, technology was moving to miniaturise the equipment of broadcasting, taking advantage of consumerism's electronic revolution to build on the almost universal availability of semiconductors, computers and CDs. Hence the wars in Wapping, the rise of Rupert Murdoch, the casuali-sation of the rest of the media workforce, the shock jock and the news bunny. Conglomerates emerged, whether within broadcasting or out-side, and the audience became one market among many. One '80s phenomenon was the fragrant postmodernity of the post-production houses, stables of nerdish geniuses who manipulated digits to make possible not merely an advertising executive's merest – or most extrav-agant – whim, but also the wherewithal of dinosaur movies. Indeed, this facility has now entered the realm of consumer electronics, and everyone can take, store and alter digital images. We have been catapulted out of the era of the television magi in their crystal caves, dictating what all should be watching, and into infinite space: un-limited access, street wisdom and hands-on capability. And as people found out how it was done, they grew tired of hype and spin even as the new means of image capture, process and marketing appeared to give them – and then tragically denied them – possession of a princess.

When today's media practitioners foregather, they agree that the most important commodity is still programmes, if only to fill the exponentially expanding spectrum now in contemplation. Proven formulae are frantically reinvented, so that we are given live dalmatians for animated, American attempts at men behaving badly, British Friends ... The independents who have survived are becoming more aware of the value of their product, and are seeking greater ownership beyond the first commissioned broadcast. Current nostrums given sage nods are that local programming is a valuable niche, Scottish accents are bankable especially speaking sweary words, there is a renaissance in Scottish film, there is a synergy across media. Then there are expectations: that the Scottish Parliament will arrogate to itself the control of broadcasting, that the Scottish media properties will escape outside ownership. The most likely outcomes are bound up with external imponderables: to make workable predictions we must identify relevant trends and factors.

One of these is the pattern of ownership in radio, the less regulated medium. This seems to indicate that it is not possible to resist a shift to outside ownership, and that audiences follow favourite performers and formats with little evidence of station loyalty.

Another is too hard to read so close to the death of Diana, Princess of Wales: in the aftermath of public disenchantment with invasion of privacy (however defined) we will have to track the pendulum of self-regulation by the popular press, and establish whether it impacts on other media, including their costs.

I have already indicated that the season of franchise (and charter) renewal concentrates the collective mind of government. Current considerations include the viability of the digital terrestrial services for which the last Broadcasting Act made provision; whether cross-media and cross-border ownership restrictions can safely be further relaxed; if positive quota requirements, whether for country of origin or for programme type, can be reconciled with European competition law. Allied with this is the vexed issue of cultural policy and the Scottish Parliament: there is controversy over the present role and accountability of the Scottish Arts Council, not least as regards film funding, with which Channel 4 and Canal + have long been involved. Broadcasting, as I have shown, is not controlled by Parliament: it is regulated, a role that might not feel comfortable to an MSP; and one of the essentials of good regulation is consistency, at present maintained over the whole of the UK by the ITC in connection with ITV.

Westminster has now to grapple with the future role and nature of all the privatised sector regulators: the high personal profiles of Don Cruickshank and Clare Spottiswoode are unlikely to be replicated, and there would be little stomach in New Labour for their Scottish equivalents to be put in post. Similarly, the BBC's current, indeed prevailing, culture is one of centralism. The economics of a separate Scottish Broadcasting Corporation with its own Governors and consultees have not been addressed, and only a strong groundswell not at present discernible, within the audience as opposed to the media observers, would move Tony Blair to change his views.

That groundswell might flow from dissatisfaction with what audiences were able to choose to see. They will be able to make their choices through all kinds of new opportunities, which render irrelevant concerns about delivery, as programmes arrive on phone lines, on miniature discs and cassettes and chips. Live broadcasting could be limited to news and events, but tailored to an individual's requirements through interactive controls. Discussions about new media assume that interactivity will transform work, shopping, banking, learning and other transactions, but I think that will depend on the speed by which the car is driven off the road. The performing arts, particularly music, will continue to be celebrated in social contexts rather than along circuits; eating out will remain in defiance of TV dinners; theme parks will pall and crumble (I have spoken).

Border Television, thirty-five years after my stint, remains a lonely independent entity, perhaps finding the border harder than ever to straddle, the twin audiences perhaps growing further apart. It must fight to maintain its local voice in the surrounding cacophony. It could do worse than employ someone with a breadth of cultural experience, a sense of being Scottish and European, a distinctive voice and a rapport with folk; someone like Maurice Lindsay.

There was also the occasion when I found myself interviewing the bird's-nest-hatted chairman of a branch of the Mother's Union. It had just expelled an unfortunate woman for being the innocent party in a divorce action.

"Is it the case", I asked, "that the Mothers' Union is a Christian organisation?"

"Certainly".

"So it follows the precepts and teachings of the church's founder, Jesus Christ?".

"Of course".

"Where, then, in the teachings of Jesus Christ is there any justification for punishing the innocent?"

For a long slow second the bird feathers quivered as if about to take off: then the good Christian mother, as purple with rage as her hat, leant forward, and in full close-up of the camera resoundingly slapped my face.

"Thank you for so complete an answer", said I.

(Thank You for Having Me, page 159)

CHAPTER SIX

Maurice Lindsay at Border Television

Mary Marquis

TO A YOUNG, nervous, would-be broadcaster, arriving in 1961 at the rather spartan building which was the new Border Television station, the stalwart Programme Controller in his tweed jacket and bow-tie carried with him a reassuring aura of warmth and geniality which seldom seemed ruffled, even through the hectic birth pangs of an infant service. Better still, here was someone who was himself a broadcaster, journalist, music-lover, and best of all, a poet.

I had no idea then, of course, just how unusual this combination in a television executive would prove to be. Indeed, the newly-hired studio-crews, accustomed to bosses with a tougher image, initially expressed a certain unease. Poetry and pragmatism together in one person was an unfamiliar concept. What would happen if he felt a poem coming on? And might not the Muse get in the way of union matters? But Maurice was perfectly well aware of the need to cope with internal politics and with balancing the books. He simply believed that quality in broadcasting mattered most, and he reflected that quality and integrity in his own work. No 'dumbing-down' for him.

When I joined Border with another young graduate of the RSAMD, Fiona Cumming, it was duly decided by Those Above that we would be given three months each in Presentation and Pro-grammes. To my chagrin, Fiona won the toss and went first to Programmes. It was small consolation to be told that mine would therefore be the first face to appear on opening night, uttering the historic phrase 'Welcome to Border Television'. I still had the sneaky feeling that I'd drawn the short straw.

Head of Presentation, Patrick Campbell, was a silvery-haired gentleman, glittering of eye and sharp of tongue, whose peppery temperament was sorely tested, I'm afraid, by an ungrateful girl who clearly longed to be on the other team, and who had difficulty finding any true creative outlet in the daily recital of the farming prices.

Maurice Lindsay's programmes, on the other hand, were going from strength to strength.

I watched enviously as his nightly news magazine covered local stories, interviewed local characters, some of them pleasingly eccentric, and whenever possible, included an item on the arts. Parish-pump matters, of course, had to be the staple fare, as was only right and proper in a regional service, but it was no small achievement to present these activities in a relaxed and interesting way, particularly when you remember that In the Beginning at Border there were no recording facilities, no proper film-editing, no such luxury as an autocue, and that the only way a producer could communicate directly with his presenter 'live on air' was by telephone. This nerve-stretching set-up was caused, of course, by the initial lack of funds, not lack of know-how. Maurice, the only experienced broadcaster among us, proved to be an admirable role-model. Studio emergencies came and went – he remained cheerfully unflappable – outwardly, at least.

From the confines of the tiny presentation studio, Maurice's world looked like much more fun. The flavours of both sides of the border were captured in a quite inimitable way, and he obviously felt it both a duty and a pleasure to transmit his own enthusiasm for people, and to 'instruct delightfully', which is at least one valid definition of entertainment. And his encouragement of young local performers, giving them a showcase programme of their own, must have been a real motivation in what was then one of the last truly rural and unsophisticated areas left in Britain. Or, as someone neatly described it, 'stunning scenery – few people – many sheep'. All this on a budget of such amazing modesty that the average controller, trying to cope with its equivalent today, would shortly need the attention of men in white coats.

The day of my own escape from Campbell's Kingdom at last arrived, a move undoubtedly hastened by making broadcasting history, of a kind, when I became the first person ever to read the football results down the way, instead of across. This wasn't exactly a Personal Best. The station had an immediate and vociferous viewer-response, in which my parentage was questioned more than once. Campbell was understandably incandescent, Maurice understanding and amused. 'Never mind – at least you've proved there's quite an audience out there! Anyway, it's about time you joined us.'

Although he produced and presented many memorable programmes himself, Maurice also believed in giving young producers their heads, within reason. Sometimes this had unforeseen results. One country-side quiz starred the naturalist and Bird Man, Robin Douglas-Home (brother of Sir Alec, Prime-Minister-to-be), together with two or three other Border notables. They naturally expected to sit quietly around a table in the traditional way, answering viewers' queries. But at the first rehearsal, Bryan Izzard, a wayward genius fresh from London and larger than life, felt moved to make a judgement: 'But DUCKIES, it's all SO tedious! MUST jazz it up just a TEENSY bit!'

Whereupon he handed out a fetching set of miners' helmets, complete with lamps. The panel were bemused but obedient, and on transmission, all became clear. As the credits rolled, the studio rocked to a small explosion. When the smoke lifted, scenery hung drunkenly from the back wall and jagged lumps of plaster lay around. The panel, shaken but not stirred, filed unsteadily out. 'There you ARE, duckies – a triumph! They'll ALL be watching NEXT week!'

So it must have been with some trepidation that Maurice invited this practitioner of the unexpected to produce Border's Burns offering that year. Possibly because of his inability as a Londoner to understand more than one word in twelve, Bryan's natural flamboyance was actually quite subdued, and he directed with touching sensitivity. Maurice himself scripted and presented, Moira Anderson sang, and John Cairney and I delivered the poems. Bryan claimed another triumph. Robert Burns, he was sure, would have been pleased.

Only one moment occurred which gave Maurice real pain. Our accompanist was a sweet young thing who taught music locally. She was willing and eager, but unfortunately given to a fairly free interpretation of the actual notation. At the first run-through, he endured these vagaries patiently. Then came a particularly inventive rendering of a beautiful song-setting by Francis George Scott, and he could bear it no longer. Clutching his brow, he uttered a heartfelt cry: 'No, no please God, not like THAT! I knew the composer!'

Robin Gill, Border's first Managing Director, clearly had some reservations about his Programme Controller's invaluable personal contributions to the output. He never really understood the artistic vision, nor the innate kindliness which so endeared Maurice to the workers at the coalface.

Looking back, it does seem extraordinary that any one individual should have had to shoulder his workload, which also included writing and producing programme 'specials', among them the Christmas panto. But the shortage of money virtually necessitated a hands-on operation from someone who would ordinarily have been tucked away in the calm of an executive suite. Nevertheless, Maurice Lindsay was a fortunate man. For all the inevitable crises, blunders and Acts of God which accompany the early years of any new television venture, he must have been aware that his own talent and sensibility were more than likely to save the day. So it was to prove. The programmes which shone like jewels in the commercial television output of the time bore his unmistakable imprint.

One such was *A Mummer's Tale*, showing for the first time on television, the story of the nativity, retold in mime, music and song. Thea Musgrave was commissioned to write the music, Maurice wrote and read the haunting words, the actor and mime-artist, Alex McAvoy, was brought from the Citizens' Theatre to choreograph, and it was beautifully directed by Janice Willett.

Possibly because of his own young family, or simply because he spotted a gap in the schedule, Maurice decided to launch a weekly children's programme. The Border area's rural nature meant that many youngsters kept pets undreamed of by city kids, and all of them – snakes, badgers, fox-cubs, ferrets, dogs claiming to be three-quarters wolf and eager to prove it – all of them, at one time or another, crept, slithered or slid into the studio with their proud owners. Added to the usual diet of what we fondly hoped were juvenile interests – serial-stories, cartoon-strips, giant train-sets and Things to Make – it proved a popular half-hour.

One star turn, however, was never bettered. A visiting circus made us an offer of their chimpanzees' tea-party. It was gladly accepted. Thus it was that Rosie and Rita duly arrived, smartly attired in frilly knickers and mobcaps. They poured tea and appeared to drink it with all the poise of a brace of Lady Bracknells. I presided over the tea-table as best I could, and Maurice stepped forward to join the fun, a move which, on reflection, may not have been such a good idea. Rosie greeted his smiling entrance with a piercing scream, bared her large yellow teeth in terror, and launched herself wildly at the first available refuge. As I sank slowly to the ground, half-submerged by several stones of chimpanzee and frilly knickers, Rosie's scrawny arm tightened in a stranglehold round my neck, and a last despairing word from me was heard to echo round the region. It was not 'goodnight'. Nor was it the most suitable expression for a children's programme. In the background, I regret to say, I distinctly heard Maurice, laughing.

When he left his home on Loch Lomondside for Carlisle all those years ago, Maurice Lindsay wrote pensively that 'the exuberance of youth had sunk beyond a lost horizon'. Not so, even allowing for poetic licence. It was exactly that ever-youthful zest that made him such a positive force in Border's beginnings, and which certainly enriched the quality of life for the young people who worked with him. As the essayist, Walter Pater, once famously observed of art and artists, 'To burn always with this hard, gem-like flame, to maintain this ecstasy, is success in life'.

When I left Border Television in 1963 to join the BBC, it was with genuine regret for a time and experience I knew would never come again. Among the farewell mementos was one from Maurice. It was his book, *Clyde Waters*, about that beautiful part of Scotland where I grew up and which he has also known and loved since childhood. More than thirty years on, the book remains a favourite. With his usual perception, he must have guessed that nothing could have given me greater pleasure.

PART TWO:
CULTURE AND IDENTITY

Tam O'Shanter, Meg and Cutty Sark.
Reproduced by permission of the Mitchell Library, Glasgow.

A VIEW OF LOCH LOMOND

Mountains open their hinged reflections on the loch,
shape and reshape themselves, grow squat or tall,
are bent by shakes of light. We never find
the same place twice; which is why picture postcards
that claim to lay the constant on the table
(the camera cannot lie) are popular;
from me to you, a reassuring fable;
what trotting tourists hoped to purchase for the shelf;
the image they'd retain, if they were able.

But landscape's an evasion of itself.

(Selected Poems 1942–1972, page 18)

CHAPTER SEVEN

The Landscape of Scotland

John Foster

I N THE EARLY POST-WAR YEARS the term Environment was little used or widely understood. Nevertheless, much was happening then which directly affected the quality of the Scottish environment, some of it good and some less so.

Comprehensive town and country planning legislation brought a degree of order to the location and design of new development and reduced the pre-war prevalence of ribbon building on roads out from towns and villages. The New Towns Act of 1946 established completely new communities away from existing urban centres, East Kilbride the first, followed by Glenrothes and Cumbernauld. People were rehoused from major towns, Glasgow in particular, allowing for redevelopment of run-down areas and providing better living conditions for many people. The Clyde Valley Regional Plan was an innovative attempt to co-ordinate development over a significant part of the heavily industrialised Central Belt.

The National Parks and Access to the Countryside Act of 1949 was a wide-ranging piece of legislation, of which sadly only the nature conservation powers extended to Scotland. Nevertheless, the Scottish element of the then new Nature Conservancy did sterling work in identifying and protecting many areas as national nature reserves and sites of special scientific interest, as well as introducing the public to the natural world through its educational services.

Despite a national survey in 1945 and a report by a government-appointed committee two years later, both chaired by Sir Douglas Ramsay and both advocating the establishment of national parks, the Westminster government of the day decided not to extend the relevant powers of the 1949 Act north of the border. On the one hand there was not the pressing demand from outdoor interests for greater freedom of access to open country, as had long been the case in England, and on the other hand many landowners feared the possibility of land being nationalised under a Labour government.

The 1947 Ramsay report contained a particularly forward-looking addendum of suggestions for planning a national park in Glen Affric, indicating the lines on which all activities might be co-ordinated. A long way ahead of its time, this perceptive document included specific proposals for the use of land for recreational and educational purposes.

A number of people remained concerned about the lack of positive government action on national parks and established the Scottish Council for National Parks. This body campaigned vigorously throughout the 1950s for appropriate legislation, but without success.

Early in the 1960s the Duke of Edinburgh, long an advocate of sound environmental policies, set up 'The Countryside in 1970'. This project sought that all relevant public and voluntary bodies in the UK should consider how to ensure conservation and seemly development in the countryside and thereafter to enter upon co-ordinated programmes to achieve that end. Three major national conferences were convened in 1963, 1965 and 1970.

For the 1965 conference study groups were set up in Scotland to examine a number of aspects of countryside. Study Group 9, under the chairmanship of the late Professor Sir Robert Grieve, concluded that misunderstanding about the role of national parks had by then so diminished as to make their establishment politically practicable. Their report also proposed a Countryside Commission for Scotland and recommended its powers and duties.

While the national park recommendation did not make progress, that for the establishment of the Commission moved forward rapidly and, under the Countryside (Scotland) Act of 1967, it came into being early in the following year, with responsibilities for '... the provision, development and improvement of facilities for the enjoyment of the Scottish countryside, and for the conservation and enhancement of the natural beauty and amenity thereof'. This was a milestone in the environmental scene, recognising the importance of maintaining landscape quality as distinct from purely scientific interest.

Contemporary with the establishment of the Countryside Commission for Scotland was the creation of the Scottish Tourist Board under the Development of Tourism Act of 1969. This took over from the voluntary tourist organisation which for many years had pioneered the promotion of Scotland to the wider world as an outstanding tourist destination.

The culmination of The Countryside in 1970 campaign coincided with the important international event of European Conservation

Year (ECY). In preparation for this the Countryside Commission for Scotland was asked by the Scottish Office to co-ordinate the activities of the many – over 100 – public and voluntary bodies involved in the national programme of events run during the year. The theme selected for Scotland was Information and Interpretation in the Countryside, designed to awaken new public interest in conservation and guide that interest towards an understanding of its vital importance in maintaining the overall quality of the environment in the long term.

Occasionally one year in history proves to be a watershed in some aspect of life. Undoubtedly 1970 was such a year, involving for the first time local authorities, national agencies such as the Forestry Commission and the Scottish Tourist Board, and a wide range of voluntary bodies, including the National Trust for Scotland and the Scottish Civic Trust, in working together with a common objective: the success of the European Conservation Year programme in Scotland.

Not only was this remarkable co-ordination of activity a success in 1970, but many of the participants continued useful joint working relationships thereafter. A particularly positive manifestation of this appeared in the year following 1970 when a dining club was established, comprising the chief executives of the national agencies and voluntary bodies, along with their opposite numbers in the Scottish Office. This unique group has continued to meet informally around half-a-dozen times a year ever since to exchange information and ideas.

Through the 1970s the needs of the environment became more widely understood in Scotland as elsewhere. When oil and gas were first discovered in the North Sea, much time was spent by public and voluntary bodies in seeking to meet the needs of this new industry while minimising the onshore impact on the character of the coastal locations required for building platforms and processing the products once ashore. This work was greatly assisted by a further coming together of the organisations involved in another new body, the Forum on Oil and the Environment, later to become the Environmental Forum, as its remit widened beyond oil and gas.

The first of a series of Scottish national planning guidelines was published in 1974, on North Sea oil and gas, in response to the pressure of an infant industry anxious to proceed speedily. A proposal to establish a rig construction site at Drumbuie, near Kyle of Lochalsh, on land owned inalienably by the National Trust for Scotland, was robustly resisted by its membership, and the Scottish Office wisely went elsewhere. Construction sites, such as those at Cromarty Firth and Kishorn, got the go-ahead only after careful planning scrutiny. Likewise the major processing sites at Sullom Voe on Shetland and Flotta on Orkney, with all their social consequences for local communities, were the subject of much heartsearching before work started.

The coming of two-tier local government to Scotland, introducing the new concept of regions, gave a fresh impetus to planning generally, with the opportunity to take a wider strategic view of land use through structure plans, supported by more detailed local plans. Further national guidelines followed, covering a broad range of planning issues where national interests were considered to be involved. These guidelines have now been part of the planning process for over twenty years, anticipating similar provisions in England by well over a decade.

The leisure explosion of the 1960s, so dramatically described by Michael Dower in his book, *The Fourth Wave*, had not extended to Scotland so intensively as had been the case in the south. However, by the mid-1970s the pressures arising from tourism and outdoor recreation were becoming so significant as to demand a thorough investigation of their nature, scale, geographical distribution and trends, and from this to seek to assess the likely social consequences and potential economic benefits to the Scottish people. To this end the Scottish Sports Council, Scottish Tourist Board, Countryside Commission for Scotland and Forestry Commission collaborated on a major project – the Scottish Tourism and Recreation Planning Studies – designed to provide reliable information and advice for incorporation in the development plans of the new regional and district authorities.

At the same time the Countryside Commission for Scotland independently developed the idea of a park system, extending from urban parks, through country and regional parks to special parks – large areas such as the Cairngorms, Glen Coe/Glen Nevis and Loch Lomond/Trossachs. While the government of the time gave general support to the system, it judged special parks to be national parks in all but name and set them aside.

Though nothing significant happened regarding the park system for almost a further decade, a closely related aspect of conservation did make progress following the accession of the United Kingdom to the World Heritage Convention in 1984. St Kilda was quickly nominated as a natural site and in 1987 became Scotland's first entry in the World Heritage List. The Old and New Towns of Edinburgh were added to the List in the cultural category just three years ago. Today the Cairngorms stand as well worthy of world heritage status except that they lack an adequate system of protective management.

The park system idea did not make real progress until 1981 when, through a successful Private Member's Bill, powers to establish regional parks came into existence. The four subsequently established, Loch Lomond, Clyde/Muirshiel, the Lomond Hills and the Pentlands, are popular recreation areas today, though now with some degree of uncertainty as to their future following the recent return of local government to a single-tier system.

Tourism and outdoor recreation were not the only pressures on the character of Scotland's countryside and rural communities in the 1970s. Building was proceeding apace, not least of new housing, much of it on the edges of existing built-up areas, and some of it with all too little regard for the long-established character of places. The Countryside Commission for Scotland, supported by voluntary organisations, particularly the Scottish Civic Trust and the Association for the Protection of Rural Scotland, worked with local planning authorities to raise standards through design guides and advice on specific development schemes.

Public awareness of environmental matters developed rapidly from the foundation laid by European Conservation Year in 1970, and the remarkable coming together of the public and private sectors in that year survived the traumas of major local government reorganisation and massive inflation in good heart. Interpreting aspects of the environment in a positive and entertaining way became extensively used as a means of managing people constructively, particularly in sensitive countryside and at historic sites and buildings. The National Trust for Scotland used interpretation to good effect in its visitor centres and out on trails, as also did the Nature Conservancy Council on its reserves, Historic Scotland at its properties and local authorities in country parks. In the case of the Culzean and Brodick Country Parks, a pioneering partnership was established between the National Trust for Scotland and the local authorities concerned.

The Countryside Commission for Scotland undertook the training of countryside rangers and others operating in the field of interpretation and, through its courses, helped to strengthen relationships between bodies previously sometimes quite remote from one another.

Interpretation, as a tool of environmental conservation, had moved a long way from its early beginnings in the Peak District National park in the mid-1960s when the technique was first introduced from the United States of America and adapted to the scale and character of the national parks of England and Wales.

As understanding by the wider public improved, so did concern about the appearance of the most precious parts of the landscape of Scotland. A report published in 1979 by the Countryside Commission for Scotland, following an extensive national survey, identified 40 areas of outstanding landscape quality stretching from Galloway to Shetland. Although planning control within these areas was tightened slightly by government, it did not offer the degree of protection that many responsible bodies and individuals felt to be essential in their long-term interest. The long-standing question surfaced again, namely the need for a top-tier designation backed by legislation strong enough to eliminate the slow erosion of quality experienced particularly on the Cairngorms and at Loch Lomond.

The eventual outcome of this concern, almost ten years on, was another report prepared by the Countryside Commission for Scotland at the specific request of the Secretary of State. This proposed four areas to be protected as national parks, with the Cairngorms and Loch Lomond/Trossachs the two most urgent. The government's response was to set up two working parties. That for the Cairngorms resulted in a partnership arrangement involving the relevant public and voluntary bodies, and that for Loch Lomond a local authority joint committee, both to operate voluntarily. The change in political government in May 1997 has altered this situation radically, with anticipation of legislation for national parks early in the life of the new devolved Scottish Parliament.

In Britain, unlike many other countries, nature and landscape conservation for many years was the responsibility of two quite independent national agencies. In the late 1980s the government in power decided that there would be merit in bringing their two separate functions within the remit of one body.

Scotland was to be the testbed, and in 1991 the Countryside Commission for Scotland and the Scottish part of the Nature Conservancy Council ceased to exist, being replaced by one agency – Scottish Natural Heritage. It was no easy task for this new body to pick up all the threads of activity of two established and busy organisations and develop forward-looking policies and a strategy for action capable of implementation with the support of the general public. That it has done this in large measure reflects the dedication of its board and staff through what have been, and still are, times of economic stringency.

Today there exists across Scotland a wide range of initiatives undreamt of in the early post-war years. Long-distance walking routes – the West Highland Way, Speyside Way and Southern Upland Way – are now well-established and popular. The Countryside Around Towns project, long supported by a variety of statutory and voluntary bodies, provides outdoor recreational facilities where most needed by urban dwellers, now with further help through Scottish Natural Heritage's recently launched Paths for All scheme. The Central Scotland Forestry Initiative, by increasing woodland cover in the Central Belt, is improving the degraded landscapes of the industrial past. Farming and Wildlife Advisory Groups, with grant support, are improving farm environments.

Within the strict nature conservation scene a National Biodiversity Network has been established to gather data on wildlife and assess trends. The management of national nature reserves, sites of special scientific interest and other special natural heritage locations is under review with a rolling programme of safeguarding and restoration activity operating. The maritime environment of the estuaries is now an important aspect of this work.

How, then, does the environment in Scotland rate as compared with the many other aspects of life in the late 1990s, only a few hundred days from the end of the millennium? There can be no doubt that what it stands for means a great deal more than it did half a century ago. The massive social changes which have taken place since the last war have allowed people to widen their horizons beyond the imperative of earning a living. In this they have been helped by the innovative activities of the national agencies working in close collaboration with an ever-growing number of powerful voluntary bodies, notable among them the National Trust for Scotland, the Scottish Civic Trust, the Scottish Wildlife Trust and the Association for the Protection of Rural Scotland.

European Conservation Year 1970 stands out as a milestone, bringing together for the first time a remarkable diversity of public and voluntary bodies to work together towards the common end of a better environment for Scotland. These organisations too have been able to get closer to central government to exchange views and develop strategies of mutual benefit, the Forum on Oil and the Environment being a particularly good example. The populace at large has also been able to become increasingly involved, either through membership of voluntary organisations or simply as concerned individuals.

Within the voluntary sector itself progress has been made in achieving a better understanding between bodies with rather different remits or priorities, as for instance the Scottish Wildlife Trust, concerned with nature conservation, and the Ramblers' Association (Scotland), promoting walking and active outdoor recreation.

In this latter connection a relatively new organisation, Scottish Wildlife and Countryside Link, representing some 23 national voluntary bodies, is doing a valuable job both in helping to clear up misunderstandings among its members and in liaising with central government on specific issues. Successful though European Conservation Year undoubtedly was in its time, those concerned with it could hardly have foreseen what by now has become accepted collaborative practice in the important field of environmental conservation.

Looking ahead, the crystal ball is inevitably somewhat cloudy. As our electronic age progresses in Scotland as elsewhere, there is likely to be less time needed for work and consequently greater opportunity for leisure pursuits. On the other hand governments keep tightening the purse-strings, making it ever more difficult to finance the facilities needed for recreation and the maintenance of environmental standards acceptable to an increasingly vigilant public. There will be many challenges ahead in the new millennium.

One thing, however, I did become certain about at this time; the enduring value of the best of the songs of the Scottish composer Francis George Scott. By chance, I found on a shop counter two of the five volumes of his *Scottish Lyrics*, all but one published by the Glasgow firm of Bayley and Fergusson at Scott's own expense. I was at once struck by the harmonic adventurousness of some of the settings of poems by McDiarmid, and in his setting of lyrics by Burns and others the recreating of a kind of folk idiom that gave the impression of emerging out of a secure tradition. Scotland, of course, has had no such continuing tradition, the flow of her art and music having been forced underground, and subsequently dissipated and dispersed, as a result of the Reformation, which allowed music no serious place in the grim Presbyterian bareboard system of worship devised by Knox and further 'refined' by Melville.

(*Thank You for Having Me*, pages 66–7)

CHAPTER EIGHT

A Survey of Scottish Studies

Alexander Fenton

THE PROFESSIONAL SHAPING of Scottish ethnology as a systematic approach to the study of the traditional ways of life of the Scots, as they were in the past and as they are now, stems largely from the 1930s. The discipline, however, has much older antecedents that laid a basis for rapid progress once the adverse impact of the Second World War had been overcome. Immediately before the War, the Scottish Anthropological and Folklore Society had been making an impact, also within international parameters, but the bitter years of the War and its aftermath seriously hindered, for a time, the development of the study of national ethnologies in Europe in general.

The establishment of folk museums was amongst the earliest signs of recovery: in Scotland, for example, the Highland Folk Museum opened at Kingussie in 1944, after a chequered history that went back to the 1930s,[1] the Glenesk Museum in Angus opened in 1955,[2] and the Angus Folk Museum at Glamis in 1950. These and others did sterling service in the local collection and documentation of objects, under the enthusiastic guidance of gifted amateurs who had been warmed by the influence of the Scandinavian folk museum movement. But only with the foundation of the School of Scottish Studies of the University of Edinburgh in 1951 did academic professionalism come to bear on the traditional and changing cultures of Scotland as a whole, especially in relation to verbal and musical traditions. Then in 1959 came the setting up of the Country Life Section of the National Museum of Antiquities of Scotland, with a remit to collect and study the material culture of all the regions of Scotland. From this flowed the Country Life Archive (later the Scottish Ethnological Archive, now known as the Scottish Life Archive), and the Scottish Agricultural Museum in which is presented the visual evidence of the background studies carried out.

To understand these post-war developments, it is necessary to go further back in time, and at the same time to take into account different attitudes to the question of Scottish nationhood. What follows provides some of the background to the professionalisation of Scottish studies or Scottish ethnology in the mid-twentieth century, and it looks at changing attitudes to the collection of verbal and musical traditions as an example.

The eighteenth century was a major formative period, when the concept of taxonomic classification based on methodical collection was beginning to lead, *inter alia*, to the formation of learned antiquarian societies, many producing journals, and to the establishment of museums. This marked a stage beyond what might be called the 'cabinets of curiosities' phase. In 1707, the year of the Union of the Parliaments, the Society of Antiquaries of London was founded, and in 1780 the Society of Antiquaries of Scotland was established by the 11th Earl of Buchan, probably under the inspiration of the older Society. Though its aims were comparable, it nevertheless put an emphasis on what would now be called 'national identity', through exploration of Scottish history and antiquities, and comparison of the ancient and modern state of the kingdom and the people of Scotland. As a matter of fact, examination of aspects of culture as a basis for the establishment of the concept of 'nation' goes back in itself to the second half of the seventeenth century, when physical bounds were being established in detail through Sir Robert Sibbald's work on mapping the country,[3] John Adair's recording of the coasts[4] and John Slezer's depictions of the built environment – castles, mansions, monasteries and townscapes.[5] Such a visual demarcation of the land of Scotland may well be construed as the shaping of an identity on the basis of the establishment of an economic, social, physical and historical geography.

To scholars of the eighteenth century, the interpretation of 'antiquities' was possibly wider than it has come to be in later times. They were seen as taking into account both the three-dimensional and documentary evidence for older ways of life, and included efforts to reconstruct ancient orders of law, political and social institutions, and economic activities and social customs.

The Earl of Buchan saw the work of the Society as proceeding along two broad lines, which he would undoubtedly have regarded as up-to-date approaches. The first was a topographically oriented 'ethnographic' survey to cover details of natural resources, their uses, population groupings, language and social customs. This proposal has left an important legacy, for example in the compilation in the

1790s of Sir John Sinclair's *First Statistical Account of Scotland*. This in turn fathered the *Second Statistical Account* of the 1840s, and then in our days the *Third Statistical Account*. These three parish-by-parish surveys, covering all of the country, have provided a reservoir of material for researchers into local history, at well-spaced intervals that allow for comparisons of change in economic circumstances and traditional ways of life, that is almost unequalled in any country.

The second was an examination of constitutional, military and ecclesiastical organisations and their associated material culture, including coins, seals, weapons and portraits of the famous, as well as the subject areas covered by Slezer in his *Theatrum Scotiae* of 1693 and in expanded later editions.

From 1781, the Society's newly founded Museum was collecting objects representing various historical periods, but it is significant that the Society itself displayed an early concern for oral and literary traditions. Following a paper of 1787 from George Dempster of Dunnichen on the present state of Gaelic poetry in the Western Highlands, ministers of the Church in the Highlands were invited to 'write down from the recital of the old Bards these songs in the Gaelic language' for the Society.[6] The concept of collection, both of objects and of oral traditions, was becoming formalised, even if the latter was particularly aimed at the language of the Garden of Eden, Gaelic, in these early days. In the early 1800s a dozen papers discussed Gaelic poetry and the authenticity of Ossian, and the Society of Antiquaries cooperated with the Highland Society of London under Sir John Sinclair in publishing Macpherson's 'originals'.[7] Similarly the Highland Society of Scotland (founded in 1784, and now the Royal Highland and Agricultural Society of Scotland) had a strong cultural remit that survived until the mid-nineteenth century, not only examining the present state of the Highlands and Islands and their inhabitants, but also paying attention to the presentation of the language, poetry, and music of the Highlands. It functioned, indeed, almost as a Gaelic academy of letters; it supported a band, a piper, a 'Professor of Gaelic', sponsored Gaelic classes, encouraged the writing and publication of piobaireachd and ran piping competitions that survived till 1844. It initiated the production of a Gaelic dictionary, which was finally published in 1828.[8]

There is no mistaking the intellectual spirit of the times, concerned as it was with logging the physical and oral evidence (albeit with a concentration on Gaelic in the latter case) for the evolution and progress of mankind. The first publication in Britain of anything approaching the nature of an ethnological 'text-book', Arthur Mitchell's *Past in the Present*, 1880, based on the first series of Rhind lectures given to the Society of Antiquaries of Scotland in 1876 and 1878, is a consummation of mid-Victorian thinking on such topics. It looks at 'neo-archaic' objects – early plough types, querns, spindles and whorls, Hebridean pottery and the like – as obsolescent survivals of old ways of life that could be used as means of understanding the past by working back from the present, and Mitchell went on in the book to propound a philosophy of civilisation.⁹ But such philosophising, even in the later nineteenth century, remained part of an all-British and indeed European pattern. Though based on Scottish material, it sought the universal, and was not in itself concerned with establishing the bounds of 'state' or 'nation'.

Nevertheless, it is likely that the Scots were very self-aware, in one way or another, as early as was the case anywhere. It has been pointed out that the word 'nation', which is to be understood in different ways at different periods, is in its modern sense no older than the eighteenth century,¹⁰ and that 'national consciousness' has an uneven development among the social groupings and regions of a country. If Scotland, 'North Britain' (as it was sometimes called after the 1707 Union), can be regarded as a region of Britain, then it appears true that such consciousness did appear early, as in the other Celtic 'peripheries' of Wales and Ireland. Three steps or phases for this phenomenon have been distinguished for nineteenth-century Europe, of which Scotland is part. The first is primarily cultural, literary and folkloric, without political or even national overtones. The second is when a group of strong supporters of the idea of 'nation', however much they are in the minority, begin to be active and to campaign politically for their ideals. The third is when the 'people below' begin to give mass support to nationalist programmes.¹¹ In practice there are likely not only to be overlaps between these three phases, but also all three can be active at the same time. The 1997 vote in favour of devolution is possibly a symbol of phase three (in spite of a degree of manipulation from above), whilst recent publications such as David McCrone, *Understanding Scotland: the Sociology of a Stateless Nation*, 1992 and David McCrone, Angela Morris and Richard Kelly, *Scotland – the Brand. The Making of Scottish Heritage*, 1995, show how sociologists can play a contemporary role in the second.

At the same time there is a mass of publication on Scottish history, languages and cultural traditions, material and spiritual, and a tremendous following for the conservation, presentation and interpretation of historical sites and monuments, typified by the activities and membership of bodies like the National Trust for Scotland and the Friends of the Scottish Monuments, that shows the strong continuation of the first, non-politically oriented phase. It is important that all three approaches and their interrelationships be taken into consideration in ethnological studies, without regarding the one approach to be too archaeologising, antiquarian or out-moded, out of line with the needs of the present day, or the others to be too political, fanatical or individualistic. All are valid aspects of the concept of national identity, and the interactions flowing from their overlapping create an exciting dynamic, the complexity of which is a challenge to unbiased research. But it can be seen that through the first phase, some elements of which have been touched on above – the mapping of physical bounds, the recording of the built environment, the establishment of museum collections, the founding of learned societies, the ingathering of oral traditions which eventually in the twentieth century began to be systematised in archives – there was a continual shaping and fostering of pride in nationhood and of Gaelic traditions as part of that nationhood, which has in some degree fuelled the more politically oriented aspirations of phases two and three. My primary concern here, however, is with phase one.

Tradition, even as it changes, is a far firmer cultural base than the changing fashions of politics whether national, regional or local, and in all its elements, including language, it deserves much fuller official attention than it has hitherto received. The asking of a question about the use of Gaelic or of Scots in census forms is not enough in itself, for though in nineteenth-century Germany some believed that language was the only adequate indicator of nationality,[12] in Scotland there is a variety of regional dialects and languages, including Eng-lish, and it is the diversity that is striking, including the diversity of registers (which makes the definition of 'Scots' as a prelude to a Census question almost impossible), though it does not appear to detract from a strong sense of nationality. The same is true of the regional variety in material culture, whether in the Northern Isles and Caithness, the Western Isles, the North-East and other well demarcated areas, or more broadly on the two sides of the Highland

Line. Language and material culture, reflecting a variety of ethnic origins and influences, and associated forms of community life; the growth of towns and villages and the interactions of town and country; the impact on the individual and his or her ways of living and thinking of central or local regulation and legislation: all of these, as they have changed in the course of history, are the real roots of the concept of nationhood or cultural community, now being increasingly well and accurately researched as the discipline of 'Scottish Ethnology' or 'Scottish Studies' perfects its techniques, in close alliance with those of Scottish history and studies in the languages of Scotland. I shall now exemplify such increasing professionalism by looking at the collecting history of song, music and oral traditions.

One of the earliest systematic collectors was not a Scot. He was Edward Lhuyd (1660–1709), born near Oswestry, who undertook a grand tour of the Celtic countries in 1697–1701. He visited parts of the West of Scotland, as well as Glasgow and Edinburgh, between September 1699 and January 1700, making the first known sketches of ancient monuments in the west and also recording information on historical and linguistic material. Many Gaelic manuscripts collected by him in Ireland and Scotland are now in Trinity College, Dublin. In many ways he pioneered research into the natural history, folklore and dialects of the Highlands, and amongst other things assembled a total of around 3000 words from native Gaelic speakers in Kintyre and East Inverness-shire – the earliest extensive vocabulary of the language.[13] Lhuyd worked over a broad geographical canvas, but his somewhat later successors were more localised in their collecting scope. They were mostly ministers of the church, people like the Perthshire-born Rev James McLagan (1728–1805), minister at Amulree, whose large collection of tales and ballads is in Glasgow University Library, and who supplied Ossianic ballads to James Macpherson,[14] the Rev Donald MacNicol (1735–1802) from Glenorchy, collector of heroic ballads and other verse;[15] the Rev Alexander Sage (1753–1824), minister of Kildonan in Sutherland, who collected heroic ballads from reciters in Strathnaver and Strathmore;[16] and the 'Apostle of the North', the Rev Dr John MacDonald (1779–1849), who in 1805 collected heroic poetry in western Sutherland, Ross-shire and Inverness-shire.[17] Thus by the early years of the nineteenth century there was an increasingly strong tradition of collecting tales and ballads by men of the cloth, who must have been inspired to do so by a sense of pride in their own past, albeit a local past, and this is a major element in the first non-political phase referred to above.

Collection by ministers, mainly of local stock and working amongst familiar people in their home or related areas, continued through the nineteenth and into the twentieth century. An example is the Rev John Gregorson Campbell (1836–1891), born in Kingairloch, and minister of Tiree from 1860. He published folktales, historical traditions and belief legends in journals, often in paraphrases with the significant Gaelic words noted, thus making the material available to a wider, not necessarily Gaelic-speaking, literary circle.[18] There were also the Rev. Dr Angus John Norman MacDonald (1860–1932) from Benbecula, minister at Killearnan, whose manuscripts on Gaelic lore and history are among the Carmichael Papers in Edinburgh University Library;[19] the Rev James MacDougall (1833–1906), born in Craignish and minister of Duror, whose material on *Folk Tales and Fairy Lore* was posthumously published in 1910;[20] the Rev Dr Kenneth Macleod (1871–1955), from Eigg, and minister in Colonsay and Gigha, who collected Gaelic folklore and song and collaborated with Marjory Kennedy-Fraser in *The Songs of the Hebrides*, 1909.[21]

Material in the Scots dialects was not ignored, but in terms of specific collecting activity, there was much less at local levels than in the Gaeltachd. The Rev Walter Gregor in the North East of Scotland is a notable example. He not only compiled and published a glossary, *The Dialect of Banffshire*, in 1866, but also wrote two valuable books of original folklore material, *An Echo of Olden Time* (1874), and *Notes on the Folk-Lore of the North-East of Scotland* (1881). His manuscript notes on the subject were given by J. E. Crombie to the library of the Folk-Lore Society in London about 1890. His account of the custom of the last sheaf, published in a French journal in 1888 and translated back into English by Sir James Frazer in *The Golden Bough*, is reckoned by a later, trained professional collector and scholar to be 'still the best and most exhaustive account of the custom'.[22] In general, however, though there is a great deal of material relating to folklore and customs in the Scots-speaking areas, much of it is embedded in the numerous local histories and books of a reminiscing nature that proliferated in Victorian times. These remain to be culled in detail, however.

It seems that the North-East of Scotland has a particularly distinguished record as far as concerns the collection of Scots songs and ballads. Gavin Greig (1856–1914), born at Parkhill, Newmachar, the son of a forester and estate overseer, became schoolmaster of White-hill in New Deer parish in 1879. He began to collect the traditional 'minstrelsy' of his area, bringing to light a tremendous and almost untapped resource. Eventually he collaborated with the Rev. James Bruce Duncan (1848–1917), son of a carpenter and millwright in New Deer parish and minister of Lynturk, Strathdon. Between them their ingathering amounted to 3050 texts (2500 by Greig) and 3100 records of tunes (2300 by Greig). The task of publishing this treasure trove as a collaborative venture between the University of Aberdeen and the School of Scottish Studies of the University of Edinburgh, in eight substantial volumes, is almost complete.[23]

There were, of course, outstanding individuals who did an enormous amount for the Scots language and for Scottish traditions of song and story, people like Scott and Burns, Leyden and Hogg, and John Jamieson the lexicographer. They were collectors who put their collecting to use in wider spheres, however, and their story must be told elsewhere.

All honour is due to the men of the cloth whose local dedication and inspiration has preserved so much. But there were also secular collectors, some of the most effective of whom had élite social status. The aristocratic John Francis Campbell of Islay (1822–85) was a man of means who, influenced by the work of the Grimm brothers in Germany and of Scandinavian, particularly Norwegian, scholars, set about collecting popular tales in 1859, teaming up with competent writers of Gaelic in order to get the exact words of the storyteller; his helpers included Hector Maclean, an Islay schoolmaster, Hector Urquhart, a gamekeeper from Poolewe, and John Dewar, a maker of fences. He also collaborated on occasion with other collectors, such as Alexander Carmichael (1832–1912) of Lismore, the excise-man for Islay, Skye, Uist and Oban, whose collections are published in six volumes as *Carmina Gadelica*.[24]

A notable local collector was the Rev Fr Allan MacDonald (1859–1905), born in Fort William, who as parish priest in South Uist and Eriskay gathered Gaelic folklore from 1887. He collaborated willingly with a number of folklorists, Walter Blaikie, Alexander Carmichael, George Henderson and others, being generous to a fault with his material, for as has been shown, the book on *The Outer Isles* published by the English folklorist Ada Goodrich Freer in 1902 was largely plagiarised from his notes (but not from his Gaelic notes, which she could not understand). In one scholar's view, the c. 350,000 words in his notebooks constitute 'one of the most important local collections of folklore ever made anywhere'.[25] Clearly, there was beginning to be a market in folklore, as also in Gaelic song, to judge by the work of the Perthshire-born Marjory Kennedy-Fraser (1857–1930), whose *Songs of the Hebrides*, 1909, attempts to 'blend traditional melody with appropriate harmonic setting'.[26] Frances Tolmie (1840–1926), born in Skye, was another collector of folksongs (as well as of folklore). In collaboration with the Folk Song Society (founded in London in 1898 and amalgamating with the English Folk Dance Society in 1932), she published in 1911 in its *Journal* 105 occupational songs from the Western Isles. These were edited by an officer of the Society, Lucy Ethelred Broadwood (1858–1929), herself a collector who worked in Arisaig in 1906 and returned in 1907 with a phonograph with which she recorded 30 songs.[27] The Society and its journal had much importance in disseminating knowledge of such material, some of which came from Scotland, as well as in fostering the use of sound-recording devices.

These widening circles of attention, however, remained essentially of a non-political nature. Traditional popular beliefs, tales, songs and music were treated as survivals of stages in the progress of civilisation, or as source-material for more fashionable literary or art forms, for which they provided a good deal of inspiration. Attitudes to the subject were not all favourable, however. Though J. F. Campbell got away with it as a man, when it came to women collectors there could sometimes be strong disapproval. A case in point is that of Lady Evelyn Stewart-Murray, third daughter of the 7th Duke of Atholl, who recorded 240 Gaelic tales, legends and songs from West Perthshire in 1891. So strongly did her mother, the Duchess Louisa, object to such unladylike behaviour that her daughter was more or less forced into exile abroad, and never returned. Her notebooks are deposited with the School of Scottish Studies.[28]

In the nineteenth and early twentieth centuries, ministers and priests, and the wealthy or leisured élite who could afford to seek helpers, all had to use notebooks, writing down the material and inevitably trailing behind and inhibiting the speakers or singers, until the new day of sound recording dawned in the twentieth century. Lucy Broadwood's use of a phonograph in 1907 in Scotland was then exceptional, and it may be that John Lorne Campbell of Canna

(1906–96) was amongst the first major users of such devices. From 1937, he built up a sound-recording archive of 1500 Gaelic songs and 350 folktales, using equipment mostly got from the United States: in 1937 a wax cylinder Ediphone Recorder, in 1938 a Presto Disc Recorder, in 1948 a Webster Wire Recorder, in 1957 a Grundig, and so on. Amongst other things, he helped to turn scholarly interest in high literary forms towards the 'real' originals, and he collaborated with a musicologist, Francis Collinson, in tracing the true, not art-form, originals of Marjory Kennedy-Fraser's Hebridean songs.[29] As a man of strong nationalist – or Gaelic nationalist – feelings, he chose to seek the 'authentic' voice of the people, and in this he was ably helped, indeed inspired, by his American-born wife, Margaret Fay Shaw, herself a fine collector.[30] As a pointer to the future it is worth noting that current efforts are being made to find and fund ways and means of keeping their collections *in situ* in Canna House, though making them available to the world of scholarship through modern electronic techniques.

The first of the trained, paid professional collectors in Scotland, and one of the best, was Calum Iain Maclean (1915–60), of the island of Raasay. He studied Celtic at Edinburgh, Irish in Dublin, and Swedish in Sweden, and was first employed in Ireland by the Irish Folklore Commission, which had been founded in 1935. Its Director, Professor James Delargy, aware of the wealth of material to be gleaned in Scotland, arranged for Maclean to undertake an explor-atory spell of collecting in his native island during December–February 1945–46, and this was so successful that he worked in the Western Isles for a further four and a half years. His manuscript notebooks for this period amount to 10,000 pages, an ingathering from Barra, South Uist and Benbecula of the largest collection of folktales yet made in Scotland, only to be compared with the work of J. F. Campbell of Islay. There was at this time no official body in Scotland responsible for investigating the traditional culture of the people, but this deficiency was remedied – with the strong support of Irish and Scandinavian scholars – in 1951, with the founding of the School of Scottish Studies of the University of Edinburgh. It is little wonder that Calum Maclean became one of its first Research Fellows, who in the nine and a half years of his employment there went on to make an enormous Gaelic collection, also making forays to Shetland and to the Borders for non-Gaelic material.[31] The School's Sound Archive, consistently built up since by members of staff such as Hamish Henderson, Donald Archie Macdonald, Alan Bruford and others, as well as by students, is now the most important repository of traditional verbal culture in Scotland. The School's magazine, *Tocher*, founded in 1971, regularly brings into the public domain material from the Archives: tales, songs, music, customs, beliefs, place-names and much else relating to Scottish cultural traditions, in Gaelic with translations, in Scots and in English. Its journal, *Scottish Studies*, founded in 1957, carries a wide range of more academic articles on all aspects of the culture of the country.

With the founding of the School, the subject of Scottish Studies came of age as a professional discipline. Even if the background of collection outlined here has a strong Celtic emphasis, nevertheless the work of the School relates to the whole of the country. There are other bodies, too, concerned with the country's culture. The Scottish Life Archive, housed in the National Museums of Scotland, was originally set up as the 'Country Life Archive' in 1959, and is now an important resource centre, not only for rural life but also for urban and industrial material. The European Ethnological Research Centre, founded in 1989 and housed also within the National Museums, but independent of them, publishes a series of volumes of oral reminiscences, 'Flashbacks', another series entitled 'Sources in Local History', and is making good progress with a massive thirteen-volume project, the *Compendium of Scottish Ethnology*. It also publishes a journal, *The Review of Scottish Culture* (founded in 1984 and taken over by the EERC in 1989). With the setting-up of an established Chair of Scottish Ethnology based on the School of Scottish Studies in 1990, and of a second Chair at the University of Aberdeen in 1996, the discipline has achieved a degree of academic status unknown elsewhere in Britain.[32]

Scottish Studies, ethnology, has thus attained maturity. It is significant that, with very few exceptions, its progress has been of a non-political nature. It is still in line with Hobsbawm's first phase, and it has kept on growing through the period of development of Scottish nationalism. Surely there is a lesson here. The country's culture, as it has traditionally been and as it is changing, with all its regional variety, has tremendous inner strength. This should be a basic taught subject in every school, and it is greatly to be hoped that the recommendations following the recent 'review of Scottish Culture and the Curriculum' by the Scottish Consultative Council on the Curriculum[33] will lead to an infusion of the subject into every curriculum. It already has a firm foothold in two of our universities, and good students now being trained would be capable teachers. The subject offers a very substantial basis for the development of a sense of community identity and belonging. Yet such a sense is also to be shared with neighbours who have comparable strands of culture, and who influence, and are themselves influenced by, now as in the past, the culture of the Scots.

References

1. Cheape, Hugh,' Dr I F Grant (1887–1983): The Highland Folk Museum and a Bibliography of her Written Works', in *Review of Scottish Culture* 2 (1986), 113–125.
2. Cant, Ronald G., 'Margaret Fairweather Michie 1905–1985: A Memoir', in *Review of Scottish Culture* 3 (1987), 1–3.
3. Sibbald, Sir Robert, *Scotia Illustrata sive prodromus historiae naturalis*, Edinburgh 1684; Sibbald, Sir Robert, *Account of the writers, ancient and modern, printed and manuscripts not printed, which treat of the description of Scotland, as it was of old and is now at present; with a catalogue of the maps and prospects and figures of the ancient monuments thereof*, Edinburgh 1710.
4. Adair, John, *The Description of the Sea-Coast and Islands of Scotland*, Pt i, Edinburgh 1703.
5. Slezer, John, *Theatrum Scotiae, containing the prospects of their Majesties Castle and Palaces, together with those of the most considerable towns and colleges, the ruins of many ancient abbeys, churches, monasteries, and convents within the said Kingdom*, London 1693: see also Cavers, Keith, *A Vision of Scotland: the Nation observed by John Slezer, 1671–1717*, HMSO for National Library of Scotland, Edinburgh 1993.
6. Stevenson, Robert B. K., 'The Museum, its Beginnings and its Development. Part I: to 1858: the Society's own Museum; Part II: the National Museum to 1994', in Bell,A. S., *The Scottish Antiquarian Tradition. Essays to mark the bicentenary of the Society of Antiquaries of Scotland and its Museum, 1780–1980*, Edinburgh 1981, 49–50.
7. *Ibid.*, 57.
8. *Prize Essays and Transactions of the Highland Society of Scotland*, I (1799), lii-liii, cxviii-cxxi; B(lack), R., 'Highland Society of Scotland', in Thomson, D. S., ed., *The Companion to Gaelic Scotland* (1983), Glasgow 1994, 121-2 [hereafter *CGS*].
9. Mitchell, Arthur, The Past in the Present: What is Civilisation?, Edinburgh 1880; Stevenson, *op. cit.*, 157-8.
10. Hobsbawm, Eric J., *Nations and Nationalism since 1780* (1990), Cambridge University Press 1995, 3.
11. *Ibid.*, 12
12. *Ibid.*, 21-2, 98-9.

13. [Watson, J. Wreford], 'Edward Lhuyd and Scottish Studies', in *Scottish Studies* 2/1 (1958), 117–9; *CGS* 149–50.
14. *CGS 179*.
15. *CGS 188*.
16. *CGS 254*.
17. *CGS 168*.
18. *CGS 33*.
19. *CGS 165*.
20. *CGS 170*.
21. *CGS 182*.
22. Maclean, Calum I., 'The Last Sheaf', in *Scottish Studies* 8/2 (1964), 193–207.
23. Keith, Alexander, ed., *Last Leaves of Traditional Ballads and Ballad Airs, collected in Aberdeenshire by The Late Gavin Greig*, Aberdeen 1925, xi–xiv; Olson, Ian A., 'The Greig-Duncan Folk Song Collection: Last Leaves of a Local Culture?', in *Review of Scottish Culture* 5 (1989), 79–85.
24. Maclean, Calum I., 'Hebridean Traditions', in *Gwerin* I/1 (1956), 21–33; *CGS* 32–3.
25. Campbell, John L. 'The Late Fr. Allan McDonald, Miss Goodrich-Freer and Hebridean Folklore', in *Scottish Studies* 2/2 (1958), 175–188; Mathieson, William, in *Scottish Studies* 4/2 (1960), 206–12; *CGS* 165.
26. *CGS 142*.
27. Bassin, Ethel, 'Lucy Broadwood, 1858–1929: Her Contribution to the Collection and Study of Gaelic Traditional Song', in *Scottish Studies* 9/2 (1965), 145–152; Bassin, Ethel, *The Old Songs of Skye: Frances Tolmie and her Circle*, ed. Derek Bowman, London 1977; *CGS* 289.
28. Bruford, Alan, 'A Scottish Gaelic Version of "Snow-White"', in *Scottish Studies* 9/2 (1965), 153–74; Bruford, Alan, 'Two More Stories from Atholl', in *Scottish Studies* 10/2 (1966), 162–70; *CGS* 275; Robertson, Sylvia and Young, Patricia, *Daughter of Atholl. Lady Evelyn Stewart Murray, 1868–1940* (Abertay History Society No 36), Dundee 1996, 13–23, 60.
29. Campbell, John L., 'Angus MacLellan MBE ('Aonghus Beag'), 1869–1966', in *Scottish Studies* 10/2 (1966), 193–7; *CGS* 34; Cheape, Hugh, 'John Lorne Campbell: scholar, folklorist and farmer', in *Review of Scottish Culture* 10 (1996–97), 1–4.
30. Shaw, Margaret Fay, *From the Alleghenies to the Hebrides. An Autobiography*, Edinburgh 1993.
31. Sanderson, Stewart F., 'Calum I. Maclean (1915–1960). *In Memoriam*', in *Gwerin* III (1960), 3–7; M(egaw), B. R. S., 'The Late Calum I. Maclean', in *Scottish Studies* 4/2 (1960), 121–3; *CGS* 189; Lysaght, Patricia, 'Swedish Ethnological Surveys in the Western Isles of Scotland, 1939, 1948: Some Data from Ireland', in *Review of Scottish Culture* 6 (1990), 27–51.
32. Fenton, Alexander, 'Phases of Ethnology in Britain with special Reference to Scotland', in *Ethnologia Europaea* XX,2 (1990), 177–88; Fenton, Alexander, 'Scottish Ethnology: Crossing the Rubicon. Inaugural Lecture for the Chair of Scottish Ethnology', in *Scottish Studies* 31 (1992–93), 1–8; Fenton, Alexander, 'The European Ethnological Research Centre', in

Scottish Local History Journal 40 (Summer 1997), 21–24; Porter, James, 'The Elphinstone Institute and the Chair of Scottish Ethnology, University of Aberdeen', in *Review of Scottish Culture* 10 (1996–97), 147–8).

33. Scottish Consultative Council on the Curriculum, *Review of Scottish Culture and the Curriculum. Report on the analysis of the Schedule response*, 1997.

I invited Sydney [Goodsir Smith] to appear with me at a poetry reading in the beautiful London home of the Poetry Society, 33 Portman Square, an institution then presided over by the Chevalier Calloway Kyle, an aged dignitary whose prejudices and mannerisms were of the minor Victorian variety. I arrived in my uniform of a captain in the Cameronians, having no civilian clothes in London than could match such surroundings. A tieless Sydney turned up in stained flannel bags and accompanied by an unannounced girl attired even more loosely. With frigid politeness the Chevalier introduced us to the audience, a collection of upper middle-class ladies in fluttering hats and chintzy summer frocks quite unprepared for the dose of Scottish Renaissance naturalism that engulfed them.

(*Thank You for Having Me*, page 73)

At one meeting Douglas Young, anxious to demonstrate the living quality of Scots, held up his empty beer glass and called to the barman 'Some mair'. To everyone's astonishment the barman presently came across carrying a long pole and pulled open an upper window.

(*Thank You for Having Me*, pages 100–101)

CHAPTER NINE

Scottish Literature:
Twentieth-Century Attitudes

Paul H. Scott

IN THE 1920S AND '30S there was a succession of books which deplored the social, economic and cultural decline of Scotland. One of these was George Malcolm Thomson's *Caledonia or the Future of the Scots*, published in 1927. He dismissed the state of Scottish literature in a short paragraph: 'There is no literature in Scotland. The country has produced none in the twentieth century, or, to be exact, since the year 1901, when the House with the Green Shutters was reared in the midst of a kailyard gone to seed. The publishing of books has been dead in the country for a very much longer period' (p. 61).

Thomson may have been right about many things when he wrote this book. It was a time when many serious observers were pessimistic about the survival of Scotland as anything more than a geographical expression. He was, however, quite wrong about literature. Hugh MacDiarmid published his first books of verse in Scots, *Sangshaw* and *Penny Wheep*, in 1925 and 1926. His major work, *A Drunk Man Looks at the Thistle*, appeared in 1926 and all of these were from a Scottish publisher, Blackwood's of Edinburgh. Neil Gunn's first novel, *Grey Coast*, was published in 1926. By 1927 Naomi Mitchison had already published five novels and Eric Linklater and Lewis Grassic Gibbon were at work on their first. Scottish literature was not dead in 1927 but in vigorous life.

Even so, there is some excuse for Thomson. It was, and is still, perfectly possible for intelligent people to grow up in Scotland and be quite unaware of Scottish literature of any period, with the possible exception of a hazy idea of a few lines of Robert Burns. For many years before 1927, and for many afterwards, the schools and universities paid very little attention to anything which had been written in Scotland. In the schools, history and literature were mainly English. This used to be true all over the British Empire while it existed, but old habits have been slow to die in Scotland.

Does this matter? After all, England has produced much fine literature and the English language is the predominant means of international communication. I think that it matters very seriously for several reasons. Firstly, there is the loss of the particular pleasure and understanding that comes from reading about the life that surrounds you and its evolution in these familiar places. Our literature is our recorded experience, our collective memory. Without it, you are a stranger in your own land. We are fortunate in having a rich and inexhaustible literature in all of our languages and it would be a sad deprivation to be left in ignorance of it. I think that you are likely to have a better appreciation of other literatures if you begin with your own. Also, if our children are encouraged to believe that every important book has been written somewhere else, and that every important event happens to other people in other places, they are being persuaded that they and their friends, family and compatriots are inferior. There are signs that this result is not uncommon.

Of course, the picture has never been entirely black. Not all teachers have succumbed to the pressures of all-embracing Englishness. I was fortunate. In the High School of Edinburgh we were not allowed to forget that we had such illustrious predecessors as Robert Fergusson and Walter Scott. One of our schoolmasters was Alexander Law, who edited Allan Ramsay for the Scottish Text Society and who was a great enthusiast for Scottish literature, especially of the eighteenth century. We had Gaels too, the remarkable Hector MacIver and a brother of Sorley Maclean. The school was generous with book prizes. Among mine were W. M. MacKenzie's edition of William Dunbar and Agnes Mure MacKenzie's book on Scottish literature up to 1714. At Edinburgh University, where I studied what was, and still is, called English, the Professor, Dover Wilson, was quintessentially English. At the same time, some of the lecturers, like George Kitchen, conveyed an enthusiasm for Scottish literature. I remember the thrill of discovering Robert Henryson in Henry Harvey Wood's edition of 1933. In the early days of the Second World War, the rediscovery of Scottish literature was already well under way.

George Davie in his great book, *The Democratic Intellect* (1961), said that the history of Scotland was marked by an 'alternation between catastrophe and renaissance in which the distinctive national inheritance was more than once brought to the very brink of ruin only to be saved at the last minute by a sudden burst of reviving energy' (p. xvi). For literature there was such a burst in the early eighteenth century when Allan Ramsay, whose anthology, *The Evergreen* of 1724, revived awareness of the mediaeval makars, and he was followed by Fergusson and Burns. Later in that century the philosophers of the Scottish Enlightenment, despite their great achievements, often seemed to forget Scotland in an atmosphere of abstract rationality. Scott, Galt and Hogg early in the next century again restored a consciousness of Scotland.

Thomas Carlyle's departure for London in 1834 symbolised another brink of ruin. William Donaldson[1] has shown that the Scottish spirit and the Scots language continued to find expression in the pages of the 200 or so newspapers which then existed, but there was clearly another burst of reviving energy in the 1880s and '90s. Patrick Geddes in his periodical, *The Evergreen*, a conscious echo of Allan Ramsay, spoke of a Scottish renaissance. It was the period of Stevenson in literature, MacCunn in music and MacTaggart in painting. The recovery of national self-confidence was evident also in political developments and in the formation of new institutions. The Scottish Text Society published the first of its volumes of early Scottish literature in 1883 and the Scottish History Society the first of its collections of historical records in 1886. The Scottish National Portrait Gallery was opened in 1889. An Comunn Gaidhealach, for the promotion of Gaelic language, literature and history, was founded in 1891. In politics, the Government responded to agitation about the neglect of Scotland by reviving the office of Secretary of State in 1885. The Scottish Home Rule Association was founded in 1886 and the Scottish Liberals first adopted Home Rule as a policy in 1888.

From some statements in the press and elsewhere, you might suppose that the revival of Scottish literature and of interest in it has been the work of the last few years. In fact, like the campaign for Home Rule, it has been a continuous process for more than a hundred years with some interruption by two World Wars. Substantial academic books on a subject are a good indication of a serious interest. T. F. Henderson's *Scottish Vernacular Literature* was published in 1898, J. H. Millar's *Literary History of Scotland* in 1903 and G. Gregory Smith's *Scottish Literature: Character and Influence* in 1919.

The First World War delayed the recovery of the Scottish Parliament because a Home Rule Bill had passed its second reading in 1913. What did it do to Scottish literature and to attitudes towards it? Apart from much poetry, the war inspired at least one major work, Lewis Grassic Gibbon's *Sunset Song*. It also seems to have been partly responsible for forming, or strengthening, the ideas of Hugh MacDiarmid about Scotland. His biographer, Alan Bold, describes how he returned from the War with a determination that Scotland should have a future (p. 95). He meant by this that the right of self-determination, proclaimed as the purpose of the Allies, should apply also to Scotland, that our literary tradition should be recognised and enhanced, and that Scots and Gaelic should be revived for serious literary use. MacDiarmid was, of course, not alone; but because of the force of his poetry, his energy and determination, he gave powerful stimulus towards the achievement of all of these political and cultural objectives. On his death in 1978, David Murison said that 'after MacDiarmid, as after Knox, Scotland will never be the same again'.[2]

From the time of MacDiarmid's early poetry in Scots in 1925 and 1926, we have been living through one of the great ages of Scottish literature in Gaelic, Scots and English. I do not have the space to discuss, or even to list, all of the poets, dramatists, novelists and other prose writers who have contributed. With apologies to many others, I mention only a few: in Gaelic, Sorley MacLean and Derick Thomson; in Scots, apart from MacDiarmid himself, William Soutar, Sydney Goodsir Smith, Robert Garioch, Robert McLellan, Lewis Grassic Gibbon, and Alexander Scott; in English, Norman MacCaig, Neil Gunn, Eric Linklater, Naomi Mitchison, Robin Jenkins, Edwin Morgan, Allan Massie, Alasdair Gray and A. L. Kennedy.

My present subject is not so much the literature itself but attitudes to it in Scotland and elsewhere. These attitudes have changed radically in the last hundred years or so. At the end of the First World War, MacDiarmid still found it necessary to assert that Scotland had a literary tradition. That has been obvious for centuries, but in some circles it was obscured by an Anglo-centric preoccupation and it has taken a long campaign to slacken its grip. By now, the reality and vitality of the Scottish tradition are beyond dispute. Scottish literature is now taught in universities in Scotland and in some in America, Canada, France and Germany. Scottish schools are increasingly paying more attention to Scottish languages and literature than in the past. Apart from many books on particular writers, histories of Scottish literature have been written by Kurt Wittig (1958), Maurice Lindsay (1977), Roderick Watson (1984), as an alphabetical *Companion* by Trevor Royle (1983) and in four volumes edited by

Cairns Craig (1987–8). The ten volumes of the *Scottish National Dictionary* were published between 1927 and 1976. Work continues on the *Dictionary of the Older Scottish Tongue. The Concise Scots Dictionary*, based on both of the two larger works, was published in 1985. A major work in Scots prose, William Lorimer's translation of the New Testament, was published in 1983. In spite of all this, Scots is still largely ignored by both the government and the media. Gaelic has been more successful than Scots in securing Government recognition and support and an established place in television programmes.

A number of organisations have helped to secure these advances. The Saltire Society was founded in 1936 in response to the concern over the apparent decline in Scottish life and culture. Its object was the encouragement of all the arts in Scotland and to restore the country 'to its proper place as a creative force in European civilisation'. One of its first actions was to publish a series of cheap editions of early Scottish literature at a time when no other editions were available. These 'Saltire Classics', along with programmes of readings, introduced many people to a literature of which they had heard nothing at school. New writing is encouraged and recognised by the Saltire Book Awards. The Society has also been involved in the creation in August 1997 of the Makars' Court in Edinburgh, a visible sign of the public acclaim of Scottish literature.

Shortly before the Referendum of 1979 on Home Rule, the Saltire Society invited some 200 organisations involved in the cultural life of Scotland to form a joint think-tank, the Advisory Council for the Arts in Scotland (now renamed the Arts and Democracy Forum). The intention was to draw up suggestions on policies towards the arts which would be put to the new Scottish Assembly, but AdCAS continued although the Assembly was denied by the 40% rule. One of its first campaigns was for paperback reprints of important Scottish books of all periods because most of them were out of print. It persuaded the Scottish Arts Council to introduce a scheme to which several publishers responded. This was the origin of the Canongate Classics which for ten years have been producing fine editions of precisely the kind needed. This was a vital step because unless the books are available, a literature might as well not exist.

Another powerful reinforcement was the formation in 1971 of the Association for Scottish Literary Studies (ASLS) which brought together university and school teachers of Scottish literature along with other enthusiasts. With the financial support of the Scottish Arts Council, it publishes a number of quarterly journals on literature and language, an annual anthology of new poetry and short stories and an annual volume which ranges from Dunbar to MacDiarmid. It organises conferences and exercises constant pressure to enhance the place of Scottish literature in the schools and elsewhere.

For most of this century there have been a number of literary reviews. Many have come and gone, but those which have been well established for some years are *Chapman, Cencrastus, The Edinburgh Review*, *Lines Review*, *Gairm* in Gaelic and *Lallans* in Scots.

Maurice Lindsay has been involved in most of these activities, quite apart from his own poetry (which George Bruce discusses in this volume). His changing attitude to Scotland and its literature is reflected in his autobiography, *Thank you for Having Me* (1983). He says that after the war he was 'totally obsessed by a desire to return to Scotland and play some part in reshaping it along, as I thought, the brave lines of MacDiarmid's vision of independence' (p. 85). At first he wrote poetry in Scots, but later he thought that the language had receded so rapidly under the impact of television it had been 'reduced to a mere matter of local accent ... a poor, wasted and abandoned speech' (p. 171). In fact, the autobiography is strongly marked by a disillusionment with Scotland generally. He speaks of its 'continuing decline' and 'all-too-evident national failure in political terms and economic terms' (pp. 212, 203). He thought that Scotland 'gave up the struggle for nationhood soon after the First World War' (p. 199). The bitterness of these words suggests to me that they were written in the spirit of despair which many people felt after the frustration of the Referendum of 1979. I wonder if he would still say the same after the impressive display of national resolve on 11th September 1997.

In an earlier book, *By Yon Bonnie Banks: A Gallimaufry* (1961), Lindsay had expressed a more qualified pessimism over the future of Scotland. The last chapter is headed, 'The death of Scotland?' and it suggests that Scotland is dying 'mainly because it no longer has any real desire to live'. It ends with this paragraph:

> So for me the love affair is over. The fervour, the obsession with Scottishness for its own sake, the strongly emotional response to whatever carried even the faintest Scottish overtone, all these things have faded to a gentle but regretful affection; an affection, however, which, I fancy, will persist to the end of my days.

I quote this partly because the definition of the love affair is the best one I know of the way many people, including myself, feel about Scotland, and from which we have no wish to escape. If it has ended for Lindsay, as he says, then we are fortunate that his 'gentle affection' has been strong enough to spur him to endeavours on Scotland's behalf which look to me very much like labours of love.

The most substantial of these is his *History of Scottish Literature* (1977), which I have already mentioned. This is a book of about 500 pages of which, he says in the Introduction, the main purpose is to encourage readers to share the 'enthusiasm and delight' which the literature of his own country has given him. His anthologies clearly share the same spirit. The earliest of these, *Modern Scottish Poetry: An Anthology of the Scottish Renaissance, 1920–1945*, first published in 1946, has travelled with me in many countries and has been one of my favourite books for half a century. *Scotland: An Anthology* (1974) contains prose as well as poetry and amounts to a generous sample of the whole of Scottish literature. It is a wonderful bedside book and so is *Scottish Comic Verse* (1981). Lindsay has written a book about Robert Burns and also his indispensable *Burns Encyclopaedia* (1959, 1979, 1980). This is an admirable work of reference, but it is much more than that. Lindsay in the Introduction again speaks of helping his readers to find 'pleasure and delight' in the poems and letters of Burns. That is surely the right approach to literature.

In addition to all this writing and editing (and there is much more about the Scottish countryside, architecture, music and painting) Lindsay has supported the Saltire Society, has been President of ASLS and editor of the *Saltire Review*. He presented radio and television programmes about literature and other arts in Scotland for more than twenty years. In his book, *Francis George Scott and the Scottish Renaissance* (1980), Lindsay says of the Saltire Society: 'A measure of the success of its pioneering efforts in the early days is the vastly improved state of all these concerns half a century later' (pp. 127–8). You might say exactly that of Lindsay himself. His contribution to Scottish literature, and to its reputation, influence, and appreciation, has been prodigious.

The greatly enhanced status and confidence of Scottish literature in the last hundred years or so is not unconnected with the long sequence of events which led on 11th September 1997 to the emphatic expression of the desire for the restoration of the Scottish Parliament.

Scotland has recovered the will to survive which Lindsay feared that it had lost. In his *Scottish Journey* of 1935, Edwin Muir said that Scotland was falling to pieces because there was 'no visible and effective power to hold it together' (1979 edition, p. 25). Now that we have met the challenge of that risk, we have every reason for confidence that Scottish literature will go from strength to strength.

References

1. William Donaldson: *Popular literature in Victorian Scotland* (Aberdeen, 1986) and *The Language of the people* (Aberdeen, 1989)
2. David Murison, quoted in Paul H. Scott, *Towards Independence* (Edinburgh, 1991 and 1996), p. 137

———————————— • ◆ ●— ◆ • ————————————

Poetry may not have been the only interest in my life, but it has always been by far the most insistent. In my own eyes my activities in broadcasting, journalism and administration have occupied a supportive role to my conviction that poetry matters supremely, and for its own sake, however it may fare with current fashion. Fortunately, when the cliques and the claques fall finally silent, posterity undertakes its own unhurried assessments and pronounces measured judgements against which, changing tastes apart, there is no appeal. Before that prospect I rest content.

(*Thank You for Having Me*, page 174)

———————————— • ◆ ●— ◆ • ————————————

CHAPTER TEN

Burns's Humanity

Kenneth Simpson

'PEOPLE POETRY' – with this term Maurice Lindsay identified 'the outstanding characteristic of Scottish poetry down the ages'[1] in his address to the International Bicentenary Burns Conference at the University of Strathclyde in January 1996. As Dr Lindsay indicated, it is a concept which explains the wide-ranging and enduring appeal of the poetry of Robert Burns. Taking its cue from Maurice Lindsay's suggestive phrase, this contribution addresses the social breadth of Burns's poetic vision, his keen sense of individuality, the humane values which he evinces towards his fellow-beings, and the extent to which he both recognises and exemplifies human complexity.

Burns typifies a tradition in Scottish poetry, stretching back via Fergusson and Ramsay to the Makars, of carnivalesque celebration of communal gatherings. These stanzas from 'The Holy Fair' are representative:

> Here, stands a shed to fend the show'rs,
>   An' screen our countra Gentry;
> There, *Racer-Jess,* an' twathree wh-res,
>   Are blinkan at the entry:
> Here sits a raw o' tittlan jads,
>   Wi' heaving breasts an' bare neck;
> An' there, a batch o' *Wabster lads,*
>   Blackguarding frae Kilmarnock
>   For *fun* this day.
>
> Here, some are thinkan on their sins,
>   An' some upo' their claes;
> Ane curses feet that fyl'd his shins,
>   Anither sighs an' prays:
> On this hand sits a Chosen swatch,
>   Wi' screw'd-up, grace-proud faces;
> On that, a set o' chaps, at watch,
>   Thrang winkan on the lasses
>   To *chairs* that day.[2]

Burns understands human nature; above all, he discerns and relishes its diverse manifestations:

> Now *Clinkumbell*, wi' rattlan tow,
>   Begins to jow an' croon;
> Some swagger hame, the best they dow,
>   Some wait the afternoon.
> At slaps the billies halt a blink,
>   Till lasses strip their shoon:
> Wi' *faith* an' *hope*, an' *love* an' *drink*,
>   They're a' in famous tune
>   For crack that day.

> How monie hearts this day converts,
>   O' Sinners and o' Lasses!
> Their hearts o' stane, gin night are gane
>   As saft as ony flesh is.
> There's some are fou o' *love divine*:
>   There's some are fou o' *brandy*;
> An' monie jobs that day begin,
>   May end in *Houghmagandie*
>   Some ither day.

Generating much of the finest of Burns's poetry is an insight into the reality of life in the rural community. It is characteristic of Burns to place the human in the over-arching context of all created life. Even in the personal mode of the verse-epistle Burns habitually begins by locating himself in relation to the natural world; witness the opening lines of 'Second Epistle to J. Lapraik':

> While new-ca'd kye rowte at the stake,
> An' pownies reek in pleugh or braik,
> This hour on e'enin's edge I take,
>   To own I'm debtor,
> To honest-hearted, auld Lapraik,
>   For his kind *letter*.

This is not mere scene-setting; rather, from the farmer's practical sense of his environment there develops a totality of vision whereby Burns finds in the duality of 'Nature' the consonance between human experience and natural setting which is integral to his world-view:

> For thus the royal *Mandate* ran,
> When first the human race began,
> 'The social, friendly, honest man,
>   'Whate'er he be,

' 'Tis *he* fulfils *great Nature's plan,*
'And none but *he.*'

This philosophy is both life-affirming and, as the moving simplicity of 'On the Birth of a Posthumous Child' indicates, consolingly life-reaffirming:

Sweet floweret, pledge o' meikle love,
    And ward o' mony a prayer,
What heart o' stane wad thou na move,
    Sae helpless, sweet, and fair.

November hirples o'er the lea,
    Chill, on thy lovely form;
And gane, alas! the sheltering tree,
    Should shield thee frae the storm.

May HE who gives the rain to pour,
    And wings the blast to blaw,
Protect thee frae the driving shower,
    The bitter frost and snaw.

May HE, the friend of woe and want,
    Who heals life's various stounds,
Protect and guard the mother plant,
    And heal her cruel wounds.

But late she flourished, rooted fast,
    Fair on the summer morn:
Now, feebly bends she, in the blast,
    Unsheltered and forlorn.

Blest be thy bloom, thou lovely gem,
    Unscathed by ruffian hand!
And from thee many a parent stem
    Arise to deck our land.

Like that of the Makars, Ramsay, and Fergusson, Burns's social vision embraces contraries and reflects a keen sense of the – often bizarre – particular. Here, for instance, in 'The Holy Fair', the hellfire sermon of 'Black Russell' is deflated by the real-life detail:

A vast, unbottom'd, boundless *Pit,*
    Fill'd fou o' *lowan brunstane.*
Whase raging flame, an' scorching heat,
    Wad melt the hardest whunstane!
The *half-asleep* start up wi' fear,
    An' think they hear it roaran,
When presently it does appear,

> 'Twas but some neebor *snoran*
> Asleep that day.

If the panoramic social canvasses of his vernacular predecessors set precedent for the recognition that society comprises a mass of individuals, another influence was almost certainly the early English novel, and above all the works of Smollett, whom Burns praised for his 'incomparable humor'[3] and Sterne, whose *Tristram Shandy*, together with Mackenzie's *The Man of Feeling*, were the poet's 'bosom favorites' (*Letters*, I, 141). Smollett's caricaturist's eye had discerned the physical and behavioural idiosyncrasies of the individual, and his epistolary novel, *Humphry Clinker*, with Sterne's *Tristram Shandy* and *A Sentimental Journey*, demonstrated the vagaries of the individual perspective. Burns warmed to Captain Francis Grose both as an antiquarian and as a Shandean original: 'I have never seen a man of more original observation, anecdote & remark', he wrote to Mrs. Dunlop, with the acknowledgement of the influence of Sterne quite explicit:

> ... if you discover a chearful-looking grig of an old, fat fellow, the precise figure of Dr Slop, wheeling about your avenue in his own carriage with a pencil & paper in his hand, you may conclude, 'Thou art the man' (*Letters*, I, 423).

Burns's capacity to render individuality is one of the vitalising elements in his poetry. In 'The Death and Dying Words of Poor Mailie' the dying ewe becomes recognisably the genteel, class-conscious mother, protective of her young and concerned that they should 'ay keep mind to moop an' mell, /Wi' sheep o' credit like thysel!'

Keats was to extol Shakespeare's 'innate universality'.[4] Burns possessed the same quality, and it found expression in the imaginative sympathy whereby he could become otherness. For Keats, 'negative capability'[5] was the essential characteristic of a poet, with Keats himself claiming, 'if a Sparrow come before my Window, I take part in its existence and pick about the gravel'.[6] Burns demonstrates precisely this capacity when he renders what it is to be the startled mouse – 'Wee, sleeket, cowran, tim'rous *beastie*,/ O, what a panic's in thy breastie!' – and when, from feigned indignation at the effrontery of the louse, his tone towards it becomes one of amused but affectionate concern, mingled with grudging admiration for its daring ascent of 'Miss's fine Lunardi'.

Of the Scottish philosophers, Hutcheson, Hume and Smith had each emphasised the moral dimension to sympathy.[7] Burns's imaginative sympathy – the essential humanity of his vision – is wide-ranging. In 'A Dream', prompted by Thomas Warton's 'Ode XVII for his Majesty's Birthday, June 4th 1786', social radicalism is fused with an awareness of the manifest frailties – and hence the ordinary humanity – of the Royal Family; for instance, what first appears to be an attack on the Prince of Wales becomes almost sympathetic identification as the poet warms to him for his weaknesses:

> Yet aft a ragged *Cowte's* been known
>   To mak a noble *Aiver*;
> So, ye may dousely fill a Throne,
>   For a' their clish-ma-claver:
> There, Him at *Agincourt* wha shone,
>   Few better were or braver;
> And yet, wi' funny, queer *Sir John*,
>   He was an unco shaver,
>   For monie a day.

Burns has the imaginative capacity to introduce the most unlikely recruits into the human family. In 'Poem on Life, Addressed to Colonel De Peyster', the Devil is identified as a revolutionary – 'that curst carmagnole, auld Satan' ('carmagnole' being a song and dance, and also a jacket, favoured by the French Revolutionaries) – and compared to a cat ('bawd'rons') waiting to catch the rat that is 'our sinfu' saul'. Familiarised in 'Address to the Deil' as 'Auld Hornie, Satan, Nick, or Clootie', the Devil ceases to be Milton's 'chief of many throned pow'rs', is enlisted in the community as, in effect, the local nuisance, and becomes ultimately the object of the speaker's compassionate concern:

> But fare you weel, auld *Nickie-ben* !
> O wad ye tak a thought an' men'!
> Ye aiblins might – I dinna ken –
>   Still hae a *stake* –
> I'm wae to think upo' yon den,
>   Ev'n for your sake.

A wider interest lurks behind the altruism here, however: if the Devil could bring himself to reform, what might be the benefits to the human community?

Epitomising the democratic thrust of his poetry, human fellowship is at the heart of Burns's value-system. Fortified by alcohol, the speaker in 'Death and Doctor Hornbook' is Burns's common man at his naturally sociable best: the grotesque figure of Death is invited to join him for a drink; when Death, pathetic and down on his luck, declines, the speaker provides him with a welcome and sympathetic listener. Burns's humanity is exemplified in his celebration of fellow-ship. In their shared penury his Jolly Beggars rejoice that 'Liberty's a glorious feast!' In 'The Twa Dogs' the fellowship of aristocrat's retriever and farmer's collie is offered as a contrasting model to the rank-riven human society; and the point is underscored by the dogs' shared vernacular.

In Caesar's criticism of the artificial lifestyle of the aristocracy – 'There's sic parade, sic pomp an' art,/The joy can scarcely reach the heart' – is a clear statement of Burns's cherishing of the natural-ness of the heart's affections. The letters regularly testify to the centrality of this notion to Burns's world-view: Mrs. Dunlop is referred to John Hildebroad's epitaph with the comment, 'This speaks more to my heart, & has more of the genuine spirit of Religion in it, than is to be found in whole waggon-loads of Div-inity' (*Letters*, II, 57); Dr. Moore is assured, 'almost all my Religious tenets originate from my heart' (*Letters*, II, 73); Josiah Walker is reminded of 'the bedlam warmth of a Poet's heart' (*Letters*, I, 155); Patrick Miller is revered as 'a MAN whose benevolence of heart does honor to Human-nature' (*Letters*, II, 190); and there is this candid acknowledgement that alcohol may help loosen the bonds of rational restraint: 'This I write to you when I am miserably fou, consequently it must be the sentiments of my heart' (*Letters*, I, 117). The morality of the heart underpins many of the poems and is encapsulated in these lines from 'Epistle to Davie, a Brother Poet': 'The heart ay's the part ay,/That makes us right or wrang'. This sense informed much of Burns's writing, including his judgements of the work of others. His 'strictures on Miss Williams Poem on the Slave trade' are revealing: '"to dare to feel" is an idea that I do not altogether like' (*Letters*, I, 428–9); and William Cowper's 'The Task' is commended for exemplifying 'the Religion of God & Na-ture; the Religion that exalts, that ennobles man' (*Letters*, II, 269–70).

It is certainly the case that Burns believed in what Keats was to term 'the holiness of the Heart's affections'.[8] Yet a reader of the collected letters of Burns might be forgiven the suspicion that the man of feeling doth protest too much. At times Burns seems intent on projecting self-images; here, for instance, with a certain bravado to James Smith:

> For me, I am witless wild, and wicked; and have scarcely any vestige of the image of God left me, except a pretty large portion of honour and an enthusiastic, incoherent Benevolence (*Letters*, I, 45).

As Carol McGuirk has shown,[9] the vogue of sensibility fostered such posturing: the man of feeling found satisfaction not just in practising benevolence but in the 'self-approving joy' that derived from contemplating himself in the role of benefactor. Accordingly, Burns flaunts his sensibility, most notably in the correspondence with Mrs. McLehose ('Clarinda'), whom he assures, 'mine is the Religion of the bosom' (*Letters*, I, 204). The literary models, of whom his words are sometimes redolent, are Mackenzie's Harley and Sterne's Yorick and Uncle Toby. According to the last-named, 'injuries come only from the heart';[10] to Maria Riddell, Burns writes, 'If it is true, that "Offences come only from the heart;" – before you I am guiltless' (*Letters*, II, 275).

Behind the posturing is a practical realism which surfaces from time to time. *The Man of Feeling* is, for Burns, 'a book I prize next to the Bible' (*Letters*, I, 17); yet in the following it is designated a 'performance' and Burns's common sense manifests itself:

> His Man of Feeling ... I estimate as the first Performance in its kind I ever saw. From what book, moral or even Pious, will the susceptible young mind receive impressions more congenial to Humanity & Kindness, Generosity & Benevolence, in short, all that ennobles the Soul to herself, or endears her to others, than from the simple affecting tale of poor Harley? Still, with all my admiration of McKenzie's writings I do not know if they are the fittest reading for a young Man who is about to set out, as the phrase is, to make his way into life (*Letters*, II, 25).

Burns recognised clearly the psychological complexity of the individual, as these lines from 'Sketch. Inscribed to the Rt. Hon. Ch. J. Fox Esq.' indicate:

> Good lord, what is man! for as simple he looks,
> Do but try to develope his hooks and his crooks,
> With his depths and his shallows, his good and his evil,
> All in all, he's a problem must puzzle the devil.

But human complexity is beyond explanation: 'For spite of his fine theoretic positions,/Mankind is a science defies definitions'.

Language fails, especially as a means of rendering the complexity of feelings.' '"Love",' Burns notes, 'owing to the intermingledoms of the good & the bad, the pure & the impure, in this world, [is] rather an equivocal term for expressing one's sentiments & sensations' (*Letters*, II, 143).

Burns exemplifies the psychological complexity which he has identified. 'Burns contains multitudes':[11] thus R. D. S. Jack in his paper to the Bicentenary Conference. Testimony is there in abundance in the diverse *personae* of both letters and poems and in the linguistic range. Recently Edwin Morgan remarked on 'how bilingual, and convincingly bilingual [Burns] must have been'.[12] One of the effects of the Union was to focus Scottish minds even further on issues of language. With the purity of expression of English to which Dugald Stewart testified,[13] Burns was able to combine the rich vein of expressive vernacular Scots, for which there was encouraging precedent in Ramsay and Fergusson. Characteristic of the various revivals in Scottish poetry, including that of the 1920s and that, more recent, to which the dedicatee of this volume has made distinguished contribution, is the rich linguistic diversity upon which poets have drawn.

Prominent in recent Burns scholarship is the recognition of the range of the poet's reading and his accessibility to influence (here the work of David Daiches and Thomas Crawford has been seminal).[14] One result has been to dispel once and for all the myth of the 'Heaven-taught ploughman' (in whose creation Burns readily participated) and replace the constrainingly reductive simplicity of the icon with the reality of a multi–voiced poet and correspondent and a highly complex individual. One of the paradoxes informing Burns is that a poet so effective in the denunciation of pretension should employ so tellingly therein the pretence of *persona*. Equally striking is the co-existence of such antithetical voices within the one poet's corpus, a point noted by Ian S. Ross in his comment that 'Burns developed a writing career that combined display of both the mocking laughter of Voltaire and the tears of Rousseau'.[15] From the pen which exulted in 'fair, candid ridicule' (*Letters*, II, 345) came the tenderness of 'Ae Fond Kiss' and 'A red, red Rose'. The versatility encompassed the use of poetic modes and stanza forms: Standard Habbie was used for, respectively, serious and comic effects in 'Elegy on Capt. Matthew Henderson' and 'Tam Samson's Elegy', with the convention of nature mourning observed in the former and totally inverted in the latter.

The rich range of the poetry should be regarded primarily in terms of the poet's formal and stylistic virtuosity. However, it may also be related to a complex individual's need to give expression to the diverse, and sometimes conflicting, aspects of his own psyche. To his brother, William, he noted ruefully:

> There is an excellent Scots Saying, that 'A man's mind is his kingdom'. – It is certainly so; but how few can govern that kingdom with propriety (*Letters*, I, 384).

Burns seems to have viewed his internal dichotomies with a curious hybrid of abjectness and fascination. He values Ainslie's friendship for his responsiveness to his extremes of mood:

> You will think it romantic when I tell you that I find the idea of your friendship almost necessary to my existence. You assume a proper length of face in my bitter hours of blue-devilism, and you laugh fully up to my highest wishes at my *good things* (*Letters*, I, 176).

In a letter of the same period (winter 1787) he writes of himself as being 'almost in a state of perpetual warfare, and alas! frequent defeat' (*Letters*, I, 185).

The flux of the mind – not least his own – fascinated Burns. The work of John Locke – 'the Great and likewise Good Mr. Locke, Author of the famous essay on the human understanding' (*Letters*, I, 212) – figures amongst his early reading as listed to Moore (*Letters*, I, 138), and in several letters (e.g. *Letters*, I, 225; II, 347) he refers to his association of ideas. In Sterne's *Tristram Shandy* Burns encountered a fictional application of Locke's thesis which must certainly have appealed to the innovatively radical side of his nature: here was the literary exemplification of the often-whimsical flux of the mental life. The Shandean *persona* pervades Burns's letters.[16] Burns is the self-conscious narrator (*Letters*, II, 16) and the Shandean free spirit, one of 'the harum-scarum Sons of Imagination and Whim' (*Letters*, I, 109); consequently, the course of his life is determined by it: 'That Fancy and Whim, keen sensibility and riotous Passions may still make him zig-zag in his future path of life, is far from improbable' (*Letters*, I, 146). In the fiction of Sterne Burns's anti-rationalist propensity found welcome endorsement. Walter Shandy's dogged pursuit of Truth by allegedly rational means leads him into ever-escalating heights of absurdity. This must have been music to the ears of Burns who was emphatically opposed to adherence to system. Perhaps there was in both Sterne and Burns a Celtic antipathy to man-made institutions and their supposed authority. Revealingly, Burns writes to George Thomson:

> But, let our National Music preserve its native features. – They are, I own, frequently wild, & unreduceable to the more modern rules; but on that very eccentricity, perhaps, depends a great part of their effect (*Letters*, II, 211).

Significantly, too, one of his most brilliant achievements, 'Holy Willie's Prayer', renders the flux of a mind imprisoned within a static value-system; sublimely detached from his creation's self-revelation, Burns allows Holy Willie's hybrid status – he is both pathetic in his limitation and awesome in his hypocrisy – to unfold.

The example of Sterne in finding a literary mode whereby the claims of creative energy, mental flux, and emotional complexity might take precedence over fixity of values was highly influential. Fluctuation in the attitude of the *persona* characterises some of Burns's finest poems, and most notably 'To a Louse', 'Address to the Deil', 'Death and Doctor Hornbook', and 'Tam o' Shanter'. But in the epistle he was to find the poetic mode which best accommodated his sense of the flux of the mind and the values which it bred. 'Epistle to James Smith' exemplifies the former point in its entirety and the latter towards its conclusion:

> O ye, douse folk, that live by rule,
> Grave, tideless-blooded, calm and cool,
> Compar'd wi' you – O fool! fool! fool!
> How much unlike!
> Your hearts are just a standing pool,
> Your lives, a dyke!
>
> Nae hare-brain'd, sentimental traces,
> In your unletter'd, nameless faces!
> In *arioso* trills and graces
> Ye never stray,
> But *gravissimo*, solemn basses
> Ye hum away.
>
> Ye are sae *grave*, nae doubt ye're *wise*;
> Nae ferly tho' ye do despise
> The hairum-scairum, ram-stam boys,
> The rattling squad:
> I see ye upward cast your eyes –
> Ye ken the road.

In a short life Burns had a prolific literary output. Begun early, the voracious reading continued throughout adulthood. In his quest for knowledge Burns was truly the child of the Scottish Enlightenment, testifying to its generalist nature. Like the mind celebrated in this volume, Burns's ranged widely in its interests. With Mrs. Dunlop he discussed French drama, Dryden's Virgil and Pope's Homer, and recent developments in chemistry and natural physics; he had an understanding of Hutton's evolutionary geology; he wrote to Archibald Alison, 'I never read a book which gave me such a quantum of information, and added so much to my stock of ideas, as your Essay on the principles of taste' (*Letters*, II, 71–2); and he longed to meet 'that extraordinary man, Smith', adding, 'I could not have given any mere *man*, credit for half the intelligence Mr. Smith discovers in his book [*The Wealth of Nation*]' (*Letters*, I, 410).

Such range of reference is beyond most of us; nor can we all be the man of 'Independent Mind' (*Letters*, II, 264) that Burns claimed to be. How, then, to explain the paradox of the universality of appeal of this unique individual? The easy answer would be that in this rich and complex diversity there is something for everyone; but the danger is that each will take from Burns only what he wishes to find, thus pinning down the chameleon or halting the flux of the remarkable mind.

'At times his energy seems almost demonic', the novelist, Carl MacDougall, wrote recently of Burns.[17] How revealing that it was with Milton's Satan that Burns so readily identified (e.g. *Letters*, I, 121, 123). Seeking an analogy for his life, Burns opted for the following: 'the resemblance that hits my fancy best is, that poor, blackguard Miscreant, Satan, who, as Holy Writ tells us, roams about like a roaring lion, seeking, *searching*, whom he may devour' (*Letters*, II, 44). Burns's 'demonic energy' – the remarkable chameleon capacity, the insatiable quest for knowledge – are, writ large, the quest of Everyman to confront his will o' the wisp identity, to come to terms with his nature, to apprehend self, a task exacerbated if one possesses the transformative power of the imagination. Here, too, Sterne set a precedent; for Yorick:

There is not a more perplexing affair in life to me, than to set about telling anyone who I am – for there is scarce anybody I cannot give a better account of than of myself; and I have often wished I could do it in a single word – and have an end of it. It was the only time and occasion in my life, I could accomplish this to any purpose – for Shakespear lying upon the table, and recollecting I was in his books, I took up *Hamlet*, and turning immediately to the grave-diggers scene in the fifth act, I laid my finger upon YORICK, and advancing the book to the Count, with my finger all the way over the name – *Me voici*! said I.[18]

Burns must have wished that for him it could be as easy; and it may be that the increasing tendency in his later letters to refer to himself as BURNS represented just that – an attempt to fix self. In Sterne, too, Burns found a precedent for the humane attitude to what he himself so exemplified – the elusive nature of the self.

The competitive ethos engendered by the Union stimulated intense literary and philosophical activity in Scotland, but the greater the range of intellectual and imaginative possibilities thereby opened up, the greater the degree of uncertainty as to identity, both personal and national. Recent Burns scholarship has penetrated beyond the icon to the complex writer and human being. Perhaps as we Scots discern the reality of national figures such as Burns, so we further the process of identification of ourselves and our reborn nation.

Notes

1. Maurice Lindsay, 'Burns and Scottish Poetry', in *Love and Liberty. Robert Burns: A Bicentenary Celebration*, ed. Kenneth Simpson (East Linton, 1997), p. 145.
2. Robert Burns, *The Poems and Songs*, ed. James Kinsley, 3 vols (Oxford, 1968).
3. *The Letters of Robert Burns*, ed. J. De Lancey Ferguson, 2 vols; 2nd edn ed. G. Ross Roy (Oxford, 1985), I, 296.
4. C. and M. Cowden Clark, *Recollections of Writers* (London, 1878), p. 156.
5. *The Letters of John Keats*, ed. H. Buxton Forman (London, 1895), p. 57.
6. *The Letters of John Keats*, p. 54.
7. See further Kenneth Simpson, *The Protean Scot: The Crisis of Identity in Eighteenth-Century Scottish Literature* (Aberdeen, 1988), pp. 149–50.
8. *The Letters of John Keats*, p. 52.
9. Carol McGuirk, *Robert Burns and the Sentimental Era* (East Linton, 1997).
10. *Tristram Shandy*, III, x.
11. '"Castalia's Stank": Burns and Rhetoric', in *Love and Liberty*. p. 112.
12. 'A Poet's Response to Burns', in *Burns Now*, ed. Kenneth Simpson (Edinburgh, 1994) p. 3.
13. W. L. Renwick (ed.), *Burns As Others Saw Him* (Edinburgh, 1959), pp. 11–12.
14. David Daiches, *Robert Burns* (Edinburgh, 1966); Thomas Crawford, *Burns: A Study of the Poems and Songs* (Edinburgh, 1960).
15. 'Burns and the *Siècle des Lumières*', in *Love and Liberty*, p. 219.

16. See, further, *The Protean Scot*, Ch 8.
17. 'Rabbietising Reality', in *Love and Liberty*, p. 41.
18. Laurence Sterne, *A Sentimental Journey through France and Italy*, ed. Graham Petrie, with intro. by A. Alvarez (Harmondsworth, 1967), p. 109.

Although I did not then know it, by 1943 McDiarmid's greatest poetry had long since been written. It was still virtually unread, even in Scotland, although in England T. S. Eliot knew of *Sangschaw* and *Pennywheep*, and spoke of their author as his equal. During another home leave I went into the once-elegant Lyons' Store – it stood on the corner of Sauchiehall Street and Elmbank Street, until a runaway lorry crashed down the opposite hill, virtually demolishing it – where Valda, the poet's wife, was then working in the book department. For two shillings and sixpence (twelve and a half pence) I bought copies of the first editions of *Sangschaw*, *Pennywheep* and *A Drunk Man Looks at the Thistle*. A mere five hundred copies of these, his three finest books, had been published a quarter of a century before, but so poor were the sales that they were still available.

(*Thank You for Having Me*, page 62)

CHAPTER ELEVEN

Scottish Poets and the National Imagination

Cairns Craig

I

IN THE 1930s Scotland's two leading poet-critics were engaged in a bitter dispute about the relationship of modern Scottish poetry to the Scottish past. For Edwin Muir, the route that had been charted by Hugh MacDiarmid, however ambitious, was fundamentally flawed: MacDiarmid's effort to recreate Scots as a language capable of expressing the totality of modern experience was, according to Muir, doomed to failure. However good MacDiarmid's poetry, it 'left Scots verse very much where it was before' and this because major poetry can never be produced 'where the poet feels in one language and thinks in another' (*Scott and Scotland*, p. 22): for Muir, 'the prerequisite of an autonomous literature is a homogeneous language' (*ibid.*, p. 19), but because of the dominance of English for all intellectual and theoretical purposes a poetry which rested on the traditions of Scots could never be the foundation of a national literature. Scots was not a language in which the totality of the national experience or the novelty of modernity could be expressed:

> Every genuine literature, in other words, requires as its condition a means of expression capable of dealing with everything the mind can think or the imagination conceive. It must be a language for criticism as well as poetry, for abstract speculation as well as fact, and since we live in a scientific age, it must be a language for science as well. A language which can serve for one or two of those purposes but cannot serve for the others is, considered as a vehicle for literature, merely an anachronism ... If Henryson and Dunbar had written in prose they would have written in the same language as they used for poetry, for their minds were still whole; but Burns never thought of doing so, nor did Scott, nor did Stevenson, nor has any Scottish writer since. In an organic literature poetry is always influencing prose, and prose poetry; and their interaction energizes them both.
>
> (Muir, *Scott and Scotland*, pp. 20–1)

The idea of a 'whole mind' as expressed in a whole language and dealing with the totality of experience is fundamental to Muir's conception of poetry and to his sense of why Scottish poetry had failed: poetry, for Muir, is fundamentally allied to national tradition, but Scottish national tradition having failed, there is no choice but for Scottish poets to escape the incapacitating environment of Scotland by joining the tradition of English poetry:

> ... Scotland can only create a national literature by writing in English. This may sound paradoxical: ... Irish nationality cannot be said to be any less intense than ours; but Ireland produced a national literature not by clinging to Irish dialect but by adopting English and making it into a language fit for all its purposes. The poetry of Mr. Yeats belongs to English literature, but no one would deny that it belongs to Irish literature pre-eminently and essentially. The difference between contemporary Irish and contemporary Scottish literature is that the first is central and homogeneous and the second is parochial and conglomerate; and this because it does not possess an organ for the expression of a whole and unambiguous nationality.
>
> (Muir, *Scott and Scotland*, pp. 178–9)

There have been many, of course, who have challenged the view that Yeats's poetry belongs 'essentially' to Irish literature rather than to English literature, and many who would not acknowledge the distinction: literature written in English in Ireland is 'essentially' a part of English literature. The relation of individual poet to a particular national tradition is much more complex than Muir allows, but Muir's argument is probably the single most influential source of later conceptions of Scottish culture and of its fundamental failure both to maintain a significant tradition and to engage with the modern world.

To MacDiarmid, committed anglophobe, the path implied by Muir was, of course, impossible. He would continue to assert the importance of challenging rather than accepting incorporation into the English tradition. But the paradox of MacDiarmid's position was that his own view of the Scottish situation was, if anything, even bleaker than Muir's. 'A Drunk Man Looks at the Thistle', the poem that was written to be the founding epic of a new Scottish identity and which, to some extent, has come to be seen as the founding document of modern Scottish literature, presented — despite its challenging and ambitious effort to recreate a vital poetic language in Scots — a view of Scottish culture which was just as negative as Muir's. In MacDiarmid's view Scottish culture is not only degenerate in its outcome but flawed from its earliest stages. His effort to recreate a Scottish culture may be founded, in linguistic terms, on going 'back to Dunbar', but the effort to re-establish connections with some fundamental origin of Scottish culture effectively denies the whole intervening history of the culture he is claiming to recuperate. MacDiarmid's 'renaissance' of Scottish culture is not a renewal of the culture's whole past in a new historical situation, or the reinvention of supposedly archetypal national myths in modern forms, but an attempted reinvention of the culture in a way that will negate all that the actual culture has been. In 'A Drunk Man' the primary focus of MacDiarmid's attack is the debased culture of nineteenth-century Scotland, an attack that has been endlessly repeated in twentieth-century Scotland by an insistent repetition of MacDiarmid's scorn for the Kailyard literature of the 1880s and 1890s and with which Scottish popular culture had become infused in the Edwardian era:

> Heifetz in tartan, and Sir Harry Lauder!
> Whaur's Isadora Duncan dancin' noo?
> Is Mary Garden in Chicago still
> And Duncan Grant in Paris – and me fou'?
>
> *Sic transit gloria Scotiae* – a' the floo'ers
> O' the forest are wede awa'. (A blin bird's next
> Is aiblins biggin' in the thistle tho'?
> And better blin' if'ts brood is like the rest!)
> (*Collected Poems*, I, p. 84)

But the denial goes much deeper: denial of such outcomes of the development of Scottish culture fundamentally undermines the origins of that culture by discerning in its conclusion originary flaws which have led inevitably to this contemporary cultural wasteland. It is not simply that the legacy of Burns has been debased by his imitators, but that Burns himself was part of a culture crippled from its inception and in its development — or, rather, in its lack of development. The need to return to Dunbar is driven by the failure of everything that has succeeded the founding achievements of Scottish culture:

> Puir Burns, wha's bouquet like a shot kail blaws
> – Will this rouch sicht no' gi'e the orchids pause?
> The Gairden o' the Muses may be braw,
> But nane like oors can breenge and eat ana!
>
> And owre the kailyard-wa' Dunbar they've flung,
> And a' their countrymen that e'er ha'e sung

> For ither than ploomen's lugs or to enrichen
> Plots on Parnassus set apairt for kitchen.
>
> Ploomen and ploomen's wives – shades o' the Manse
> May weel be at the heid o' sic a dance,
> As through the polish't ha's o' Europe leads
> The rout o' bagpipes, haggis, and sheep's heids!
>
> The vandal Scot! Frae Brankstone's deidly barrow
> I struggle yet to free a'e winsome marrow,
> To show what Scotland micht ha hed instead
> O' this preposterous Presbyterian breed.
>
> (*Collected Poems*, I, p. 106)

The actuality of Scottish tradition has to be set aside in order to make space for a Scotland that might have been, a Scotland that MacDiarmid will *will* into existence entirely out of the resources of his own consciousness, a Scotland in the image of the poet himself.

The paradox of MacDiarmid's 'renaissance', in other words, was that it required first the execution of the culture that had actually existed in Scotland for the previous four hundred years, an erasure of identity even more radical than Muir's resigned acceptance that the story of Scottish literature was one of the 'disintegration' of the possibilities of a real literature. While Yeats in Ireland could contemplate the portraits in the National Gallery and see in them a world his poetry had brought into existence, MacDiarmid would complain that

> Just as Frenchmen, loathing war,
> With the intelligent distaste of that paradoxical nation,
> Fought for Anatole France and the Louvre,
> Germans for Bach, Beethoven, and Bierhalle,
> Italians for Verdi and the Sistine Chapel.
> We Scots have nothing to fight for like any of these.
>
> (*Collected Poems*, I, p. 628)

MacDiarmid's nationalism was not a passion for an existing Scotland or even for a lost Scotland but a *cri de coeur* at its absence.

MacDiarmid and Muir may have been deeply opposed on a personal level but their views of Scottish tradition, far from being in opposition to one another, shared a deep similarity: Scottish culture was a failure, an emptiness, its artists and writers people who could not escape the destructive effects of their cultural context. Muir's analysis of Walter Scott in *Scott and Scotland* provided the rationale for the failure:

... men of Scott's enormous genius have rarely Scott's faults; they may have others but not these particular ones; and so I was forced to account for the hiatus in Scott's endowment by considering the environment in which he lived, by invoking the fact — if the reader will agree it is one — that he spent most of his days in a hiatus, in a country, that is to say, which was neither a nation nor a province, and had, instead of a centre, a blank, an Edinburgh, in the middle of it. But this Nothing in which Scott wrote was not merely a spatial one; it was a temporal Nothing as well, dotted with a few disconnected figures arranged at abrupt intervals: Henryson, Dunbar, Allan Ramsay and Burns, with a rude buttress of ballads and folk songs to shore them up and keep them from falling.

(Muir, Scott and Scotland, pp. 11–12)

If MacDiarmid thought that he could radically overstep the Scottish tradition by a declaration of 'precedents not traditions' and simply overleap all the intermediary failures by going back to Dunbar, Muir insisted on pointing out that the whole tradition had failed to provide the basis on which Scottish writers could, now or in the past, build successful works of literature. That deeply negative conception of Scottish culture was to be recorded in one of Muir's most powerful poems, 'Scotland 1941':

> ... smoke and dearth and money everywhere
> Mean heirlooms of each fainter generation,
> And mummied housegods in their musty niches,
> Burns and Scott, sham bards of a sham nation.
>
> (Collected Poems, p. 97)

Sham bards were all that a sham nation could provide, and however heroically MacDiarmid exerted himself, he could not create a substitute for the real traditions which his country had failed to provide or for its failure to develop a language adequate to his own imaginative purposes:

> God gied man speech and speech created thocht.
> He gied man speech but to the Scots gied nocht
> Barrin' this clytach that they've never brocht
> To onything but sic a Blottie O
> As some bairn's copybook micht show.
>
> (Collected Poems, I, p. 115)

Far from being, as Mallarmé had envisaged, 'a purifier of the language of the tribe', Scottish poets in the early part of the twentieth century were the elegists of their languages, a position given its most intense expression in Gaelic by Sorley Maclean:

I do not see the sense of my toil
putting thoughts in a dying tongue
now when the whoredom of Europe
is murder erect and agony.
                    (*Collected Poems*, p. 157)

It is a fear, however, which echoes in all those who struggle to maintain the distinctness of a Scottish tradition founded in the distinctness of its languages. In the work of MacDiarmid's major successors in Scots, Goodsir Smith and Robert Garioch, the poet's effort is under continual threat of elision by the death of the tradition of which he is a part. In the case of Goodsir Smith, this leads to a fantastical inflation of the poetic persona matched by a deep self-mockery: in 'Under the Eildon Tree' the whole of European culture is assembled to reveal the fundamental emptiness of the poet's situation:

Defeatit by his ain back-slitherin
Efter lang strauchle wi the serpent slee
Lea him at least outgang wi mockerie,
The Makar macironical!
A sang on his perjurit lips
And naething in the pouch
        – Or in the hert, for that!

                    Music, maestro!
                    (*Collected Poems*, p. 185)

And in Garioch's case, despite the constant fun and wit of his poetic imagination, the sense of a tradition has to be maintained by a personal commitment of the poet to his predecessors, a commitment which no longer connects with the culture around him. 'To Robert Fergusson' celebrates the earlier Edinburgh poet in a language which unites eighteenth century to twentieth:

Pechan, I turn, whilst aye your leid
of lowan Scots sounds in my heid
wi levan braith, tho ye ligg deid;
        I glowre faur doun
and see the waesome wrak outspreid
        of your auld toun.

The unity between past and present enacted in Garioch's language is, however, a personal commitment, a commitment of the poet who must rejoin a modern world that has no need of the linguistic riches he or his great predecessor have to offer:

Syne trauchlan up the brae yince mair,
frae Canogait, I leave ye there,
whar wee white roses scent the air
      about your grave,
and til some suburb new and bare
      gang wi the lave.
      (*Collected Poems*, p. 26)

The tradition which MacDiarmid sought to re-establish survives, but it survives not as the flowering of a renaissance but as a sustained act of resistance, a refusal to accept that the 'auld sang' should be allowed to end or that the speech of the streets and fields cannot still be translated into the words of the poet. Among contemporary poets, Raymond Vettese's 'My Carrion Words' might stand as commentary on this tradition of poetic of resistance:

In deep
o dairk sleep
I dreamt my words
gaithert like stairvin birds
on a bare tree
and skreiched owre me
wi carrion hoast:
Lost! Lost!

...

Whaun I woke
the day spoke
wi anither voice
that croodled douce choice:
give up this nonsense,
this pretence;
what's gone is gone, here's
English for contemporary ears.

But ach, I doot
I'm no cut oot
for sic mense
(that's dowit leid for 'common sense');
the auld coorse Scotland's in me,
an the bare tree
an' the stairvin birds:
frae sic as them, frae yon, my carrion words.
      (Dunn, *The Faber Book of Twentieth Century
      Scottish Verse*, p. 362)

These poets might be exploiters of the linguistic resources that Mac-Diarmid had made available but they were also inheritors of the deep pessimism about Scottish traditions which MacDiarmid, far from challenging, had encouraged. A deeply negative nationalism was born of MacDiarmid's renaissance, a nationalism which, given the Scottish nation in all its historical complexity, was a failure that required to be swept aside so that a new – or a very old – Scotland could be established in its place.

II

This way of understanding the Scottish cultural situation has been deeply influential: MacDiarmid and Muir are defining figures whose analyses of Scottish culture and whose struggle to overcome what they understood to be the difficulties of their own specific situation have been accepted at face value as the reality of the cultural world that they inhabited. Scotland's failed cultural traditions, and the struggle to reinvent a language in which a fundamental Scottishness – whether 'coorse Scotland' or 'synthetic Scots' – could express itself, have become accepted ways of reading what was happening in the first half of the twentieth century in Scotland. But such analyses are deeply influenced by what was happening in the development of literary criticism in precisely this period, for it was in the years between the wars that the modern discipline of literary study was established in the universities, and that discipline was a fundamentally national one. That the rise of literary criticism goes hand in hand with the reinvention of nationalities across Europe in the aftermath of the First World War and, in the English-speaking world, with the re-ordering of the relationship between Britain, the world's leading cultural power of the nineteenth century, and the United States, as the dominant force in the twentieth century, is no coincidence. The task of literary criticism is to establish a national identity through literature that will be a bulwark against the internal threats to western societies from the alienated masses of the industrial cities, while at the same time justifying the nation's sense of its own historic significance in the increasingly competitive world of capitalism in the first half of the twentieth century. In this context the social task of literary criticism in Britain was the construction of a cultural superiority which would provide a counterbalance to the country's loss of economic and military power, both in relation to its old enemies in Europe and in relation to its upstart cousins in the New World. Whereas in the eighteenth century, as Linda Colley has demonstrated in *Britons* (1992), cultural processes were central to the construction of a new national identity – a Britishness in which all the elements of Britain could participate – in the twentieth century literary criticism provided a line of resistance to the fragmentation of British power by presenting English culture and, specifically, English literature, as a whole which, unlike the pasts of other cultures, was shaped by an unbroken unity and coherence, presenting a model of a complete culture which others had never achieved and could only strive after. The emphasis on 'tradition' – of the unfolding of a single national consciousness through the various stages of literary development – in the literary criticism that was dominated by Eliot and Leavis from the 1920s to the 1950s constructed an ideal of English culture that also made England the ideal of culture. All other cultures were failed versions of this culture whose unity was the glass in which others would see their own fragmented and deformed visages.

It was through the prism of this way of understanding 'culture' and 'literature' that Scottish literature was seen by Muir and Mac-Diarmid as such a deformation of a real culture. Even George Davie's *The Democratic Intellect*, which was, from 1961 onwards, to exert such an influence on the reinterpretation of Scottish culture, accepts that the 'tradition' which he is describing foundered in the 1870s, the decade before Muir's and MacDiarmid's births, leaving them in exactly the kind of vacuum and absence which Muir had ascribed to Scott's environment. It is hardly surprising, therefore, that in the aftermath of the Second World War a new generation of Scottish poets – MacCaig, Graham, Crichton Smith, Mackay Brown – should accept that the language which was appropriate to their writing was one that did not tie them into the specifics of this failed Scottish culture. So little did their language make calls upon that Scottish tradition that Al Alvarez's influential anthology *The New Poetry* (1962) simply refers to them as English poets.

And yet their dislocation from a tradition did not leave their poetry unmarked: rather it cast in doubt the whole nature of the language in which they wrote. In these poets the nature of language itself becomes a major concern, and particularly the breakdown between the languages we inherit from the past and their applicability to the world in which we now live. The poet is continually forced to adopt a language which no longer has purchase on the world beyond language, or which cannot help turning the world into a human construction that denies us access to the fundamental meanings that we seek in nature. In MacCaig's 'Porpoises', for instance, the speaker

> ... looked to see on their backs
> or in the carved car they might well be pulling
> some plump mythical boy
> or sea-green sea-nymph
> or Arion himself, twangling from his lyre,
> audible spray
>
> But not
> these days.
>
> All the same, I myself
> (in a mythical sort of way)
> have been drawn over metaphorical waters
> by these curving backs, till,
> filled with an elation
> I don't want to have explained to me,
> I lifted a pagan face and shouted
> audible nonsense.

> (*Collected Poems*, p. 149)

The 'mythical' language of classical art is juxtaposed against a world in which such differentiation is impossible because the world is 'all the same', and the only myths are those the poet constructs in the isolation of the self – 'audible nonsense' to anyone else. The metaphysics of the isolated self left rootless by the destruction of a communal tradition is, equally, the burden of Crichton Smith's long debate with the destructive effects of Calvinism on his culture, in its negation both of poetry and of the Gaelic language into which he was born. In the title poem of his early volume, *The Law and the Grace* (1965), the challenge to the powers of the religious community around him can only be made by the invention of a personal version of that external authority:

> Do you want me, angels, to be wholly dead?
> Do you need, black devils, steadfastly to cure
>
> life of itself? And you to stand beside
> the stone you set on me? No, I have angels. Mine
> are free and perfect. They have no design
> on anyone else, but only on my pride,

my insufficiency, imperfect works.
They often leave me but they sometimes come
to judge me to the core, till I am dumb.
Is this not law enough, you patriarchs?
(*Collected Poems*, p. 54)

The line ends structure the poet's dilemma: 'to cure/life of itself' is poised between assent to external authority and finding a cure in 'life of itself', in an isolation that leaves his values – 'Mine/are free' – standing in an absolute separation whose liberation is no less silencing than those of external authority, since it leaves him 'dumb'.

The most insistent explorer of these limits of poetic language's inability to root itself in any communal vision is W. S. Graham. Graham's poetry enacts the sense of the poem itself as radically alienated from the world, a meeting place of absolute isolation in which the selves of both poet and reader are discarded for the making of a new but utterly transient identity within the false eternity of language itself. In 'The Nightfishing', for instance, the realistic poem about a fishing expedition is riddled with the sense of the poet's persona being trapped not in the darkness of a night at sea but in the black of type, and the fishing is not a trawling for a living catch but a trawling into the eternity which the poem mimics in its stasis:

So I have been called by my name and
It was not sound. It is me named upon
The space which I continually move across
Bearing between my courage and my lack
The constant I bleed on. And, put to stillness,
Fixed in this metal and its cutting salts,
It is this instant to exact degree,
And for whose sake?
(*Collected Poems*, p. 97)

The poet is 'named upon' the space of the book rather than on his person; he has become fixed in the 'metal' of type as well as in the metal of the ship; the instant of autobiography, the instant of the composition of the poem and the instant of the reading of the text are set in ambiguous confrontation one with another, so that the poem undermines the certainty of any reference to a 'real' world or an inner world of personal experience. In Graham's poetry the written poem becomes a space in which the poet's life is transformed into the life of the reader, but with no certainty that there is any meeting ground of their identities or any common world by which they can recognise each other's experiences. The reader becomes the only interlocutor of the poem, but an absent one to the writer:

> Meanwhile surely there must be something to say,
> Maybe not suitable but at least happy
> In a sense here between us two whoever
> We are. Anyhow here we are and never
> Before have we two faced each other ...
>   ('The Constructed Space', *Collected Poems*, p. 152)

Reader and writer face each other across an abyss of language, a language which is 'Mainly an obstacle to what I mean'.

If, for MacDiarmid, Scots was a way back to a revitalised language for poetry and, thereby, to the possibility of a revitalised nationality, the failure of that enterprise left younger poets struggling with the English language, each in some way tormented by the impossibility of that language having anything but a destructive relationship with meaning, each seeking some space, some element in the natural world or in the national world that can be brought over into meaning in defiance of the fundamental limitations, both social and epistemological, of language.

III

In the United States, in the very period in which Hugh MacDiarmid and Edwin Muir were struggling to come to terms with the meaning of their national identity, the 'tradition' of the academy, still rooted in the sense of American literature as an outgrowth of English literature, was opposed by what is best described as a 'nativist' tradition, one which sought to establish not only the independence of an American literary tradition, rooted in the specific cultural forms of American life and language, but also of a nativist poetry that sought expression for a contemporary American voice, for a writing which would enact not its sense of relationship to the English literary past but its sense of relationship to a demotic present. The great precursor in this tradition, MacDiarmid's contemporary, was William Carlos Williams, whose influence was to be felt in the 'Beat' poets of the 1950s as well as in the transformation of Robert Lowell's poetry in *Life Studies* (1956). Williams's poetry celebrates the present within a deeply local sense of culture rather than within the culture of the high art tradition. 'A Negro Woman', for instance, celebrates the anonymous wonder of the ordinary:

What is she
       but an ambassador
              from another world
a world of pretty marigolds
      of two shades
           which she announces
not knowing what she does
      other
           than walk the streets
holding the flowers upright.
                  (*Selected Poems*, p. 156)

The 'two shades' – the ghosts of the poet and the woman held in the poem – hold 'the flowers upright' against the passage of this world in a language which insists that it is not part of an art opposed to the ordinary world but simply a part of it.

In the world of multinational media and of multinational popular culture, Scotland's relations with England seemed, from the 1950s onwards, less and less significant in comparison with its relations with America. It was to such American examples rather than English examples that writers like Edwin Morgan, Tom Leonard and Liz Lochhead were to turn in the 1960s and '70s for an alternative language for their poetry. Even Douglas Dunn, so often connected because of his early studies with Philip Larkin with the traditions of English poetry in the 1960s, shows the strong influence of such American writing. Edwin Morgan's 'The Second Life' might stand as allegory for this rebirth of a nativist Scottish writing out of the influence of American nativism:

But does every man feel like this at forty –
I mean it's like Thomas Wolfe's New York, his
heady light, the stunning plunging canyons, beauty –
pale stars winking hazy downtown quitting-time,
and the winter moon flooding the skyscrapers, northern –
an aspiring place, glory of the bridges, foghorns
are enormous messages, a looming mastery
that lays its hand on the young man's bowels
until he feels in that air, that rising spirit
all things are possible, he rises with it
until he feels that he can never die –
Can it be like this, and is this what it means
in Glasgow now ...
              (*Collected Poems*, p. 180)

An American spirit rises through the revitalisation of Glasgow to reveal an alternative relationship of language to reality, one that passes not through the Scottish dictionary nor the English tradition but through the living voice of this particular place.

It is that voice that Tom Leonard celebrates in one of the poems from 'Ghostie Men', which starts from the acceptance that 'right inuff/ma language is disgraceful' and ends by denying the limitations ('ma maw tellt mi/ma teacher tellt mi/ ... even thi introduction tay thi Scottish National Dictionary tellt mi') which seek to impede the living voice that is the medium we live in and through:

> ach well,
> all livin language is sacred
> fuck thi lohta thim.
> (*Intimate Voices*, p. 120)

For Leonard the lesson of William Carlos Williams lies in listening to the present voice but being deeply aware of how problematic is its transcription into written form. Each poem is an effort not to deny the 'livin' language in the permanently dead world of type. Similarly, Liz Lochhead's poems are the effort to extract the living voice from the dead world of cliché in which our individual existences are trapped:

> I'll get all dolled up in my gladrags, stay
> up till all hours, oh
> up to no good.
> It'll amaze you, the company I keep –
> and I'll keep them at arm's length –
> I've hauled my heart in off my sleeve.
> (*Dreaming Frankenstein*, p. 76)

The 'livin language' that we all inhabit is in fact a dead language, but a dead language which has to be transmuted by the energy of the poet to reveal the living person who inhabits both the linguistic and cultural social stereotypes that deform us.

This is a poetry whose initial energy comes from its apparent refusal of tradition, a liberation into the immediacy of the present. But it is, of course, deeply conscious of the extent to which it can only achieve its aim by consciously challenging the reader's awareness of the traditions which it refuses, traditions which remain the context of the poem precisely to the extent that they are denied. The anti-tradition of the poem in fact implies precisely the power of tradition against which the poems are working: what these poets

confronted was the outcome of that establishment of literary criticism in the early part of the century in a highly formalised and
imposed canon of great works disseminated within an educational
system that presents poetry not as the voice of the people but as the
language of a class, a class whose fundamental commitments are to
English culture.

IV

If the American example provided an alternative route for Scottish
poets from the 1960s onwards, the culture in which they were writing
was being radically transformed. The final 'end of Empire' with Suez
in 1956 and the granting of independence to the remaining colonies
in the 1960s, Britain's joining of the European Community in the
1970s, and the destruction of the traditional Scottish heavy industries
together with the discovery of oil, created a Scotland suddenly en-
meshed not into the economic lineaments of the British Empire but
reshaped in the relationships of European and multinational capitalism. Filled with Japanese and European and American companies,
this was a Scotland whose identity might seem under threat by its
lack of autonomy but which, paradoxically, was driven to try to
define exactly what kind of culture remained in this place riddled
with international influences, and even more how that culture related
back to its past. From the failure of the devolution referendum in
1979 till the success of its second effort in 1997, Scottish culture
underwent a transformation, but one which was the absolute antithesis of MacDiarmid's 'renaissance', for what it sought was to
discover, behind the apparent discontinuities of Scottish culture, the
structures which held the diverse strands of that culture together. In
the histories of literature, painting and music which were produced
in this period; in the new attention given to the significance of the
Scottish Enlightenment and to the fundamental continuities of Scottish philosophy; in the re-evaluation of Calvinism's relation to art;
in all of these areas what was being established was a sense of a
continuing culture behind whose apparent fractures and fissures
could be discerned a fundamental identity, an identity founded not
on Muir's idea of a 'homogeneous literature' but on its antithesis –
the intellectual and artistic power that is generated out of the ex-
changes between the various languages and cultures which
participate in the space that is Scotland. As criticism began to accept

that the notion of autonomous and homogeneous cultures was a fiction of the nineteenth and early twentieth centuries, and that the bilingual and multicultural was in fact the norm for all but the most 'backward' parts of the postcolonial world, so Scotland's culture could be seen not as a failure to *be* a culture, but rather as an immensely successful engagement in which the various languages acted as stimuli to each other, and in which the relationship to English culture forced a continual resistance to domination which made even English-language culture in Scotland very different from English culture itself.

The divisions to which MacDiarmid and Muir had pointed in the failures of Scottish tradition were to be transformed: the continuities across the divides of the Reformation and the Union were to be re-established by the historians, and where a writer like Burns had been seen as the antithesis of the anglicising Enlightenment philosophers of his day, Burns came to seen as himself a figure of the Enlightenment. It is this realignment that is celebrated in Edwin Morgan's 'Sonnets from Scotland', in which Burns and the Enlightenment author James Hutton, author of *The Theory of the Earth* (1797), become the joint inhabitants of a culture that is both vernacular and scientific: Burns's metaphors from his most famous love lyric, 'My Love is Like a Red Red Rose', are revealed as infused with the new scientific knowledge of Hutton's geology, which was predicated on the fact that what are now rocks were once molten ('and the rocks melt wi' the sun') and that they emerge out of the seas ('Till a' the seas gang dry'):

> They died almost
> together, poet and geologist,
> and lie in wait for hilltop buoys to ring,
> or aw the seas gang dry and Scotland's coast
> dissolve in crinkled sand and pungent mist.
> ('Theory of the Earth', *Collected Poems*, p. 443)

Morgan's poem reunites the divided traditions of Scottish culture, just as in many of his poems he exploits both the vernacular and the traditions of poetry in standard English. The poet is the comfortable inhabitant of multiplicity rather than the dogged creator of singularity; but a fundamental part of that tradition is MacDiarmid himself. MacDiarmid's later career, when he veered off into writing in an English which was as little related to any actual spoken English as his Scots had been to any specific dialect of Scots, becomes a model of a sense of the interaction of multiple cultures and spheres of linguistic activity – of the poet's ability to make language happen out of all the resources available to him rather than out of any specific tradition:

> ... and out of scraps of art and life and knowledge
> you assembled that crackling auroral panorama
> that sits on your Scotland like a curly comb
> or a grinning watergaw thrown to meteorology,
> your bone to the dogs of the ages.
>
> ('To Hugh MacDiarmid', *Collected Poems*, p. 153)

Morgan's own language, mixing MacDiarmid's Scots ('watergaw') with his penchant for abstract English ('auroral panorama'), creates a single texture out of what, in MacDiarmid, had been a linear development. As we draw to the end of the twentieth century Morgan's amalgam of Scots, American, and English traditions, together with the influence of East European poetry and the concrete poetry with which he experimented so effectively in the 1960s and '70s, looks to be the cultural equivalent of MacDiarmid's 'synthetic' Scots – against the synthetic cultures of multinational capitalism Morgan creates a synthesis of cultures which yet could only happen in this place, in this cultural space, in sonnets that are 'from Scotland' and form Scotland.

Douglas Dunn performs a similar inclusion of MacDiarmid into the English-language tradition of Scottish poetry when, in 'St Kilda's Parliament', he adopts the language of MacDiarmid's 'Eemis Stane' into the texture of his own poem. MacDiarmid had presented an image of the earth as a gravestone on which some meaning might have been inscribed

> Had the fug o' fame
> An' history's hazelraw
> No' yirdit thaim.
>
> (*Complete Poems*, I, p. 27)

'Hazelraw' is usually glossed as 'lichen' and the connection appears in 'St Kilda's Parliament' where Dunn imagines how

> It was easy, even then, to imagine
> St Kilda return to its naked self,
> Its archaeology of hazelraw
> And footprints stratified beneath the lichen.
>
> (*Selected Poems*, 144)

Words made suggestive of each other by MacDiarmid's poem in Scots have come to inhabit the language of a poetry in English. MacDiarmid has become part of the tradition his own poetry sought to negate. A dialogue opened between Scots and English, between emotion and reason, between the demotic and the elite: these poems enact the possibility of a new kind of tradition capable of encompassing and uniting all the diverse elements of the Scottish past. Instead of a search for some fundamental unity which requires the exclusion of vast tracts of Scottish history and Scottish culture, the poetry of modern Scotland is an exploration of how the diverse cultures of Scotland speak to one another, of one another, with one another, an intertwining of the potentialities of a place full of voices, the absolute antithesis of the 'nothing' in which Edwin Muir imagined Sir Walter Scott writing:

> Micro-nation. So small you cannot be forgotten,
> Bible inscribed on a ricegrain, hi-tech's key
> Locked into the earth, your televised Glasgows
> Are broadcast in Rio. Among your circuitboard crowsteps
> To be miniaturised is not small-minded.
> To love you needs more details than the Book of Kells –
> Your harbours, your photography, your democratic intellect
> Still boundless, chip of a nation.
>   (Robert Crawford, 'Scotland', *A Scottish Assembly*)

In contemporary Scottish poetry the national imagination has been re-formed not by erasing Scotland's pasts but by recognising that the nation's identity is founded on the multiplicity of its intellectual and linguistic currents: Scotland could not and cannot be constructed into the homogeneity of a single tradition, not because of the failure of its dialects but because the Scottish tradition is a series of intertwined strands whose uniqueness is the dialogue which this engenders: rather than an imagination undermined by dialects, Scotland's is an imagination in dialogue, a dialectical imagination.

Bibliography

Robert Crawford, *A Scottish Assembly* (London: Chatto & Windus, 1990)

George E. Davie, *The Democratic Intellect: Scotland and her universities in the nineteenth century* (Edinburgh: Edinburgh University Press, 1961)

Douglas Dunn, *The Faber Book of Twentieth-Century Scottish Poetry* (London: Faber and Faber, 1992)

Douglas Dunn, *Selected Poems, 1964–1983* (London: Faber and Faber, 1986)

Robert Garioch, *Collected Poems* (Edinburgh: MacDonald, 1977)

W. S. Graham, *Collected Poems, 1942–1977* (London: Faber and Faber, 1979)

Hugh MacDiarmid, *The Complete Poems of Hugh MacDiarmid*, ed. Grieve and Aitken (London: Martin, Brian & O'Keefe, 1978)

Tom Leonard, *Intimate Voices, 1965–1983* (Newcastle upon Tyne: Galloping Dog Press, 1984)

Liz Lochhead, *Dreaming Frankenstein & Collected Poems* (Edinburgh: Polygon, 1984)

Norman MacCaig, *Collected Poems* (London:Chatto & Windus, 1993)

Sorley MacLean, *From Wood to Ridge: Collected Poems in Gaelic and English* (Manchester: Carcanet, 1989)

Edwin Morgan, *Collected Poems* (Manchester: Carcanet, 1990)

Edwin Muir, *Scott and Scotland* (London: Routledge, 1936)

Edwin Muir, *Collected Poems* (London: Faber and Faber, 1963)

Iain Crichton Smith, *Collected Poems* (Manchester: Carcanet, 1992)

Sydney Goodsir Smith, *Collected Poems* (London: John Calder, 1975)

When I arrived at Hamilton Terrace Alec Robertson had begun work on his study of Dvorak for Dent's Master Musicians series. It was to become the first systematic biographical and critical work on Dvorak written originally in English. The series, with advice on the techniques and responsibilities of music criticism, was of great value to me. He laid emphasis on the importance of the integrity of a defenceless dead composer's indications and intentions, a principle to which I have held firm throughout my own career, and which accounts for the intensity of my dislike for that late twentieth-century phenomenon, the tasteless opera producer who takes a selfindulged visual ego-trip at the expense of the composer.

(*Thank You for Having Me*, page 64)

CHAPTER TWELVE

Opera in Scotland, 1725–1997

Michael T. R. B. Turnbull

OPERA IN SCOTLAND, to some extent, has been a tale of two cities. While Edinburgh spent decades dithering over the famous 'hole in the ground' at Castle Terrace – once the site of Poole's cavernous Synod Hall – Glasgow seized the hour and established the headquarters of Scottish Opera at the Theatre Royal across the road from the Royal Scottish Academy of Music and Drama, now with its new Opera School.

Once a year Edinburgh revels in a feast of operatic entertainment fleshed out with recitals. Most of the great contemporary operatic names have trod the boards at Edinburgh's King's Theatre during the annual International Festival, whose initial impulse came from a widespread need for political and cultural reconciliation at the end of the Second World War. Music and opera still bring enormous pleasure and consolation.

Opera, indeed, has been popular in Scotland for more than 250 years.

Quantitatively, if not qualitatively, perhaps Scotland's greatest contribution to the world of opera comes in the more than forty operas whose libretti are based on the works of Sir Walter Scott. These include Boeïldieu's *La Dame Blanche* (1825), Bellini's *I Puritani di Scozia* (1835), Donizetti's *Lucia di Lammermoor* (1835) and Bizet's *La jolie Fille de Perth* (1867).

One could go a stage further and include operas derived from Scottish history such as Verdi's *Macbeth* and Shostakovich's *Lady Macbeth of Mtsensk* (1934), both taking as their inspiration Shakespeare's 'Scottish play'.

If opera can be described as 'stories set to music', then Allan Ramsay's ballad opera, *The Gentle Shepherd* (1725), takes the nod over John Gay's better-known *The Beggar's Opera*, first performed three years later and thought to have been influenced by Ramsay's earlier work. One would have liked to have been a fly on the wall when the temperamental Sienese castrato, Giusto Tenducci, shared lodgings with the poet Robert Fergusson in Edinburgh's Tolbooth.

Fergusson wrote two songs for Tenducci which he performed in Arne's *Artaxerxes* at the Canongate Theatre in 1769.

During the nineteenth century, opera continued to draw on the Scottish genius for music. On one of her visits to perform in Edinburgh, Jenny Lind, the 'Swedish Nightingale', paused during a summer concert at the Assembly Rooms. Through the open window drifted the call of a fishwife, 'Caller Ou'. The Swede drew her rapt audience's attention to the purity and naturalness of production of the street seller's voice. Later, in 1873 Edinburgh-born Euphrosyne Parepa, wife of the Hamburg violinist, Karl Rose, founded the Carl Rosa Company which toured Britain until its demise in 1957.

Ernst Denhof, an Austrian living in Edinburgh, founded the Denhof Opera Company whose aim was to present Wagner's *Ring Cycle* outside London, using local orchestras. The Denhof Company went bankrupt in 1913 and its touring commitments were taken over by the Beecham Opera Company until December 1920 when it too failed, to be succeeded by the British National Opera Company under the leadership of Sir Thomas Beecham which lasted until 1928. Other touring companies which made their mark in Scotland were the Quinlan, the O'Mara and the Moody-Manners. Their productions, often rough and ready and using a limited repertoire, kept opera alive north of the Border.

During the nineteenth century Christina Bogue's *The Uhlans* (1885) was thought to be the first opera composed by a Scotswoman, although Jane Smieton had published a lyric opera in 1874 in Dundee. Hamish McCunn (1868–1916), a pupil of Parry at the newly-opened Royal College of Music, London, wrote his *Jeannie Deans* (1894) based on Scott's *The Heart of Midlothian*.

A significant watershed for opera in Scotland came in 1962 with the birth of Scottish Opera, the brainchild of the conductor, Sir Alexander Gibson, Richard Telfer (an Edinburgh teacher and organist) and Ainslie Millar, a Glasgow chartered surveyor. From its beginning the company went from strength to strength, taking over the Theatre Royal, Glasgow in 1974 as its base. Scottish Opera established a tradition of permanent opera in a way no amount of magnificent visiting productions at the Edinburgh Festival ever could. Today, its outreach programme builds a present and future audience which will be its lifeblood.

From the 1960s to the late 1970s the publisher John Calder helped to provide opera at Ledlanet House in Kinross-shire. Having studied at the Royal College of Music, June Gordon, the Marchioness of Aberdeen and Temair, had founded a choral society in 1945 with her husband at Haddo House, some 20 miles north of Aberdeen. This formed the nucleus of a fine tradition of opera production, beginning with Bizet's *Carmen*.

The importance of amateur opera companies should not, however, be forgotten. In 1929 Sir John Barbirolli conducted the Edinburgh Opera Company with the Edinburgh-born tenor Joseph Hislop. Sir Thomas Beecham used the stage of the Empire Theatre (now the Festival Theatre) to appeal for funds for his Imperial League of Opera. In the west, Glasgow's Grand Opera Society gave the British première of Berlioz's *Les Troyens* in 1935. The practice of hiring professional opera stars to sing with amateur companies often bore spectacular fruit – in 1957 Sir Alexander Gibson conducted the Edinburgh Opera Company in Verdi's *Nabucco* with one of the finest Scots singers of all time, the towering bass David Ward (1922–83), in the title role. It should not be overlooked that amateur companies not only keep, cultivate and develop the general public's interest in opera (so building an audience for the professionals to harvest), but they also often tackle works seldom performed by professional companies. In recent years, Ayr Intimate Opera has achieved an enviable reputation with some 16 operas produced since 1972. In 1968, as Opera West, they presented McCunn's *Jeannie Deans*. Under the guidance of the company's honorary president, the soprano Elisabeth Schwarzkopf, Mozart's *Cosi Fan Tutte* was given in 1987 and *Carmen* in 1988. Over the following years the company has continued to exert a lively presence on the operatic scene.

Opera in Scotland over the last thirty years was dominated by the work of Robin Orr. Particularly noteworthy are his *Full Circle* (1968) with a libretto by Sydney Goodsir Smith, *Hermiston* (1975), based on Robert Louis Stevenson's unfinished novel and, in collaboration with the dramatist Tom Stoppard, *On the Razzle* (1986). The literature of other cultures inspired composer Iain Hamilton. His operas include *The Catiline Conspiracy* (1974), based on a play by Ben Jonson; *The Royal Hunt of the Sun* (1977) after the Peter Shaffer play and *Anna Karenina* (1976), taken from Tolstoy's novel. Of the same generation is Thomas Wilson, best known for his opera *The Confessions of a Justified Sinner* (1976), and Thea Musgrave who wrote her *Voice of Ariadne* in 1974 and *Mary Queen of Scots* two years later.

Among composers who are Scots by domicile, one of the earliest was Domenico Corri who presented his *The Wives Revenge* in Edinburgh in 1778. Donald Tovey (1875–1940), Professor of Music at Edinburgh University, wrote one opera, *The Bride of Dionysus*. Written in 1912, it was not produced until 1929 and failed to live up to expectations. Gian Carlo Menotti (1911–) settled in Scotland in 1973. His *Juan la Loca* (1979) was partly written in Scotland, while his children's opera, *The boy who grew too fast*, and *Goya* (1986) were composed wholly in Scotland, as was his *Il Matrimonio* (1988). Sir Peter Maxwell Davies (1934–) made his home in Orkney where he has been the driving force behind the St Magnus Festival. His operatic works include *The Martyrdom of St Magnus* (1977), *The Lighthouse* (1980) and *Miss Donnithorne's Maggot* (1974).

Since the late 1980s at least twenty operas have been composed by Scots. These include Judith Weir's *The Black Spider* (1989), *Il sogno di Scipione* (1991) and *Blond Eckbert* (1991); Ian Balfour's *Scenes from the People's Paradise* (composed in the early 1990s); Ian McQueen's *Line of Terror* (1987) and *Fortunato* (1992); Edward McGuire's *Loving of Etain* (1990) and Edward Harper's *The Mellstock Quire* (1987). Probably the two operas which have achieved the widest critical acclaim are Judith Weir's *The Vanishing Bridegroom* (1990) and James MacMillan's *Ines de Castro* (1996).

As well as providing libretti, indigenous opera and a number of opera companies, Scotland produced two great singers in the golden age of singing – the Aberdeen-born soprano Mary Garden (1874–1967) and the Edinburgh-born tenor Joseph Hislop (1884–1977).

Mary Garden made an astonishing first appearance on the stage of the Opéra-Comique in Paris on 10 April 1900. Born in Aberdeen, raised in the United States and trained in Paris, her debut at the Opéra-Comique, looked to the general public as if it had been a lucky break, the result of chance. In fact, it was quite the reverse. Garden had last rehearsed Charpentier's *Louise* in March, a month previously, with the whole cast under composer/conductor André Messager. She had been careful to keep everything fresh in her memory by continual study of the role, as her coach, the baritone Lucien Fugère, had previously advised. Director Albert Carré had had a phone call from the soprano Marthe Rioton to say that she would try and complete the performance that evening, but that she might be forced to pull out because of a severe cold. The official understudy, Mlle Mastio, was also ill. Carré told Garden to be at the theatre by seven o'clock.

Garden arrived at the Opéra-Comique accompanied by her friend, the American soprano Sibyl Sanderson, with whom she was lodging. She dressed in the first act costume, hidden under a cloak. She and her companions were shown to groundfloor box 17, at the back of the auditorium, directly facing the stage. She squeezed herself into as small a bundle as possible. Her eyes and nose, swollen with weeping for the death of Sibyl's dog, might easily have frightened Albert Carré off. 'One minute I felt hot all over', Garden remembered, 'then it seemed as though someone had run an icicle down my back.'

To a full house, the curtain opened on Louise. Marthe Rioton made valiant efforts to sing, in spite of her obvious discomfort. She struggled through the first two acts without giving up and then, finally breaking under the strain ('très énervée, émouvée', as the Register put it), admitted defeat. During the performance, Garden kept her eyes glued to the small stage door that opened into the orchestra pit. As the curtain fell on Act Two, she was aware of the white head of a little old man, peering about with near-sighted eyes. It was the stage manager, M. Vizentini, looking over his spectacles for her. As he approached her seat, she got up to meet him and he hurried her backstage through a side door.

There, pandemonium reigned as the management and stage crew milled about. Carré rushed towards her: 'Are you ready to finish the third Act for me?' 'Certainly', Garden answered. In spite of the conductor Messager's misgivings Garden was taken up to a dressing-room, her cheeks rouged, her eyes outlined with black. Her costume was adjusted and she was then shown onto the rear of the stage, where she took up her position with a final quick adjustment of her dress. Her teacher, Lucien Fugère, stepped out to face the packed theatre and announced the substitution to the audience.

'My first realisation of what I was doing', Garden confessed later, 'came with the curious whirring sound of the rising curtain, and when I saw over the footlights the black coats with the gleaming white shirt fronts, I felt as though I were facing a row of white tombstones. But I had no time to think. I remember turning my back on the audience', she continued, 'walking upstage, saying to myself: 'Now, Mary Garden, here is your chance'.

Then she turned calmly and walked downstage, steeling herself, but trying to be as relaxed as she could. She positioned herself behind the chair where Léon Beyle (the tenor who was singing the part of

Julien) was seated. With a glance at Messager in the pit, she began to sing 'Depuis le jour, où je me suis donnée'.

When she finished the aria, the applause was incredible. To Garden's ears it sounded like rain torrenting onto a tin roof. 'When the curtain fell at the end of the Act, the audience went into a frenzy', she said. 'Men and women stood shouting "bravo", waving handkerchiefs and programmes and even, in their excitement, throwing them up onto the stage. Some were calling out *"Marygardenne!"* in the French fashion.'

Messager stood transfixed. He rose, and, baton in hand, turned to his orchestra and ordered: 'Debout!' As they silently rose to their feet in salute, he held his baton high in the air – the greatest compliment a chef d'orchestre and his staff could pay.

In 1902 came another lucky break for Garden. She was chosen for the role of Mélisande in Claude Debussy's avant-garde new opera, *Pelléas et Mélisande*. Garden was elated at the announcement. A few days later, all the artists who had been picked for *Pelléas et Mélisande* assembled at Messager's home on the Boulevard Malesherbes to hear the work played by the composer himself. Each singer was given a proof copy of the score to follow. Oblivious of the cast around him, Debussy sat down at the piano. Sensuous chords sprang from the instrument. He intoned the vocal parts in his deep, hollow voice which forced him sometimes to transpose the notes an octave down. The music unnerved Garden. But, as the third Act unfolded, it began gradually to fascinate her. By the time Debussy reached the fourth Act, she was filled with emotion she had seldom experienced. And when it came to the death of Mélisande, it was more than she could bear. Suddenly she and Madame Messager (the Irish composer, Hope Temple) were racked by uncontrollable sobbing and had to leave the room until they could regain their composure.

Some days later, Garden was called to the Opéra-Comique to be heard by Debussy. He greeted her with an air of resignation born of a long and fruitless search to find the ideal interpreter of the role of Mélisande. 'Sing, Mademoiselle', said Debussy and his long, thin fingers, weighed down with rings and tipped with unbelievably long nails which rattled on the keys, began to race up and down the keyboard. Debussy chanted the other roles for her. 'I sang the first two acts; he didn't say a single word', recalled Garden later. 'Then we began the third Act, the balcony scene. When we had finished, he suddenly buried his head in his hands and sat in silence for over a minute. Then, without a word, he got up and left the room.'

Mary could not think what had happened. She waited some time for him to return, but nobody came. Then, just as she had decided to leave, a boy came upstairs with a message from Albert Carré, saying he wanted to see her immediately. She went into the director's office. There was Debussy. He came towards her, took both her hands in his and asked (in an echo of the text of *Pelléas et Mélisande*): 'Where do you come from?' She told him and he stared at her with his deep mysterious eyes: 'Scotland! You have come all the way from the cold North to create my music'.

But singers sometimes find themselves in situations where fate seems to stand between them and success. The often inexact nature of vocal tuition is well illustrated in the case of Joseph Hislop. Hislop's former choirmaster at St Mary's Episcopal Cathedral, Edinburgh was the University organist, Dr Thomas H. Collinson (1858–1928). Hislop, who had been studying in London, came up to Edinburgh in 1907 hoping to receive a favourable opinion as to his future prospects as a professional singer. Dr Collinson listened to Hislop's voice and then remarked: 'My dear boy, you sing with fine expression but I'm afraid your voice will never take you into the professional ranks'. Fortunately, Hislop was not easily put off. He eventually trained in Sweden and launched his international career at the Royal Opera, Stockholm before going to Covent Garden. In 1922, Hislop gave a concert at the Usher Hall. Collinson and his pupils at St Mary's were all there. 'Joseph Hislop is simply one of the marvels of the twentieth century', wrote Collinson in his day-book; 'his genius even transforms a poorish song into a thing of beauty and significance!'

Others of Hislop's career decisions were not so happy. Young singers are at times at the mercy of an agent. In America in 1921 Joseph Hislop had been managed by Paolo Longone, a former violinist and friend of Caruso. Hislop had been kicking his heels in New York, waiting for Longone to clinch a new deal with Mary Garden's Chicago company where he had just spent the season. However, the Chicago company under Garden had run up a $1 million loss. Garden cut back on singers and Hislop, who had held out too long (he was really hoping to be signed up by the Metropolitan Opera), was one of the casualties.

Once in a lifetime a singer is offered an opportunity which he or she would be foolish to let pass. In the following year (1923) Hislop, once tipped in New York as a possible successor to some of Caruso's roles, made his début at La Scala, Milan, singing the role of Edgardo in *Lucia di Lammermoor*. He was the first male British singer to sing a leading role in the opera house since its construction in 1778. Under the baton of Franco Ghione, Hislop took over from Aureliano Pertile, in a cast that included the soprano Toti dal Monte and the bass, Ezio Pinza, and made a huge impression on the discerning audience. After four performances he was offered a contract for 45 more. However, it appears that he had allowed his wife to overspend in the local shops. Hislop asked for a fee the La Scala authorities would not meet and the opportunity was lost – either through an over-estimation of his own worth or as a result of financial mismanagement on his part.

As Scots, both Mary Garden and Joseph Hislop have one circumstance in common – they had to go abroad for their ability to be discovered. In America, Garden was fêted like royalty and known as 'Our Mary'. Both their host countries honoured them nobly. Garden gained the Légion d'Honneur and the Médaille de la Reconnaissance for her services to France during war and peace. Joseph Hislop was given one knighthood by the King of Denmark and another by the King of Sweden. Sadly, neither singer received any similar honour from their own country!

Over the years Scotland has consistently produced singers who have made their mark. Probably the first was the tenor John Wilson (1800–49), to be followed by another tenor, John Templeton (1802–86), who was once embraced by Donizetti after a performance and known as 'Malibran's tenor'. Other tenors have included Canon Sydney McEwan (1909–91), Murray Dickie (1924–), William McAlpine (1925–) Kenneth McKellar (1927–) and Neil Mackie. Among the baritones and basses are Ian Wallace (1919–), Bill McCue (1934–), Peter Morrison (1940–) and Joseph Hislop's final pupil, Donald Maxwell (1948–).

But it is in the soprano department that Scotland seems best gifted at present – Linda Ormiston (1948–), Margaret Marshall (1949–), Linda Finnie (1952–), Marie Slorach (1952–), Isobel Buchanan (1954–) and Marie McLaughlin (1954–), all singers who have put an individual stamp on their art.

With the construction of a new Opera School at the Royal Academy of Music in Glasgow the finishing touch will be put in place in the training of young singers for the stage. The coming generations of Scottish singers will no longer have to rely on chance or the perspicacity of teachers abroad. But they will inevitably be able to look back with great pride on the many fine Scottish singers who have preceded them.

Percy Gordon, my former teacher of the thirties, was then still music critic of the *Glasgow Herald*, a post he had held for more than quarter of a century. He disapproved strongly of his pupil's appointment to the *Herald*'s sister paper on the grounds that a critic should have behind him a long and wide experience of listening. He was not, of course, aware of the extent to which I had made use of my wartime opportunities for hearing music. Undoubtedly, though, he had a point. To set against it there was, however, my refusal to acquiesce in his acceptance of what I called 'the tradition of pretence'.

A famous pianist gave a recital in St Andrew's Hall, during the course of which not one but three strings of the instrument broke. Next morning, I suggested in the *Bulletin* that it was high time Glasgow secured for itself a concert grand that measured up to international standards. A director of Paterson's, the firm of piano sellers who hired the instrument, wrote to the paper protesting that I had broken a long-standing convention, 'whereby the instrument itself is never mentioned'. Percy Gordon shook his head sadly and hoped that I would soon 'learn'.

(Thank You for Having Me, page 123)

CHAPTER THIRTEEN

Visual Arts in Scotland over Half a Century

Cordelia Oliver

IT WAS LATE in June 1978 that I responded, with understandable reluctance, to a request from the Scottish Arts Council to assemble for that year's Edinburgh International Festival an art exhibition intended to display some fifty years of Scottish painting. Twelve months, at the very least, would normally be allowed for research on such an enterprise, but the situation seemed desperate. Edinburgh College of Art had been booked for an entirely different exhibition which had somehow failed to materialise. So I conquered my reluctance: this was a challenge that anyone like myself, as an artist and critic whose adult life had covered more or less the period in question, would have found it hard to resist.

And here I am, twenty years later, accepting another irresistible invitation to survey the post-war Scottish scene in the visual arts. Now, however, an even greater challenge presents itself. Already in the late 1970s the old staple fare of painting and sculpture – representational or abstract on the one hand, modelling or carving on the other – was just beginning its long fight against that invasion of other forms of visual art which we have witnessed ever since. New media began to take over: acrylics, for example, had entered the field even of water-colour painting, leading to a notable change in scale and density and so transforming the appearance of the annual RSW exhibitions. And sculpture, or rather three-dimensional artwork, began to suffer an even more disturbing sea-change. Even in the most prestigious open exhibitions, the Royal Scottish Academy not least, 'installations', so-called, might be found in the Sculpture Court among the modelling and carving of old.

Conceptualism, new to Scotland except as something to read about in art history books, was first encountered at full strength in 1970 during a momentous irruption from Germany led by the now legendary Joseph Beuys. The exhibition was Richard Demarco's contribution to the Edinburgh Festival and it was given a palindromic title, Strategy-Get-Arts. Most of the exhibits were site-specific works which inspired an increasing number of young native artists to look beyond the long-accepted art media and subject matter for their inspiration. Being 'up to the minute' does not, of course, automatically endow an individual with real creativity. And there is no doubt that the peaks are still attainable through more familiar means.

Even for those who seldom travel, twentieth century European art at its best is no stranger to Scotland, since the quality and range of our collections both national and regional are exemplary. And while it cannot be said that the Edinburgh International Festival has ever fervently embraced the visual arts as part of its official programme, the important exhibitions mounted each August at the RSA galleries – Delacroix, Degas, Cézanne, Rouault, Braque, Modigliani, Soutine and many more including the German Expressionists of *The Blue Rider* – but not least, our own William McTaggart – have offered a great wealth of experience to enthusiasts, and novices, of all ages. Indeed, the latest such display, of portraits by Raeburn, reminds us of the peaks which have been reached in painting by a Scot working in his native country. Art from beyond the Iron Curtain – introduced, once again, by Demarco – had the effect of stimulating many young Scottish artists including Ainslie Yule and Will McLean. And after it was opened in 1960, the Scottish National Gallery of Modern Art became a very important influence with its focus on twentieth-century art from Scotland and beyond. Brainchild of the late David Baxandall, then Director of the National Galleries of Scotland, and ably developed by Douglas Hall, the gallery had its first home at Inverleith House in the Royal Botanic Garden. Now, of course, with a greatly enlarged collection, it occupies the former John Watson's School in Belford Road.

For someone who, like myself, was a wartime art student as well as a regular exhibitor at the open exhibitions which, by and large, offered almost the only opportunities to show our work, senior figures in the Scottish art world were still very much to the fore. James Cowie, a painter of unique quality whose inspiration lay in the *quattrocento* (he was a draughtsman without equal in our time in Scotland), is remembered as a formidable presence commanding great respect. Cowie was trained at Glasgow School of Art where draughtsmanship and classical concept traditionally reigned supreme. But it was, above all, the magic of colour that became widely associated with Scottish painting and which certainly informed most of the work from the East, the so-called 'Edinburgh School'.

Edinburgh, as the home of the Royal Scottish Academy, the Royal Society of Painters in Water-colours and the Society of Scottish Artists – not to mention the all-important National Galleries themselves – has had a head-start, so to say, on other major Scottish art centres like Glasgow and Aberdeen, although I suspect that the West remains, what it always was, an important cradle of creativity, and during his long regime as Director, Ian McKenzie Smith brought Aberdeen Art Gallery into the forefront as a showplace for contemporary as well as traditional art. It also must be said that many gifted Scots artists have continued willing to work within, rather than against, the established art societies. The more innovative exceptions include Glasgow-born Mark Boyle who, with his family, set out on a so-called Journey to the Surface of the Earth, thereafter presenting exhibitions of astonishingly realistic casts taken worldwide and wall-hung in a valiant attempt to make us see as art the very good ground we walk on in its infinite and fascinating variety.

But there is no doubt that throughout the 1950s and 1960s painting, and especially the work of colourists, was paramount. In passing it is perhaps worth mentioning that the term 'colourist' was first used by Dr Tom Honeyman in the title of his book, *Three Scottish Colourists*, about Cadell, Peploe and Hunter, the first two being Edinburgh-trained. So, too, were the younger William Gillies and John Maxwell who led the 'Edinburgh School' in the 1940s and 1950s. As painters both were highly creative, the one poised between his passion for the lowland landscape and his admiration for Georges Braque, the other equally in touch with the land but also fired by mysticism. And close behind was Anne Redpath, home in Scotland after years of life in the south of France, charming all and sundry with her paintings of decorative domesticity (her warm personality, too, cast its spell over all who knew her), but developing remarkably in later life as a painter of truly potent vision inspired, in part, as she herself admitted, by foreign travel.

There has been a long tradition in Scotland, which still continues, for genuinely gifted artists to combine teaching the current generation of art students with a life's work in the studio. Gillies and Maxwell are both remembered with great affection and regard by their students at Edinburgh. Robin Philipson and James Cumming, artists utterly different in style and outlook, the one a romantic colourist, the other a genuine visionary, also continued to teach throughout their lives like David Donaldson in Glasgow and Alberto Morrocco in Dundee. To teach the young, after all, for an experienced artist whose craft and philosophy may well have reached a dangerous point of balance, can be a profitable two-way experience.

One of the most impressive painters of the older generation, William Johnstone, as Head of the Central School of Art and Crafts in London, might be said to have been as influential as any. He it was who, believing in what he called 'tangential teaching', persuaded the young Alan Davie to take a class in jewellery design and, likewise, gave to budding sculptor, Eduardo Paolozzi, the task of overseeing a class in ceramics. Johnstone, always a painter of stature (arguably, he was the first Scottish surrealist), came fully into his Kingdom, as such, during his long retirement in the Borders.

I count myself fortunate to have studied under two exceptional masters. First of all, at Glasgow School of Art was Hugh Adam Crawford, to my mind among the most inspiring and least hidebound of teachers, and later, at Hospitalfield, I had James Cowie to contend with; he enjoyed serious argument, but only when he was allowed to emerge the winner. Hospitalfield, that summer art school in a grand Victorian mansion near Arbroath, was of enormous value to several generations of students graduating from the four Scottish art schools, not least because, during the war years and those hardship times immediately following, when continental travel was out of the question, that was the place where one could escape from the boring familiarities of home. It was there that Ian Fleming (another fine Glasgow-trained draughtsman) followed James Cowie as Warden, and afterwards continued to teach and inspire the young as Head of Gray's School of Art at Aberdeen.

By the 1950s and '60s travel became possible once again, and younger artists, like Elizabeth Blackadder and John Houston from Edinburgh, Jack Knox from Glasgow and Ian McKenzie Smith from Aberdeen, shared the inspiration that foreign travel can offer. As painters, they have never had much in common except dedication and high quality of their work. With Blackadder – as indeed with the older Anne Redpath – the visual impact of European places, in form and colour so different from Scotland, offered a fresh impetus (more recently, of course, a visit to Japan has added a new element to Blackadder's painting). For Knox and McKenzie Smith in the '60s,

Paris and the contemporary exhibitions seen there, giving, for example, a first taste of abstract expressionism 'in the flesh', were rich stimuli to open-mindedness. Those were exciting times for budding artists.

But most of them faced the problem of finding outlets, places in which to exhibit and sell their work over and above acceptance in open exhibitions like the RSA, the RSW, the SSA and the Royal Glasgow Institute, all of which societies, it must be said, have made attempts to move with the times. Such commercial galleries as were still in operation after the war – the most prestigious, Aitken Dott's, was also the most senior by far – tended to err, not on the side of adventure, but of conservatism. So in 1957 the first move was made towards the founding of small galleries run by artists themselves. The '57 Gallery was, in fact, an artist's studio in a top flat in Edinburgh's George Street, where a small group of painters took it in turn to man the gallery, and where exhibitions were held of interesting work by Scottish artists as well as others from south of the Border. Bet Low, whose fondness for coastal landscape was even then apparent, had her first important solo exhibition at the '57; likewise Ian McKenzie Smith, then, as always, a passionate explorer of potent simplicity. Joan Eardley's work, too, was first seen in Edinburgh in that same small space which, before long, was bursting at the seams. Inevitably the '57 Gallery was forced to move, first of all to Rose Street and eventually, with the help of the Scottish Arts Council, to the upper level of the former fruitmarket in Market Street, the building which is now, years later and after radical refurbishment, the much more prestigious Fruitmarket Gallery. But there were some young painters like John Bellany, full of confidence – with justification it has to be said since his mastery was evident even then – who gained permission to hang their outsize paintings on the National Gallery railings.

Early in the 1960s three Glasgow painters, Bet Low, John Taylor and Tom Macdonald, combined to create the next artist-run gallery, in a rented loft in Sauchiehall Street. This enterprise was highly successful for a time with a blend of exhibitions from Scotland and beyond. And indeed, although closure became inevitable on the sale of the building, the New Charing Cross Gallery, as it was called, might be said to be still functioning under another name, since Cyril Gerber, one of its directors, promptly set about acquiring a better space in West Regent Street and continues to run it as the non-profit-making Compass Gallery, concentrating as before on contemporary talent. Since those early days the gallery scene has proliferated in all the Scottish centres to the point where there is even an annual art fair in George Square, Glasgow, with London as well as Edinburgh dealers eagerly participating. Throughout the '70s and '80s, indeed, until the abrupt demise of the aptly named Third Eye Centre, Glasgow became one of the most lively arts centres in Britain.

Although, as I have said, many fine Scottish artists have always found themselves able to work and develop within the art schools, others, among them some of the most gifted, have found it necessary to devote all their time to making art. Joan Eardley, for example, refused to be corralled in any way, and her work became her life, whether in recording and responding to the street activity of Glasgow's Townhead urchins or, increasingly, through her own emotionally charged relationship with the environs of the Kincardineshire fishing village, Catterline, where, latterly, she spent most of her time, with the seasonal 'theatre of the elements', both on land and in the seascape below the high clifftop.

This single-minded attitude is uncommon, and it is interesting to find that I can think of two Scottish women painters who have always shared it with Eardley. Patricia Douthwaite is an artist forever feeding on her own volatile, not to say histrionic, temperament, whose work, driven by a heightened imagination, dances on paper or canvas in a way that many find disturbing; the other is Carole Gibbons, a true colourist with a penetrating vision that continually demands release. Both are, to my mind, underestimated if only because their work seldom, if ever, coincides with current fashion.

In the first post-war decades studio space in the cities was easy to find. The old rooftop studios in central Glasgow, for example, which seemed to come straight from La Vie Bohème, were both plentiful and remarkably inexpensive. But when things began to change, with galloping inflation and the need for new office buildings, different, less romantic spaces had to be found for young impecunious artists. To its credit – inspired, it has to be said, by the dedicated activities of artists like Bridget Riley in London – the Scottish Arts Council helped to create workshops and studio complexes in disused buildings in all major Scottish centres. The popularity of printmaking led to the founding of print studios and galleries; photography, too, gained acceptance as a genuine art form (some would say that 'art photography' is merely another form of printmaking); the art-crafts also began to make themselves felt, not least in textiles which at times have assumed the status of soft sculpture. Printmaker Jacki Parry's knowledgeable enthusiasm for creative papermaking, born of a visit to Japan, led to the founding of a paper work-shop in one of Glasgow's studio complexes; nor was sculpture overlooked.

Eventually even the commercial art galleries began to display and sell craftwork at its best and most ambitious. The opening of the Burrell Collection in Glasgow, and the continuing exhibitions at the Royal Museum of Scotland in Edinburgh, undoubtedly helped to stimulate interest in creative craftwork ancient and contemporary. The older universities, too, have established their own prestigious galleries for the display of modern as well as traditional work.

The new availability of large working spaces, while undoubtedly beneficial, has had the effect of encouraging the use of vast canvases even where the blend of vision and painter's craft is pint-sized at best. Large photographic collages in full colour preclude the need for ability to draw and paint, demanding, instead, the admittedly imaginative skills of a scene-setter. Moving images on video screens can mesmerise or fail to hold the viewer according to the power of the work. In all those fields, of course, genuine talent may be found, but, as with the increasingly popular computer graphics, it now seems easier than at any previous time to conceal a lack of creativity behind a surfeit of cleverness.

The seal was surely set on scale as a priority by an exhibition of contemporary art which was mounted in the National Gallery of Modern Art at the 1987 Edinburgh Festival. It was called 'The Vigorous Imagination' and it brought together a number of young Scots artists some of whom have become household names. Among the most gifted, to my mind, are painters: June Redfern, for example, whose richly imaginative imagery is matched by an expansive, but always sensitive, technique, and Philip Braham, who has developed a powerful imagery of landscape charged with symbolism. David Mach's is also a unique, inventive talent, creating three-dimensional work, often on a very large scale using, you feel, almost anything that comes to hand from old newspapers to discarded rubber tyres. But somehow he manages to cross genuine power with whimsical satire in a way that touches a deep, responsive chord in many viewers. By comparison the so-called 'New Glasgow Boys', the figurative painters Howson, Currie and Campbell, seem to me, for all their pop star acclaim, to be little more than clever illustrators, albeit on a monumental scale. But undoubtedly that exhibition did provide a springboard to fame and fortune for a number of young local artists.

In Scotland, as everywhere, we are now at a crossroads, in art as in much else. Technology is in danger of taking over completely unless some other factor intervenes. Yet there are signs that handwork plus imagination is not entirely *déjà vu* even among the *avant garde*. Some years ago the two Scottish winners of a UK competition to create a work of art aimed at complementing existing landmarks in Edinburgh and Glasgow were essentially hands-on artists, albeit entirely different in background and style. Both looked to the past for inspiration. On Edinburgh's Calton Hill Kate Whiteford created her elegant, Celtic-inspired dance of lines cut into the green turf and filled with white pebbles; and high up on the huge Finnieston Crane that still dominates the north bank of the Clyde, cheek-by-jowl with Norman Foster's new Glasgow Conference Centre (nicknamed the 'Armadillo', isn't that just another vast contemporary artwork?), George Wyllie hung his full-scale Straw Locomotive in memory of the real Springburn railway engines that were once lowered on to ships from that same hammerhead crane and sent to the far corners of the globe. Art? Perhaps not, in any sense that a Victorian visitor would understand. But as with the best of contemporary art, in all its richly imaginative variety of form and imagery, there is no other word that fits.

PART THREE:
SECURING THE HERITAGE

St Bernard's Well, Edinburgh, 1975
by John Knight

From 'TRAVELLERS' TALES'

According to our childhood expectations
landscape should wear the look of history,
and island waters lap soft wordless legends.
    No place, wherever it may be,
preserves impersonal objectivity.

(Selected Poems 1942–1972, page 19)

CHAPTER FOURTEEN

Environment: A Developing Groundswell of Concern

Michael Middleton

FORTY years ago the word 'environment' was not in wide usage. Of course the same period has seen many shifts in public attitudes as old frameworks, old certainties, have been replaced by new challenges, new alignments. But what has brought to the fore in particular the present concerns with the rational use and enhancement of land, the protection of landscape and wildlife, air and water pollution, the safeguarding of irreplaceable historic sites and monuments, the nature of our new construction – indeed the very nature of change and the quality of life that goes with it? For different people the word 'environment' has come to cover some, or all, of these things. And more. How has it come about?

At one level the reasons are self-evident. The pace and scale of change have accelerated to a degree unknown to previous generations. Since the end of World War II mechanised farming and forestry have radically changed the appearance of the countryside. Hundreds of thousands of miles of hedgerow have been grubbed up. Conifer plantations have replaced indigenous forests. Lakes and rivers have become grossly polluted. Toxic chemicals, used with abandon, have entered the food chain. The development of atomic energy has posed daunting problems in how to deal with atomic waste. Arable land everywhere has fallen under the concrete of roads, airstrips, industry, housing – in England, it has been estimated, to the equivalent extent of maybe three counties.

In built-up areas, where four-fifths of the population now live, change has been perhaps even more evident. Loved buildings, streets, whole quarters of towns – familiar landmarks which had been the community's reference points for generations – have been obliterated; what has taken their place has too often been crude, banal, brutish, ugly. The surge of high-rise development between the 1950s and 1970s, at first welcomed, came to be hated (often, it has to be said, because maintenance was scandalously neglected, while the promised landscaping of surrounding areas was never undertaken at all). Traffic grew to choke the arteries of settlements big and small, to the point where its fumes have become the major urban pollutant and journeys can take longer than they did at the beginning of the century. The squalor of advertising, wires, filling stations and grab-you commerce, haphazard street structures, has never in this country reached the rampant apotheosis of the American 'strip', but it has degraded once seemly towns to the point where they have become non-places. The second half of the twentieth century has not, overall, been kind to Britain's cities, towns and villages.

All these things are now the concern, in some measure, of governments, local authorities, public utilities, quangos, commerce and industry. International institutions – UNESCO, the Council of Europe, the European Union and others – struggle to find means by which they may be brought under more purposeful control. This, however, is a development of recent decades. Though France took steps in the 1830s to list and care for her historic monuments, it is only since World War II, broadly speaking, that officialdom has felt impelled seriously to intervene in such matters. That environmental values were brought to public attention at all was, for generations, due to the work of unofficial, non-governmental organisations: the 'voluntary movement'.

The roots of such associations go back, in Britain, at least 170 years. It was in 1826 that a group of citizens in York issued an appeal for funds with which to restore the thirteenth-century walls – one of the glories of the city but then threatened with demolition. About £3,500 was raised – then an enormous sum – as a result of which the walls still stand today. The oldest civic society in England with an unbroken history was formed in Sidmouth in 1847. Three years later, in Edinburgh, Lord Cockburn concerned himself with the public subscription to save John Knox's House, and gave his name a quarter of a century later to the oldest conservation body in Scotland, the Cockburn Association.

Over the next seventy years a diversity of national and local organisations came into being to promote the protection of the countryside and open spaces, waterways, historic buildings, the creation of new towns, the concept of planning, and much else. Memories are short and the movement (if such it can be called, for although memberships often overlapped, these associations tended to go their own way) has lacked historians. Most of the hard-won victories of our forebears are, in ignorance, taken for granted today; the battles fought in a *laisser-faire* world without serious planning legislation, forgotten. Nonetheless Britain was ahead of other countries in this concern for our surroundings, and we owe these pioneers much.

It might have seemed, after World War II, with the passing of the Town and Country Planning Act, the creation of the National Parks in England and Wales, and legislation to bring into being a string of New Towns, that these unofficial bodies had had their day. In fact, the explosive growth of the movement lay ahead. And the most significant development of these post-war years was surely the arrival on the scene of the Civic Trust.

*

The Civic Trust was created by Duncan Sandys, the then Minister for Housing and Local Government. When I joined it early in 1957 he had obtained for it a covenanted income of nearly £40,000 a year, promised by a small group of the largest industrial companies, but it had as yet neither staff nor premises. It was launched publicly that summer at a conference held in the Library of Lambeth Palace (the Archbishop of Canterbury being one of its distinguished trustees), at which national and local government, the professional institutions, the voluntary bodies and notables of every kind pledged their support to this new, unknown and wholly untried organisation.

What was our role to be? Two special issues of *The Architectural Review*, 'Outrage' and 'Counter-Attack', had recently focused attention on the creeping banality of the post-war environment we were creating, but Duncan's own thoughts, it has to be admitted, were nebulous. There was no 'mission statement'. The tiny staff was totally amateur. What differentiated us from existing associations was, then, the fact that we enjoyed a healthier income. This gave us greater freedom and clout. We saw ourselves as a UK body. We saw ourselves as covering both town and country, as much concerned with planning as architecture pure and simple, with new development as much as the care of the old. We sought to compete with no one. We did not wish to set up as an arbiter of taste, nor as mere protesters but to be as creative as possible – to demonstrate the possibilities of excellence by practical means and then to publicise the results nationwide. Arrogantly I said that our job was to shift public opinion across the board, and create a much wider public

concern with, and understanding of, environmental potentials. Without this, fundamental progress would remain impossible.

But how, lacking any formal status, were we to get a foothold in
the system? What should be our priority? The early days of the Trust
were pretty chaotic, and I have often wondered since then what the
early days of other comparable organisations may have been like.
To some extent we were pushed along by others. A day or two after
our inaugural conference I was rung by Jamie Stormonth-Darling
(now Sir James), who asked if we could send the most expert planner
available to help save the Close round Dunblane Cathedral. But *now*
please. *Instantly.* We sent Thomas Sharp on the night train, the
proposals were killed, and we did good business with the National
Trust for Scotland ever after.

In retrospect, our first ten years have the look now of an heroic
decade. We spearheaded (and won) the Piccadilly Circus Inquiry,
the first *cause célèbre* in planning. We created the Lea Valley Regional Park, an unprecedented consortium effort by eighteen local
authorities. We drafted the Civic Amenities Act of 1967, which
amongst other things brought the concept of the conservation area
into the planning system. These were important highlights, but there
was much else as well. We started our Awards scheme, still going
strong forty years later, the biggest of its kind in the world. We
pioneered the use of volunteer labour to clear eyesores in the
countryside. We re-introduced the idea of moving big, semi-mature
trees with which to soften the lines of new development, something
now taken for granted, with a range of specialist equipment available for the purpose. We achieved immense publicity through our
co-operative improvement schemes in Norwich, Burslem, Windsor
and Haddington, to the point where hundreds of places all over
Britain were following suit. It was at the inauguration of the Haddington scheme, in 1962, that I first met Maurice Lindsay,
ricocheting around the town with a TV film crew, being then with
Border Television. And all the time we were nurturing the growth
of the civic society movement. When we set up shop in London in
1957, one of our first tasks had been to find out what local societies
existed in the UK. After considerable research we were able to list
about one hundred; with hindsight we now know there were nearer
two hundred. These we set out to inform, advise, encourage and
develop (in those days even with small grants). Ten years later the
number had grown to 630. Today there are maybe around one

thousand, formed into the National Council for Civic Trust Societies.

It was at the end of this first decade that Duncan persuaded Lord Muirshiel – surely one of the nicest people to become involved in Trust affairs – to head up a Civic Trust for Scotland; his inspired choice of Director was Maurice Lindsay. A regional Trust for the North West of England had already been formed; Trusts for the North East and for Wales followed. The four Associate Trusts, though based on comparable trust deeds, have found their own sources of finance locally and, rightly, have developed their own personalities. Their Chairmen sat upon the London Board, their Directors were in irregular but frequent contact. For Scotland we chose Glasgow as the new Trust's headquarters, and at the University we organised an appropriately impressive launch for it. The dramatic resurgence of central Glasgow over the past fifteen years has been a particular pleasure to watch.

Others describe in these pages particular aspects of the Scottish Trust's first thirty years, with some of which, like the great conservation campaign for Edinburgh New Town, we were happy to be associated. In London we pushed ahead with our own new initiatives – the reclamation of derelict land, campaigns to tame the environmental impact of the heavy lorry, environmental education in the schools. We made films which were translated into eighteen different languages, and gained clutches of national and international awards. We were a founder member of the European association of non-governmental conservation societies, Europa Nostra (which had, indeed, been brought into existence by the Council of Europe on the evidence of the Civic Trust's example). At the end of the 1960s Duncan became its President.

In the 1970s we were asked by the Government to administer, in the UK, the Council of Europe's campaign for European Architectural Heritage Year, 1975. This was aimed at alerting the Council's member nations to the steady erosion of Europe's architectural heritage, and was essentially an inter-governmental programme: in only one other country (Switzerland, where no appropriate federal department existed) was it handed over to a non-governmental agency. For us, ahead of the rest of Europe, this was a four-year programme. We set up an impressive framework, with the Duke of Edinburgh as President, covering every sector of public life. (Against the inclination of the Department of the Environment I insisted on the need for national committees for Scotland, Wales and Northern Ireland.) There is no doubt but that the UK, with the possible exception of the Netherlands, led the field and was the amazed envy of the other twenty or so nations participating. It is nice to be able to note that, among the permanent legacies we were able to leave from the campaign, the Architectural Heritage Fund, now worth some £11 million, was largely based upon the National Trust for Scotland's 'Little Houses Scheme'.

At the end of the 1970s we embarked upon the first of our regeneration schemes, in Wirksworth in Derbyshire. This was followed by a ten-year programme for Halifax and the Metropolitan District of Calderdale. The Trust's Rehabilitation Unit is today active in scores of towns and cities in all parts of England.

What did all this amount to? Much of the Trust's work has taken place behind closed doors, out of sight. Through all its activities, however, it seems to me that three broad strands can be identified. The first was the Trust's insistence that the environment has to be seen as a whole; that architecture, planning, landscape, conservation and new development, town and country, are indissolubly interlinked. The environment, as Molotov used to say of peace, is indivisible. Quality is the touchstone.

Secondly, we demonstrated, long before 'partnerships' became a buzzword, that nothing of environmental significance can be achieved without purposeful co-operation between the many parties necessarily involved. This was the essential lesson of those early street improvement schemes, when, for the first time, authorities, utilities, property owners, the professions, civic groups, all sat round a table deciding jointly what they hoped to achieve and how to do it. So too the creation of the Lea Valley Regional Park; so too EAHY, the regeneration schemes and all else.

Thirdly, surely, the establishment of the great network of civic societies, bringing to bear upon decision-making processes the full weight of informed public opinion. It is impossible to generalise about these societies. Some are big, some small. Some are rural, more are urban. Some are immensely active, others are moribund, all tending to wax and wane depending on their local problems and the leadership of the moment. The good ones are very good indeed and signal the enormous potential of this 'movement'. The view has been expressed within the assemblies of Europe that its potential is greater than that of the housing association movement.

With others the Civic Trusts have, it seems to me, indeed done much – as we hoped in 1957 – to shift public opinion over the post-war decades. And not only in Britain, but, through its films, lecture tours, conference contributions, far overseas.

*

So what now? Nothing stands still. The problems at the start of the new millennium are not those of 1957 or 1967. New organisations, some of an international character, have come into being – better funded some of them, more aggressive in some cases. Will the Civic Trusts come to be seen as a phenomenon of a certain period? What, if anything, should be the role of the environment movement in the years to come?

Some of the needs are obvious enough: the need for rational transport policies, for the better management of mass tourism, for a full acceptance of the levels of investment necessary to keep our towns and cities in good working order, for environmental education in schools, for greater imagination in the way we handle change. Decline has fuelled nostalgia and the heritage industry; now we have to learn to love the future.

Underlying any specifics, however, are some important generalities. Though important battles have been won, the war has not. As Duncan used to say: 'The gardener can never regard the job as done. Next week the fruit trees will need pruning, the grass will need mowing again'. The need for watchdogs has not disappeared. Although the basic machinery remains, much of the steam has gone out of the planning process. A primary purpose of the Thatcher/ Major years was to reduce the degree of government intervention in public life (though ironically, in administrative terms it increased). Decision-making was to be governed by the discipline of the market. The result, environmentally, was to relax the planning disciplines. Cash-strapped local authorities gave up refusing planning permission for undesirable developments because they knew that, on appeal, the application would be allowed by the Minister and the costs of the appeal, therefore, would be spent fruitlessly. After fifty years the basic purposes of planning have to be spelled out afresh, the rights of the public domain re-stated, enthusiasm and creativity rekindled.

Short-termism has become endemic in every corner of life. Its dangers bear particularly heavily on how we deal with our surroundings. Environmental change takes place over long timespans, but the pendulum of political policy swings wildly from administration to administration, from Minister to Minister; new fashions are promoted, key players disappear from the scene, boredom sets in. Flexibility in the detailed implementation of programmes and policies is essential, but continuity and commitment to the objectives are no less essential. There has to be a long-term keeper of the vision if imaginative concepts are not to become blurred, resources dissipated in half-realised, half-abandoned projects. Here, surely, is a role for the non-political, non-governmental associations?

The Civic Trusts' experience shows how greatly independent agencies can contribute to quality and imagination in all forms of environmental improvement – provided they are given adequate resources. Some forms of charitable work require little more than a personal commitment of time. Substantial change to our surroundings, however, nearly always calls for substantial investment. If that investment is to be attracted, professional expertise of the highest calibre has to be available to shape the project concerned. To realise its potential for positive, creative work the non-governmental movement must somehow be put upon a more orderly financial footing. Private donations and annual subscriptions can never pay for more than the paperclips. Commercial sponsorship has become the approved source of funding in recent years, but it is not without its dangers. When the Civic Trust was formed, its covenanted income was without strings of any kind. Today, as costs escalate alarmingly and competition for charitable funding becomes ever more acute, industrial and commercial companies, not unnaturally, look for some sort of return from their investment in terms of kudos and publicity. The result is that, while the projects they finance may well be worthwhile, they are not necessarily the projects that *most* need doing (some of which might even cut across sponsors' commercial interests). 'Core' funding – i.e. for basic administration, working libraries and so on – is notoriously difficult to obtain. Long-term funding, for anything lasting more than a year or two, is seldom to be looked for. Over and above these considerations, the continual search for possible charitable sources, often fruitless, siphons off time and talent which could more usefully be devoted to the purposes of the charity concerned. In all environmental work stable, continuing funding, free of political and commercial pressures, is a prerequisite of effective action.

Somehow, perhaps at the hands of the Press, environmental groups are now lumped together with all sorts of special interest pressure groups as just another 'lobby'. This surely, is a misnomer. 'Lobbies' – and today they are without number – in my understanding of the word represent the special interests (often financial) of a single-issue sector of society: farmers, the heavy-lorry industry, house builders and so on. The environmental movement works, not for its own interests, but for the community, the nation, as a whole. Its funding needs to reflect this.

Of course life will be more pleasant for all of us, in every walk of life, when town and countryside, the places where we live and work, are seemly, dignified, beautiful, enriching to the spirit. But there is more to it than that. Unless we halt their slide into squalor and disarray, unless in our surroundings we can demonstrate a clear faith in the future, investment in those places will dry up, they will represent the fading face of a dependent society. We shape our surroundings, but in some measure they shape us. What is at stake is in fact the future of civilised society.

M   Maurice, musician, makar, monifauld
A   Anthologies you plan and execute,
U   Urbane, warmhertit, catholic, astute,
R   Radiant o hope, wi sweirties unappalled,
I   In spite of kiaughs an comitees untauld
C   Castan your nets for renascential loot,
E   Editor, critic, eident to recruit

L   Leal Scots for our Kulturkampf, slee and bauld,
I   I scryve this thrawn acrostich raw on raw
N   No cataloguan aa the credit due,
D   Dear Maurice, to your zest for tune and rhyme.
S   Scotland's Renaissance awes a feck to you,
A   Anither Allan Ramsay come in time.
Y   Your wark's weel ruitit, as its fruct sall shaw.

Douglas Young

CHAPTER FIFTEEN

The Scottish Civic Trust

John Gerrard

S CENE: the University of York, summer of '68. Its brand-new campus was staging a major conservation conference, intended to set the pace for solving the growing physical and economic problems of the nation's historic towns and cities.

The event drew in participants from the length and breadth of Britain, among them Maurice Lindsay, then hardly a year into his task as the first Director of the Scottish Civic Trust and, by chance, myself as a humble delegate from my then employer, Oxford City Council.

By such encounters are whole lives changed. Thirty years on, the contrast remains vivid between the steady routine of the junior local government officer and the vast, unpredictable range of activity demanded of this still tiny fledgling of the Civic Trust movement.

Tiny, certainly, but already vigorous in the hands of Maurice and its most wise and human of Chairmen, the late Lord Muirshiel. Projects already under way ranged, geographically, from organising an intensive professional survey of the Park Area of Glasgow, soon to become one of the City's, and Scotland's, first Conservation Areas, to a successful battle to defeat the schemes of Orkney County Council to demolish one of Kirkwall's most historic buildings, Papdale House, in order to free its site for school building.

After experiencing only a day or two of this strange new career, a trick of coincidence took me back with Maurice to the same University of York and a gathering of British civic amenity societies organised by the Civic Trust. If the strength of this emergent popular voice on behalf of the built environment was not already apparent, it became so then, as, more gradually, did the essential differences between the roles of the original parent and its autonomous family of associate Civic Trusts in the North of England, Wales and Scotland. Maurice expressed it well in one of his writings at that time: 'This focal point of the Civic Trust movement makes possible the pooling of experience and ideas and the provision of certain common services but leaves the component parts complete responsibility for developing according to the needs and character of the area they serve'.

So the special and peculiar needs of Scotland – 'this knuckle end of Europe' – and its distinctive character have, from its birth, provided constant reference points for the activity of the Scottish Civic Trust and the justification for its separate existence.

It was asked then, and sometimes since, why it seemed right to found a new Scottish environmental body to attend to these needs. Well-respected cultural organisations had, after all, been at work for many years in much the same field, notably the National Trust for Scotland, the Saltire Society and the Association for the Protection of Rural Scotland. The Scottish Georgian Society had by then established itself as a bonny fechter in the cause of architectural preservation, and civic amenity societies such as the venerable Cockburn Association and the *parvenu* New Glasgow Society were highly active on their own territories. Encouragingly, however, it was some of those very organisations, and in particular the National Trust for Scotland, which helped to welcome the new Trust into being at Glasgow University in May 1967.

Its place of birth was no accident, nor was it coincidental that its first Chairman and Director were both men with long West of Scotland pedigrees, nor that its office was set up in Glasgow rather than further east. This decision may have contributed to its welcome at the hands of its Edinburgh-based counterparts. It is certainly why its efforts have often been directed particularly towards those areas, many of them in the Glasgow conurbation, which during and after the industrial revolution had failed to keep up high standards of civic housekeeping.

The Trust's *raison d'être* has always been based on that of its parent, with its insistence on the importance of high quality in our surroundings, whether through careful protection of the past or the encouragement of the best in contemporary planning and environmental design. Here, its effective promotion simply needed a Scottish dimension through the appointment of trustees and staff familiar with the important institutional differences north of the Border and at ease with the governmental, commercial and cultural networks vital to securing sound funding and making its initiatives work for the widest common good.

For the first two or three years the Trust's lines of action diverged little from those familiar to colleagues in England and Wales. First priorities included encouraging the public to become involved in local environmental issues by developing the small Scottish network of existing civic amenity societies, as the Trust's autonomous battalions in the field. At times, indeed, matters could seem akin to a state of war. Almost unimaginably, the word 'heritage' then crossed few lips, while most Scots would forgivably have confused 'Conservation' with the manufacture of jam. It was, simultaneously, still a time of immense and often poorly controlled change, particularly in those areas of high population suffering from over-comprehensive urban redevelopment and ambitious traffic plans which badly needed the criticism and, frequently, the vehement opposition of an alert and well-informed public.

Scottish planning law and practice were, however, slowly adjusting to the need for greater sensitivity to local character, especially through the operation of the Civic Amenities Act. This radical measure had been approved by Parliament in 1967 as an all-party response to a Civic Trust initiative led by its founding Chairman, Duncan Sandys. By this Act was born the now familiar but then original concept of the Conservation Area, which the new Scottish Civic Trust saw as essential to its cause of maintaining an abiding 'sense of place' within every sensitive area of change. Its initial practical involvement in Glasgow stood it in good stead. By the end of 1975, when it was chosen by Government to co-ordinate a generous Scottish contribution to European Architectural Heritage Year, more than two hundred Conservation Areas had been designated by local planning authorities in places as different as commercial city centres, remote Highland villages and planned industrial communities.

One of the Trust's most valuable functions has been as the catalyst for a number of well-known and urgently needed long-term environmental projects. Occasionally there may have been a suggestion of jackets held and recalcitrant heads knocked together. Usually, however, the Trust's involvement has been invited and maintained through belief in its reputation as honest, independent environmental broker.

Two of its more significant ventures into these waters began almost at once. The famous campaign for the conservation of the Georgian New Town of Edinburgh, described more fully in a later chapter, was sparked by the concern of one of the greatest Scots of recent times, Sir Robert Matthew, at that time a Trustee of both the London- and Glasgow-based Civic Trusts. His energetic drive and the hard work of the voluntary survey teams which confirmed the true depth of neglect prevailing in the New Town were a revelation to one arriving on the scene in the midst of such activity. The evidence collated for presentation at the subsequent 1970 International Conference was sufficient to convince the Scottish Office and Edinburgh Corporation of the need for urgent action, the benefits of which, through the New Town Conservation Committee, continue to this day. That conference can also be seen as a landmark in the perception of the Trust as a national body, one capable of co-ordinating such a major international event albeit, then, with assistance from Civic Trust colleagues.

Perhaps this publicity encouraged the appearance in the Trust's office one afternoon of a university lecturer in Economic History who suggested that the Trust should now turn its attention to stimulating the regeneration of New Lanark. John Hume, now Historic Scotland's Chief Inspector of Historic Buildings, together with Harry Smith, the Provost of Lanark, thereby helped to initiate an ongoing twenty-five year saga of heroic proportions. New Lanark may have seemed then the most hopeless of Britain's industrial sites of undisputed world importance. Now its revival can appear to have been almost too effective, especially on a Glasgow holiday weekend. The occasional huge influx of visitors masks, however, the underlying success of one of the project's main guiding principles, that the village must no longer be dependent on a single type of venture but should be a place where new businesses and a varied social mix of permanent residents balance the demands of the tourist industry. The Scottish Civic Trust can feel justifiably proud to have been instrumental both in the campaign's beginning and in helping to steer its subsequent course.

This enabling role has carried on in numerous ways. Occasionally graceful retirement seemed proper, once an initiative had begun to settle down. In other cases the Trust has kept up its original involvement, on the boards and committees formed to take the projects forward. The list of such bodies only emphasises the breadth of the Trust's expanding interests. In the 1970s and '80s they included the funding of church repair (Scottish Architectural Heritage Trust), the rescue and transfer to new ownership of redundant railway viaducts (British Rail Scottish Viaducts Committee), environmental education (the Scottish Environment Education Council which originated in an approach to the Trust by teachers in Strathclyde Region) and, in this decade, island management (Iona Liaison Group). An outstanding instance has been the Trust's collaboration in starting and developing the Glasgow West Conservation Trust, conveying across the central belt the exemplary experience of its Edinburgh New Town and Old Town predecessors. The operation formally began with a deputation to Glasgow's Lord Provost, led by the Trust and the Glasgow Institute of Architects. As at New Lanark, however, it was seeded by the persistence of a University lecturer, Dr James Macaulay, and his awareness that a major combined effort was required to stop and reverse the insidious erosion of the quality of Scotland's largest and finest nineteenth-century suburb. This Conservation Trust has naturally developed its own Glaswegian flavour and ways of working, and its energy may soon be put to practical use over a wider area of the City.

A further strand in the Scottish Civic Trust's web of activity concerns the physical improvement of smaller communities. Far from commonplace in the Trust's early years, urban regeneration is now a standard item in the armoury of local authorities and enterprise trusts. The Civic Trust bequeathed an already well-defined role to its offspring in the form of the 'Street Improvement Scheme', a good example of which it had masterminded in Haddington a few years previously. Relying strongly on the Civic Trust's guiding motto, 'sense of place', such comprehensive, if mainly cosmetic, facelifts had already proved popular in various parts of England when the Trust was approached by Brian Lambie, the last Provost of Biggar in Lanarkshire, to design and carry through a similar scheme in the burgh's unusually wide High Street. Two years of hard work and great personal pleasure ensued before the street scene was initially judged to be complete, its enhancement heightened by the anonymous donation of a permanent sundial sculpture by the internationally famous artist, Ian Hamilton Finlay. Travelling through Biggar today, it is remarkable to see how the spirit of that first redding-up has survived the vagaries of twenty-five years, thanks to the continuing care and respect of the community.

While the Biggar project was progressing, the Trust was invited by Glasgow Corporation to run a pilot campaign to brighten up the appearance and image of the city. 'Facelift Glasgow' became responsible for the first concerted attempts to remove the century-old layers of grime from its sandstone frontages and monuments, beginning symbolically with the statue to Sir Walter Scott in the centre of George Square. The jury remains out on the long-term physical effect of most methods of stone-cleaning but there can be no doubt of its benefits in revealing Glasgow as a city of magnificent architecture, to its own citizens and in the eyes of the rest of the world. Without this long-term effort, would Glasgow have been given the prized accolade of the 1990 European City of Culture? It seems doubtful. 'Facelift Glasgow' was also remarkable for engaging the energy of young people in local tree-planting and clean-up campaigns and in other works of physical improvement, all co-ordinated from the Trust's George Square office by specially recruited colleagues. Among them was Sadie Douglas, who stayed with the Trust to become its friendly and much-respected Administrator after Maurice Lindsay's retirement.

Nevertheless, the Biggar and Glasgow enterprises hardly constituted 'regeneration' as it is known today and practised, for instance, by a special unit of the Civic Trust. A second Lanarkshire small town initiative followed at Lesmahagow, this time intended to make the community more attractive to incoming industry. More recently the Trust has contributed its experience to a more substantial area regeneration programme focused on the East Ayrshire lace-making town of Newmilns where the local economy has long been in decline. Here its growing competence in the art of historic building re-use has been put to practical effect in stimulating the conversion of an architecturally important but redundant listed school and the restoration of a ruinous but now bijou example of a mediaeval tower house, both at the centre of the town. Such positive progress has encouraged the new local authority to extend the initiative outwards to embrace a number of other towns and villages in the Upper Irvine Valley, and the Trust remains committed to its support.

In spite of the range of all these projects and the effort spent on them, few varied radically from the established pattern of Civic Trust activity in other parts of the Kingdom. The trigger which changed the major emphasis of the Trust, giving it to this day a role all its own, was the passing into law of the 1969 Town and Country Planning (Scotland) Act and the effect of the official regulations that went with it. Amongst its other provisions this Act bestowed legal protection, for the first time, on Scotland's amazing array of individual historic buildings. With the exception of Ancient Monuments and a few other special cases, this tremendous stock of cultural assets could previously have been altered or demolished virtually at will. Suddenly, the situation was very different. A new requirement for public advertisement of all such schemes meant that any group or individual was entitled to comment on them and, if so desired, to lodge formal objection with the Local Planning Authority, which, with the Secretary of State as long-stop, would judge the matter on its merits. Now we tend to take for granted what was then a huge advance in cultural damage prevention and limitation and, by extension, in demand for higher standards of foresight, care and skill in historic building conservation. Furthermore, by the unheralded stroke of some official pen, planning departments were required to consult the Scottish Civic Trust on every plan proposing the demolition of any one of the country's then approximately twenty thousand listed buildings. So began an uninterrupted stream of 'casework' which soon expanded into an expectation to respond to many other individual proposals affecting listed buildings and Conservation Areas and which shortly required the Trust to take on extra help in the form of a succession of newly qualified graduates working on two- or three-year training contracts.

Soon the Trust was plunged into the first of many public local inquiries, resulting from the refusal of applicants to accept a decision in favour of retaining their listed property or from the wish of the Secretary of State to make his own judgement where there was a sufficient body of objection. Fortunately not all of these tribunals were as strangely motivated as that triggered by the decision of the Council of a small Fife burgh that its ancient castle should be destroyed as a symbol of former feudal oppression. Lasting good, however, followed when the same Council was persuaded to sell its unwanted asset for restoration to the architectural practice of Ian Begg, whose evidence greatly helped the Trust, the (then) Scottish Georgian Society and other objectors to win their case.

The Trust has always and rightly jealously preserved its independence from officialdom in any form. Nevertheless its acquired specialism in historic building and area conservation led quickly to a comradely relationship of mutual respect with the officials of the responsible department, now agency, of the Scottish Office. This relationship has flourished in a number of practical ways, starting with a commission in 1980 to compile a pioneering manual of guidance on the re-use of historic buildings. Long out of print, it may nevertheless have served its purpose in stimulating the prolonged life of all kinds of interesting buildings, up and down the country, which had exhausted their existing purpose. This completed, the Scottish Office turned to the Trust to take over and develop what was then a minor function of its property division, the Register of Buildings at Risk. As a further extension of the Trust's concern for building re-use this role seemed only natural and, supported by one hundred per cent funding from Historic Scotland, it has become perhaps its most important year-round missionary task. Comprising a database constantly averaging over a thousand threatened or otherwise redundant properties in Scotland alone and with a dedicated and expert member of staff to run it, the Register's practical success in promoting their availability has already established it as a model for similar projects in other parts of the United Kingdom.

Likewise unequalled by our companion Civic Trusts in recent years has been the Scottish Civic Trust's involvement in matters European, which may in part reflect Scotland's long history of mutual links with countries across the North Sea and further abroad and its distance from certain Anglocentric political attitudes to 'Europe'. The Scottish Civic Trust can, therefore, be proud of its constant commitment to the cause of Europa Nostra, the pan-European federation of voluntary amenity organisations founded by Duncan Sandys and certain influential friends as the trans-national counterpart of the Civic Trust and National Trust groupings in the United Kingdom. This commitment was strikingly reinforced when Maurice Lindsay became its Secretary General, soon after retiring in 1983 as Director of the Scottish Civic Trust, at a time when the whole future of Europa Nostra was in very grave doubt. That it flourishes again today is in no small measure due to his canny native perseverance and, where necessary, powerful directness of mind.

The second notable jewel in the Trust's international crown is its championship of European Heritage Days, the September event popularly known in Scotland as Doors Open Day. When Glasgow was setting out its stall as the European City of Culture for 1990, the Trust encouraged its arts organisers to try out this simple idea, pioneered in President Pompidou's France, whereby the owners of good buildings with interesting interiors are invited to open them without charge to the public as part of a concerted programme. This free-for-all celebration of the nation's architectural riches has since spread to over forty member-countries of the Council of Europe and to the rest of the United Kingdom. Scotland's own programme has grown to ensure free entry to over six hundred buildings annually, from cottages to power stations, along with related displays, activities and archaeological events. All of this is co-ordinated centrally by the Trust with generous support from Historic Scotland and the enthusiasm and efficiency of numerous local organisers, including public authorities, civic societies and building preservation trusts. It has not always been easy to find ways of contributing so directly to the gaiety and cultural enjoyment of the nation, given so many more re-active demands on the Trust's services. It is to be hoped that other such opportunities will continue to arise and that the Trust will be able to grasp them as securely. Such ambitions may prove less difficult to fulfil now that the Trust at last owns its own small part of Scotland's built heritage, the beautifully conserved 'Tobacco Merchant's House' of 1774 which is one of Central Glasgow's very few elegant survivors from that era, providing more space and greater opportunities for contact with the public.

The age of information technology is well and truly upon us and its possibilities and consequences will surely lead the Trust along new routes unsuspected by those who joined it in its early years. Even so, the purpose of those journeys must surely remain the same, to recognise and serve Scotland's contemporary needs to the Trust's best ability and to ensure that the immense quality and variety of its landscapes and its built environment are never overlooked in the process. A new millennium dawns, with the prospect of a closer, more approachable and perhaps more responsive system of government. Maurice Lindsay's successors have interesting times ahead.

To attempt such a survey, in short order, has been to omit so much of interest which, one day, should be set down at greater length. Maurice himself needs no reminder of how greatly the Trust's achievement, to date, is due to him and to successive Chairmen with vision, tact and good judgement, who, with a doughty band of Trustees from many walks of life, have steered the Trust on course past many rocks and shoals which could have grounded its progress. Nor has there been space to do justice to the succession of close colleagues, chosen as much for their good humour and willingness to lend a hand at almost anything legal as for their genuine professional or secretarial abilities.

The Trust's place in the philosophy of Maurice himself, that remarkable embodiment in one person of so many aspects of Scottish cultural life, might best be summed up in his own words, composed as a contribution to another publication: 'At this stage of our evolution toward the good life, the imagination satisfied through the arts and an environment that both stimulates and refreshes should be regarded not as luxurious fripperies but as a basic human right'.

On our way back to Carlisle we made a detour through Biggar to take MacDiarmid and his wife to dinner. We had a pleasant meal in a former mansion house converted to a country hotel. MacDiarmid was at his most gallantly engaging. Over coffee Valda suddenly said:

'I can't think why I'm accepting your bloody middle-class hospitality.'

'I don't think you need worry too much,' I laughed. 'You've already eaten it'.

As usual on such occasions, the poet looked embarrassed and annoyed.

(*Thank You for Having Me*, page 176)

CHAPTER SIXTEEN

The Conservation of Biggar

Brian Lambie

MY FIRST KNOWLEDGE of the newly formed Civic Trust in the early '60s came from a newsreel in which I spotted an uncle, Mayor of an English midlands town, in the party of dignitaries walking through Windsor at the opening of one of the first street improvement schemes. The scheme which later materialised in his own town was no doubt a reflection of the degree to which he had been impressed by this inaugural project.

A few years later I found myself in a similar situation walking through the streets of Haddington, deputising for our own civic head at the first such scheme in Scotland. It too was organised by the Civic Trust, shortly before its Scottish counterpart was launched with Maurice Lindsay as the first Director.

The new Scottish body's first street improvement scheme turned out to be Biggar. I'm not sure who made the choice, but initial discussions had taken place between Maurice and Provost Jimmy Telfer in 1969. The latter's sudden death propelled me into the Chair, and into the welter of arrangements for all the proposed renovation of road surfaces and shop fronts.

Biggar has one of the widest streets of any town in Britain. It straddles the old route from Edinburgh to the south and to the south-west where lay the shrine of St Ninian and Whithorn. Outwardly Victorian, the buildings cling to the medieval lay-out of 1451 when the town received its first charter as a burgh from King James II. The north side is on an incline from the road, providing the early inhabitants with plenty of room for markets and fairs, and their twentieth-century successors with ample parking spaces. Only this central portion, which includes the principal shopping area, was chosen for the scheme.

We were very lucky to have advice and support throughout from John Gerrard who, at that time, had only just come to the Scottish Civic Trust. His enthusiasm won over the doubters, the grumblers and the downright opponents of the scheme, his youthful figure became a very kenspeckle part of the streetscape, and his open approach disarmed all those whose natural attitude was to resist change.

Much was achieved by subtle colours, in harmony with the local plum-coloured stonework and by the upgrading of fascia signs with quality lettering: very little was required in actual structural alterations. The main road surface, like so many in Lanarkshire, had originally been clad in red Cairngryffe gravel, quarried only 10 miles away from the town. This now failed the exacting standard required for a trunk road and was replaced with grey. Happily, John saw to it that Cairngryffe stone was used to surface the vast area of the sidelines, and the parking areas were marked with neat studs instead of lined-out boxes. When finished, the whole road surface was a masterly blend of good design and indigenous materials. The 1950s lamp standards were fitted with more elegant heads and painted an unobtrusive grey.

Biggar's High Street had been lined with an avenue of forest trees to mark Queen Victoria's Jubilee. While most of these had survived the injudicious pruning of former Councils, some just had to be replaced. The locals got together and paid for this as a contribution to the scheme. Unfortunately at that time, the supply of semi-mature trees available was limited and several ash trees were included which have a very short season in leaf.

A handsome jubilee fountain, once a focal point on the crown of the High Street, had been removed after the war as a relic of imperialism, and the gap left in the streetscape had never been filled. As it was European Conservation Year, this was remedied to some extent at least by commissioning a sundial from the poet Ian Hamilton Finlay, whose garden at Little Sparta, a few miles north of Biggar, was then just in its infancy. I picked up the slate slab, which came up from a quarry in Wales on the back of a friend's lorry, and transported it to Dunsyre on the roof of the car. At Little Sparta, Michael Harvey was waiting to carve Ian's poem on it, in brand new typography which he had specially created for the work.

Back in Biggar, the burgh's 'works department' (two handymen bricklayers) cast the circular plinth and laid down a surround of secondhand cobblestones. The local engineer provided an aluminium gnomon rod to Ian's specifications. One of Stephen Bann's interpretations of the terse inscription of just three lines –

AZURE & SON
ISLANDS LTD
OCEANS INC

– speaks of the relevance to the situation in a town where the time of opening and shutting of shops – human time – is linked with solar time, the time of the stars.

Fourth September 1970. The big day dawned, and Maurice, with impeccable bow tie, was there along with Lord Muirshiel the Chairman and other representatives from the Civic Trust, the Scottish Office and Lanarkshire County Council. In the party was Miss Mitchell, late of Langlees, Biggar. Then 90 years of age, with another ten years of activity before her, she had come to see that we hadn't done anything amiss with her beloved town. A former member of Biggar Town Council and the only woman on the East Kilbride Development Corporation, her studies in Canada before the First World War had borne fruit in that most successful of Scottish New Towns and earned her the Town and Country Planning Association's highest award, the Ebenezer Howard Medal.

On the platform in front of the High Street's Victorian Corn Exchange, I stood between Lady Tweedsmuir, the Minister of State, who was performing the inaugural ceremony, and the Lord Lieutenant, Lord Clydesmuir. Thus I was able to quote quite accurately, being the Provost, from a local poem of the last century, each verse of which ends with the lines 'Biggar stands, mid pleasant lands,/ Betwixt the Clyde and Tweed'. Ian's sundial was then unveiled by four children from the High School and Primary School, and it has been stimulating comment and questions ever since.

The party walked round the bounds of the new scheme, the car parking areas briefly empty for the occasion and the shop fronts resplendent in gold leaf and new paint. Two small council house schemes of improvement were inspected, both designed by Larry Rolland and Ian Begg. One replaced a former shop and had a three-storey gable to the street, the other had been a very derelict seventeenth-century property at the townhead which still retained an attractive stair tower at the back. Both schemes were in accordance with the Town Council's policy of restoring or rebuilding rundown property in the townscape instead of adding to existing council house developments which sprawled over the farmland around the town.

(The result is now taken for granted but has preserved an inner townscape of indigenous integrity.)

On the officials' tour list that day was a visit to Gladstone Court, the small street museum off the High Street, then just a couple of years old and at that time only opened on request for the key from my ironmongery shop. In it were the shopfronts and street furniture saved from a different age, later to be joined by a bank, telephone exchange and other symbols of civic confidence.

Just a very few years after the completion of the street scheme, Biggar lost its own living civic symbols, its Provost and Town Council, and found itself in Strathclyde Region as a minor part of Clydesdale District. Thoughts of extending the scheme to the rest of the town were conveniently dropped, although the planning department of the new District did succeed in having the High Street declared an Outstanding Conservation Area with over 100 listed buildings. This hasn't always been a blessing: we now for example have a commercial garage canopy disguised with a slate roof and, to date, no good honest modern work has emerged.

Much worse than these minor irritations was, however, the inability of the one national and two local authorities to agree upon responsibility for repairs to the not inconsiderable surface areas of the wide High Street. Local pressure brought forth one official from the Scottish Office with a plan for an island down the middle, lit by the ubiquitous round glass globes. After being soundly criticised at a public meeting in 1988, this plan disappeared from sight, perhaps down one of the numerous potholes which were becoming a feature of the street. As the potholes deepened, the various authorities did get together with a consultancy group and, heedless of what might have been learned from the previous occasion, launched plan number two in 1992. A courtesy exercise was held later for the benefit of the lieges, who were not impressed by the fact that little if anything had been suggested to offset the vast loss of street parking facilities by providing an adequate alternative elsewhere. The sham Victorian lamp posts, the other street furniture and the suggested textured surfaces proposed were all of the type which distant policymakers and planners have used to create town centres nationwide of consistent banality.

Having been told that this was it or nothing, Biggar decided to do without meantime. Within a very short time a Business Group was formed, and also (something which I ought to have seen to after the

1970 scheme) the Biggar and District Civic Society. These and other local organisations have since met with a much better response from the new South Lanarkshire Council which, fortunately, is now in charge of all the major services and has nobody else to argue with over responsibilities. A Town Centre Consultative Forum has provided a meeting place for all interests, and a new scheme has been worked out which faced up to the all-important parking question.

This new scheme will be upon us soon. Will we like it? Will the many visitors who enjoy watching the world go by seated in their cars in the free parking areas like it? There have been compromises but, despite some official replies to comments by the public ('there can't be anything wrong with the new lamp posts; they were designed by an internationally famous architect'), South Lanarkshire appears most willing to DO the Right Thing. Miss Mitchell, after all, had called it the finest street in the County, and for a short time after 1970 it continued to be so.

Soon after the inauguration of the scheme, Gladstone Court, the wee museum off the High Street, became the nucleus of the Biggar Museum Trust, which has since expanded into a mini-state of buildings and artefacts saved from destruction or loss. It had been opened in 1968 by Hugh MacDiarmid, who lived in a cottage near the town with his wife Valda. It was to be one of the supreme achievements of the Trust to secure this cottage, Brownsbank, and renovate it in time for MacDiarmid's centenary in 1992. Since then, three young writers have been given accommodation there, in a joint venture supported by the Scottish Arts Council and the local authority. The enthusiastic local committee, which runs the writers' fellowship on behalf of the museum, is backed by a circle of writers, academics and poets, one of the first of whom was Maurice Lindsay.

Biggar's museum ventures are never complete – a Motor Museum commemorating Scotland's only successful commercial motor manufacturers, the Albion company, is on the cards. This firm was founded in 1899 by a local engineering genius, Thomas Blackwood Murray, and his brother-in-law Norman Fulton, and it is ironic that these two were part of the revolution responsible for the clogged-up road system of today and the problems arising from the decline of the rail system in favour of motorways after the war.

Perhaps by the time we start putting Albion lorries into our museum, the nation's attitude to the roads and transport of the future will take better account of the places we live in. The generation of

2098 may see our street, again a handsome tree-lined boulevard, as good, if not better than the one which was created out of the old market place by the visionaries of the 1880s. Perhaps too, Joly Mitchell's plaintive song reminding us, 'You don't miss what you've got till it's gone', when you *'pave Paradise and put in a parking lot'*, and *'put the trees in a tree museum'*, will no longer need to be sung. I hope so.

***

ANON

They are excavating the mound at the foot of the village
young men with gentle eyes and curious beards,
and names like Brown and Soutar, and soft-breasted girls
on whom they'll one day stamp their borrowed image,
name upon name. What else have they to preserve?

They are digging for signs. How like were the other Browns
and Soutars, ripening out of the nameless soil
and having to leave their names when it took them under?
Turning anonymity over and over,
they are finding only shards and pieces of bone.

(*Selected Poems 1942–1972*, page 43)

***

CHAPTER SEVENTEEN

The Revival of New Lanark

Harry Smith

D EAR MAURICE,
It's Happy Birthday to you from an old friend, who celebrated *his* 80th, in the Musicians' Gallery in New Lanark, in Robert Owen's world famous 'Institute for the Formation of Character'. You will remember well that Robert Owen had the Institute built for his mill workers and their families, at considerable cost, and thereby caused some disquiet to his partners in the Mills' ownership.

You will recall, too, that you and John Ford, of our Scottish Civic Trust, and your ladies, were coming to the 80th party, but failed to make it because of a car breakdown. A great pity indeed, for we had a very happy evening, but in your case, Maurice, you missed the wonderful choice of quality red wines which were available. Of course, to explain this last remark, I have to reveal that over the last several years I have observed your obvious enjoyment of good red wines. A weakness of will, which Joyce, your good lady, must surely be aware of, and be concerned about.

Today, a Sunday, I have just returned home from New Lanark; the village was alive with several thousand visitors. There were stalls of so many kinds, music, dancers, young children playing their guitars and singing, bouncy castle, Punch and Judy, and so many other entertainments. It was another successful New Lanark Victorian Fair, with most of us dressed in the appropriate apparel of the time.

Why am I recalling this day to you, Maurice? Because, in thinking about my Birthday Greeting, I remember with gratitude the long and strongly supportive role you have played over the last twenty-five years. Ever faithful, influential, reliable and innovative in your suggestions and particularly so in those early difficult years of rebuilding New Lanark.

It was in April 1972 that we first met. A day which, not to be over-dramatic, really did change the course of my life, through your enthusiasm and that of Viscount Muirshiel, your Chairman of the Scottish Civic Trust, about the conserving of New Lanark.

The Government of the day had asked you and the Trust to call a public meeting of interested parties and organisations to discuss the possibilities of reviving New Lanark as a historic reminder of Robert Owen and David Dale's work. It was held (as you will recall) in a hotel in Kirkfieldbank, on the banks of the River Clyde, about one mile from Lanark, an appropriate setting for a beginning.

We had a most encouraging cross-section meeting of conservation-minded delegates. The aim was to find the will, the desire, the organisation to revive a historic village, which at the time was almost derelict. This was likely to be a huge task, as those of us who were local knew that the Mills were then in the ownership of a local scrap metal industrialist. However, your enthusiasm that day – and I can remember it vividly – played a major part in carrying forward the decision to seek means to restore the village for posterity. You were powerfully persuasive that day, and assured us that you would play your part, as would the Scottish Civic Trust, in giving us the maximum advice, support and technical advice.

Thus, from this meeting, a fairly rookie Provost of the Royal and Ancient Burgh of Lanark was 'landed' (and I use the word literally) with the Chairmanship of what was to prove a highly profiled conservation committee. And it's fair to say, Maurice, and you will agree, that the work done by this committee over the years had European and indeed world-wide publicity for Robert Owen's social reforms, and David Dale's mill village.

Then in 1974, when Jim Arnold was appointed, came the massive clean-up job, before we even began conservation. From the previous mills' occupant, tons and tons of scrap of all kinds, metal, aluminium, parts of aircraft bodies, old lorry bodies, even old boats, and tons of old metal slag dust had to be moved. As well as that, some buildings had been so long out of use that trees were growing through the broken roofs. So, as we often indicated to each other, in those early days it was somewhat of a nightmare. But we worked on and started the real conservation and, you remember, we finished up with a workforce of 260 Manpower Services Commission manual, and about 60 supervisory and administrative, staff. They certainly did a great job over ten years' work, and without them we would have had great difficulty in achieving the success that New Lanark is now so well known for.

Later, when you were appointed Secretary-General of Europa Nostra from 1983 to 1991, already, among your many heritage memberships, you were also a member of the Historic Buildings Council for Scotland and it seemed you were able to highlight the outstanding conservation work being achieved at New Lanark. This resulted in no small way in our being awarded the Europa Nostra Medal in 1987. This achievement had been preceded by New Lanark being proposed as a World Heritage Village. These were proud moments for us, especially those who had been involved since the very early days of near dereliction.

I can recall for you that in those years up to 1985 I too was a member of the Historic Buildings Council for Scotland, and constantly I was aware of your kindness, your advice and technical help for me and New Lanark, which was always graciously and ungrudgingly given. At no time did I have fears or inhibition about 'lobbying' you, or asking for the 'inside' information.

Happily, and due to the national and international publicity, our awards increased and they included Tourist Board Awards, Travel Writer Awards, and awards from the Royal Institute of Town Planning, Urban Re-generation, the Robert Owen Society in Japan, the Royal Institute of Architects and many others.

To add to this, Maurice, our team at New Lanark was chosen by Government, along with Wanlockhead Mining Museum, to carry out a feasibility study for the marketing and financial operation of the world-famous salt mine of Wieliczka in Poland. This was really quite an honour for us, and further European recognition of our continuing, acknowledged and respected role in industrial heritage conservation. The Salt Mine later became a World Heritage Project.

Despite your continuing and constant role in so many conservation bodies, and your literary outpourings, you were always available to us in New Lanark; you were there if needed, with that final piece of advice, technical, finance-seeking or grant-pursuing. In addition, when I look at the list of your activities during your lifetime, your writings, books, poems, such a variety of publications, it makes me wonder where your time came from, and despite all of this you invariably had time to help us.

As you now know, Maurice, the Annie McLeod Ride has been updated, and the Mill Hotel in Mill One was completed in May 1998, with an official opening ceremony on May 14th, Robert Owen's birthday, with all the facilities of an upmarket hotel in a conserved mill building. We have plans, but not the money yet, for a Millennium Ride alongside Millennium New Lanark celebrations. The Robert Owen School is wind and watertight, but our plans for the internal refurbishment towards an outdoor educational centre, for the many thousands of school pupils who come here each year, have yet to attract the substantial grant required. However, we are confident that money for this internationally famous Robert Owen School will come one day.

There are, too, other exciting projects, part of New Lanark's vision for the complete restoration of the village: bridges across the River Clyde to the wildlife conservation area, the restoration of Mantilla Row, and the last of the housing in Double Row to be restored.

Dear Maurice, you were there alongside us at the rebirth of 'our' social experiment. Your contribution has been, and is, greatly appreciated. I can only hope that you and I, in our eighties, can live to see the final and complete restoration of the work that you began.

I end this letter by sending the sincere regards of your fellow Trustees and of Jim, our Director, and all the staff here, in appreciation of your help over the past twenty-five years. For a man so highly ranked in the field of Scottish literature and in conservation, you were always notable for the manner in which you offered sound advice, in the most quiet and un-self-important way.

I send my regards to your dear wife Joyce, to your girls, and to all your families, and to you, my friend of many years, the most unassuming of unassuming men, I accord my humble appreciation and thanks for all you have done for New Lanark.

Yours sincerely,

Harry Smith, MBE, JP
Chairman of the Trustees of New Lanark Conservation Trust and ex-Provost of the Royal and Ancient Burgh of Lanark, 1971 to 1975.

HURLYGUSH

The hurlygush* and hallyoch† o the watter
skinklan i the moveless simmer sun
harles‡ aff the scaurie mountain wi a yatter
that thru ten-thoosan centuries has run.

Wi cheek against the ash o wither't bracken
I ligg at peace and hear nae soun at aa
but yonder hurlygush that canna slacken
thru time and space mak never-endan faa:

As if a volly o the soun had brocht me
doun tae the pool whaur timeless things begin,
and e'en this endless faa'in that had claucht me
was ilka ither force was gether't in.

(Selected Poems 1942–1972, page 16)

    * *Hurlygush*: the sound of running water
    † *hallyoch*: the noise made by water on stones
    ‡ *harles*: peels

CHAPTER EIGHTEEN

The Historic Buildings Council
for Scotland

Professor David Walker

OVER ITS FORTY-FOUR YEARS of existence the Historic Buildings Council for Scotland has had a far greater impact than
anyone unconnected with it ever realises. The historic buildings which have survived tend to be taken for granted. Few pause
to think how architecturally impoverished Scotland would have been
if the Council and the statutory provisions for grant aid had not
been brought into being. Edinburgh would not be the great centre
of cultural tourism it is today since two-thirds of the Old
Town would have vanished and the New Town would have been
fragmentary with nothing left north of Great King Street. At least
half of the best towers and spires would have disappeared from the
Glasgow skyline. In the wider Scottish countryside such places as
Dunkeld, St Monance and Inveraray would at best have been little
more than post-war housing estates, while New Lanark would have
been a deserted heap of overgrown ruins. Two-thirds, if not more,
of the greater country houses would have gone and the National
Trust for Scotland would not have been what it is today.

What has been achieved has not cost a lot of money in terms of
government expenditure as a whole. The Council has never been
able to recommend the Secretary of State to offer very large grants
in any one year. From the tiny sums in the early days the grants
offered have risen to £12.4 million in 1996–97, generating about £40
million in repair work. But the Council's achievements should not
be counted in terms of simple expenditure. Traditional building
skills, so threatened with extinction thirty years ago, have been kept
alive and the standards of building repair raised throughout the land.
Most importantly, in the 1970s the larger planning authorities were
encouraged to start grant schemes of their own, a development

unthinkable in the '50s and '60s, and for the first time the finances of the more difficult repair schemes began to stack up. The historic building trust movement came into being. And finally through its policy recommendations on the listing of historic buildings the Council did much to secure the conservation of city-centre commercial areas ineligible for grant.

When the Council, of which Maurice Lindsay was a member from 1976 to 1987, was set up on 17 November 1953 under the provisions of the Historic Buildings and Monuments Act of that year, few had such high hopes for it. Like its sister Councils for England and for Wales it was seen at the time as an inadequate response to the Gowers Report which had proposed a far wider raft of measures to ensure the survival of the nation's country houses and landscape parks; and again like those Councils, it was for its first twelve years administered by the Ministry of Works – through its Scottish head-quarters at 122 George Street in Edinburgh – as an adjunct of its Ancient Monuments service. The Council's responsibilities were to advise the Minister of Works on repair and maintenance grants for historic buildings; on the acquisition of such buildings and their contents by the Minister, or on grants towards acquisition by local authorities and the National Trust for Scotland; and to advise the Secretary of State for Scotland on the preparation of the lists of buildings of architectural and historic interest and the exercise of his functions in respect of them under the Town and Country Planning (Scotland) Act of 1948. The Council thus reported to both Ministers, the advisory rôle on listing having particular significance as it had been decided not to have a Scottish counterpart to the Maclagan Committee which had determined policy and advised on such mat-ters in England and Wales since 1945.

If the Council first met on 4 December 1953 in an atmosphere of some disappointment, knowing that the non-implementation of the Gowers recommendations would result in the flood of post-war country house demolitions remaining substantially unchecked, at least it had a membership determined to make the most of such opportunities as it offered. The Earl of Dundee was Chairman and, along with the Countess of Haddington, provided the necessary experience of estate and country house management, together with useful contacts; Ian G. Lindsay, part-time Chief Inspector of Historic Buildings and the country's leading conservation architect, and Sir Robert Matthew, then just returned from London, represented the architectural profession; Sir John Imrie and Archibald Templeton local government interests; Douglas Johnston Q.C. the House of Commons and the legal profession; and Lord Polwarth the business community. Within a year the Minister added to their number the Earl of Cawdor, later to become its longest-reigning Chairman. It was a spread of membership which was to prove enduring and which is in some degree still recognisable today. The Council was also fortunate in its first secretary, the outstandingly sympathetic David Watson, its assessor Stuart Cruden, Principal Inspector of Ancient Monuments, soon to be aided by Iain MacIvor, and its architects, headed by Horace White, all of whom provided advisory reports. Also in attendance as an assessor was the Secretary of State's principal in charge of listing, D. M. MacPhail, who was present more to seek advice as and when required than to assess. In practice he tended to come with rather negative proposals which he hoped that the Council would be persuaded to rubber-stamp, as it duly did in the case of David Dale's house in Glasgow at its first meeting and that of the proposal to make Category C non-statutory at its second.

Although the Council had been set up with country houses in mind, the smaller local authorities were quick to see it as a source of financial assistance for their historic tolbooths and town houses, and it was with some relief that the Council was able to report that the Minister had accepted its recommendations in respect of them. 'Little Houses' (i.e., medium-sized urban houses of the sixteenth, seventeenth and eighteenth centuries), the listing of which had been pioneered by the 4th Marquess of Bute and Ian Lindsay in 1935–39, and which had been a particular interest of the National Trust for Scotland since its inception in 1931, were soon to prove a more contentious area. The extensive discussion of the interpretation of the word 'outstanding' and the reference to periodic meetings of the three Councils to ensure consistency of standards in the second annual report (1954) reflected serious disagreements over which types of building the legislation was intended to cover. Nevertheless, in the earlier lists of grants offered the Weaver's House in Kilbarchan, the Tannahill Cottage in Paisley, and the Square and Cathedral Street in Dunkeld, were to be found alongside such great castles and country houses as Kellie, Craigievar, Craigston, Traquair, Winton, Yester, Newliston and Culzean. Most country house grants were to houses which were either in continuing occupation or owned by the National Trust for Scotland but a few were pioneer rescue operations such as Carnsalloch, organised for Cheshire Homes by John Gladstone, Balbithan heroically saved from ruin by Mary McMurtrie, Menstrie Castle incorporated into a housing estate and Dr Harrowes's sadly failed attempt to restore Mavisbank to its original form.

In the report for 1955 Lord Dundee was able to report that in its third year the work of the Council had passed from the formative to a more mature stage in its development, and within another year or two it had begun adopting a more pro-active rôle. In the spirit of the Gowers Report it began taking an interest in the conservation of historic house chattels and endeavoured to pre-empt the demolition of a very few of the more important houses by seeking to persuade the owners of their value, at that date a sensitive exercise which only the composition of the Council made possible. As part of that exercise it had also begun to forge links with the National Trust for Scotland with a view to joint action on matters of common concern, notably at the ducal village of Dunkeld. But by far the most adventurous undertaking of those early years was the extension of the pioneer interest in 'Little Houses' to the grander ducal burgh of Inveraray. In 1957 the Council persuaded the Minister (Hugh Molson) to acquire all the properties owned by the Argyll trustees and convey them to the Town Council. The transfer was accompanied by its largest grant up to that date, £26,000, with a further £500 per annum for the following twenty years, a step made possible only by the esteem in which that formally-planned town was held by the town planners of that time. Lady Haddington's attempt to extend the Inveraray principle to Haddington in furtherance of Frank Tindall's pioneer conservation scheme there was resisted by both the Ministry's senior administrators and the Minister himself on the grounds that the houses were not individually outstanding and did not constitute a formal composition. In its report the Council avoided airing its differences with the Minister and expressed only concern, and implied regret, that its restricted funds prevented it from undertaking more burgh and village conservation schemes even although the sums involved were small.

The National Trust's rescue of Kirkwynd at Glamis had in fact cost as little as £500. Looking back, it remains astonishing that so much could have been achieved for so little money, even allowing for inflation. In 1957 the Council's largest single country house grant had been only £5,000, although over a period such grants could soon add up, Dunvegan being the most expensive case. In Edinburgh Old Town the problems were, however, beyond any finance the Council could recommend and the old difficulties about which buildings could be regarded as 'outstanding' again arose. The Council's rôle was limited to consultation and a few projects, notably Mylne's Court, Brodie's Close, Riddle's Court and Bakehouse Close. Much of the remainder of the Royal Mile was largely rebuilt as a façade exercise by Robert Hurd, who had been the Marquess of Bute's architect at Acheson House before the War. Although Hurd did well by the standards of those days at Chessels Court, the overall result led to a final parting of the ways with Ian Lindsay, a friend in his Cambridge days, who remarked of it icily that it was 'what Mr Hurd was pleased to call restoration'. But without Historic Buildings Council support Hurd was left at the mercy of the requirements of the housing department, the firemaster and, worst of all, the highways department which demanded, and got, street widening at the best-preserved section of the Canongate.

The Council had in fact been moving into a more difficult period generally. Lord Cawdor was a happy choice as successor to Lord Dundee in 1958 as he had a deep personal commitment, evident on his own estates, but Douglas Johnston had been replaced by 'Uncle Arthur' (Arthur Woodburn, Secretary of State for Scotland, 1947–50) who, although kindly enough personally with a great fund of rather droll old-fashioned similes, was much more politically correct and could be awesomely forbidding, at times almost taking over the chair and exercising a veto which brooked no further discussion. Moreover Molson was less willing to accept the Council's recommendations than his predecessor and the number of recommendations rejected rose to twenty per cent. Representations were made by both the English and the Scottish Councils on 'outstanding group value', in Scotland arising mainly from dissatisfaction over Haddington, and on the need for local authorities to co-ordinate their relevant departments and play a greater rôle. An unsympathetic Select Committee on Estimates examined the work of the Councils and was generally unhelpful, particularly on two counts. First the English members did not see the more traditional Scottish buildings, great as well as small, as outstanding in their terms; the Council did not agree but was forced to accept that the merit-threshold would have to be raised. Secondly the Committee took exception to the number of municipal projects assisted, tolbooths, town houses and such schemes as Inveraray, ruling that local authorities should have to meet the cost themselves without recourse to the Secretary of State's funds. The Committee's recommendations did not have too much effect at first as the then Minister of Works, Lord John Hope, proved in Ian Lindsay's words 'very understanding in relation to Scottish problems, both architectural and financial', and after a first difficult year he came round to trusting the Council's recommendations. But the Committee's strictures did result in a steep reduction in the Council's allocation from £68,550 to £50,200 in 1962, when the number of grants offered fell to as low as nine. Hope's successor Geoffrey Rippon also tended to accept the Council's recommendations; Haddington at last got a grant, the restoration of the core of Culross was virtually completed, and in 1964 Lord Cawdor was able to report that with the Secretary of State's help the New Lanark Association had come into being, that the first discussions towards the founding of the Edinburgh New Town Conservation Committee had taken place, and that local preservation societies were now receiving grants towards 'revolving funds' (i.e., buy, restore, sell and buy again), a concept pioneered by the National Trust for Scotland under the direction of Hew Lorimer, following the advocacy of Michael Crichton-Stuart, its then Chairman, for 'the ordinary homes of ordinary people'.

In that same year (1964) the Council recognised that it would have to take a wider view of merit criteria. From the very beginning it had been wary of any architectural style labelled 'revival'. Culzean had got through the net on the strength of its classical interiors and Abbotsford on that of its association with Sir Walter Scott, but Richard Crichton's brilliant picturesque fantasy at Abercairny did not and its owner duly demolished it in 1960. The Council's assessor did not attach much, if any, importance to such houses, and a recommendation for a major Lorimer house had previously been rejected by the Minister. Its merit had not been disputed, it had simply not been old enough to be historic. But the Council did now venture across the 1800 barrier into the period of revivals, both Greek and Gothic. Greek did not cause the Council members any difficulty but Gothic did. By 1964 the number of major Georgian Gothic and neo-Tudor country houses lost since the War had begun to cause concern, the merits of the survivors were more widely appreciated and several owners had applied. The Council found these difficult and their assessor still lacked enthusiasm for them. The applications were temporarily put on ice as there were 'no accepted criteria for such houses', Iain

MacIvor being instructed to produce an illustrated catalogue and assessment of the survivors, which is still a testament to his analytical skills. Regrettably it did not succeed in saving Millearne where the owner felt she could not maintain the house even with the massive grant aid the Council was prepared to recommend.

Iain MacIvor's study was undertaken against a background of continuing difficulty. Although grant offers had been raised from £68,895 to £109,050 in 1965, the Council was obliged to appeal for an increase in funds to cope with expensive cases, particularly Culzean and Hopetoun, and the now-accepted expansion of its work in the burghs and villages, particularly in Edinburgh, New Lanark, Cromarty, Falkland and perhaps most notably Portsoy where the elderly Provost Wood had initiated a remarkable local authority housing conservation scheme for the whole of the harbour area which was happily complemented by some privately financed ventures. But although, wisely, Cawdor and Crane did not refer to it in their reports, their main difficulties were with the Minister, Charles Pannell, and the Works under-secretary advising him, neither of whom trusted the experts. The number of recommendations turned down rose to twenty-five per cent. In particular their southern eyes did not see the later tower houses as castles, or indeed as buildings of any merit whatsoever. The recommendation on Hills was accepted because it had a crenellated parapet, that for Balfluig was rejected. Even the great Dr Douglas Simpson, Chairman of the Ancient Monuments Board for Scotland, was informed that his views were mistaken. His memorable reply on Balfluig, like a prolonged roll of thunder, will be found in Maurice Lindsay's *The Castles of Scotland*, a by-product of his work for the Council.

It was thus initially with some relief that the Council became the sole responsibility of the Secretary of State for Scotland on 1 July 1966, regretting only the loss of its secretary, the wonderfully sympathetic Geoffrey Crane who had handled a bad situation with remarkable skill and diplomacy. The secretariat was transferred to the listed buildings section of the Scottish Development Department at Old St Andrew's House under Tom Rarity but the professional advice, both at inspector and at architect level, remained with the Ministry of Public Building and Works at Argyle House. An allocation of £255,000 was fixed for the three-year period 1967–70. Balfluig now got its grant, inaugurating a long series of restorations of semi-ruined or completely roofless tower-houses. But administratively there were teething problems as the listing staff had no experience of grant-work whatsoever and had difficulty in coming to terms with the fact that the standards required were quite different from those for listed building consent. That came to a head with the conversion of Capelrig House as part of a new school building and was quickly remedied, but the death on 28 August 1966 of Ian Lindsay, architectural historian and premier conservation architect as well as Chief Inspector of Historic Buildings, was a severe blow. James Dunbar-Nasmith regrettably declined an informal approach to succeed him although he was in fact always on hand to give advice.

The loss of the New Club and the Life Association buildings in Edinburgh, against its advice, deepened the Council's depression. As Secretary of State for Scotland Michael Noble had given away the first, William Ross the second, even although J. Dickson Mabon had done his best to dissuade him and James Dunbar-Nasmith had both a scheme and a client for it. Its opulent Venetianism offended Ross's Presbyterian soul. But in other respects the foundations for the future were laid. The political representation on the Council had brightened up immensely with the appointment of Betty Harvie Anderson, enabling a more adventurous approach to be taken. The Civic Amenities Act of 1967 led to the establishment of a Scottish Civic Trust with Maurice as Director. It also extended to Scottish local authorities the powers those in England already had to make grants to historic buildings which ultimately had crucially important results in both Edinburgh and Glasgow and gave the Council the power to offer loans, a power it decided not to use as the interest charges would have eroded its allocation. The Act was also to have important results in the designation of conservation areas, a subject which appears in embryo form in a number of the Council's early reports. It was quickly followed by the Town and Country Planning (Scotland) Act of 1969 which at last made statutory listing a reality, even if the difficulties in achieving regulations acceptable to the Scottish Office lawyers came near to breaking Rarity and represented an appalling distraction from Council business. Even the annual reports could not be written. But in other respects great progress was made in the 1967–70 three-year period. Gunsgreen House and Robertson's Court in Edinburgh were saved from demolition. The owner of Robert Adam's Kirkdale was dissuaded from demolishing it, even although he would not accept a grant. And from 1966 onwards the Council had felt able to offer grants to Victorian buildings of real quality, a shift in opinion which owed something to Geoffrey Crane, who had persuaded the Council that it should offer a grant to the great Venetian palazzo warehouse at 37–57 Miller Street, Glasgow in 1966. It did not in the end save the building as Glasgow for its own reasons championed the owner and played on being too hard to please, but it was a significant precedent. Grants to Butterfield's Cathedral of the Isles at Millport, and to Alexander Thomson's Holmwood at Cathcart and his double villa at Langside, followed hard on its heels.

In December 1969 the long chairmanship of Lord Cawdor came to an end. He had brought to it outstanding qualities of quiet firmness and tact, with at times an effective use of silence. One knew it was time to shut up if one saw the blood pressure rising in his face. And in a quiet unobtrusive way he tried to fulfil Ian Lindsay's rôle, keeping in touch with the professional staff, taking soundings, exercising influence through friends, and giving support and encouragement. The writer will always remember him with affection, gratitude and the most profound respect. His last meeting, held on a dark winter's day in the new office at 25 Hill Street, Edinburgh was a very emotional one. He reviewed past successes and failures, the most recent of which had plainly upset him. Most of the cases of which he spoke were very different from those which would have been mentioned a few years earlier: the New Market in Aberdeen, demolished by private parliamentary legislation, and the Edinburgh Café Royal, threatened by Woolworth's; Burnet's McGeoch warehouse and Alhambra, and Spence & Kennedy's Randolph & Elder's engine shop, all in Glasgow. Although characteristically he avoided mentioning the fact, he had presided over the most momentous shift in Council policy. And at the end of it all he spoke of his hopes for the future and quietly mapped out the route he believed the Council and its staff had to follow. It was a future he did not himself live to see. A few weeks later he was dead, almost on the eve of much of his vision being fulfilled.

Lord Cawdor had nominated as his successor another Campbell, Lord Stratheden. He did not at first strike the staff as an auspicious choice as he had demolished his own Bryce house, Hartrigge, but he proved an excellent Chairman, as Cawdor had promised he would be, and during his period of office great advances were made, aided and indeed encouraged by the incoming Secretary of State, Gordon Campbell, and most particularly George Younger who had succeeded

Lady Tweedsmuir as his Under Secretary of State. Viscount Younger, as he now is, swiftly responded to the call for action on Edinburgh's New Town from the Scottish Civic Trust's international conference in 1970 by setting up the present Edinburgh New Town Conservation Committee with an initial annual grant of £50,000. In parallel Sir Robert Matthew, one of the prime movers in the setting up of the Committee, was appointed his adviser on conservation (in belated succession to Ian Lindsay) and re-appointed to the Council in November 1970. With him at last came Ronald Cant, greatly strengthening the architectural and historical representation on the Council. Administratively there were further important changes: Ronnie Cramond replaced Bob Butler as the responsible assistant secretary and Harry Graham succeeded Tom Rarity as Council secretary. Together they set about giving practical effect to everything that had been planned or legislated for, and in their aims they were greatly assisted by the provision for grants to conservation areas in Section 10 of the Town and Country Planning (Amendment) Act of 1972, incorporated into the consolidated Act of that same year. On the financial side, the necessary augmentation of their funds, £50,000 per annum for Edinburgh and a similar sum for conservation areas in the rest of the country, most certainly helped, and to speed processing the Council agreed to the professional and administrative staff taking greater responsibility at the in-principle stage. Thus although of the buildings mentioned by Lord Cawdor at his final meeting all but the Café Royal were ultimately lost, conservation as we know it today began to take shape, the abandonment of the exclusion from grant aid of buildings in ecclesiastical use with a pilot scheme in 1972–73 completing the present pattern of grant provision.

With Sir Robert Matthew's appointment the Council began to assume an increasingly influential rôle. It advised on the Secretary of State's purchase for the National Trust for Scotland of Kellie, Haddo and Brodie; it recommended the purchase of the Hill House, and when that initiative failed the Royal Incorporation of Architects in Scotland was motivated to buy it in 1971, passing it to the National Trust for Scotland in 1982; it advised on the acquisition of the nearly-demolished Inveraray courthouse; and it made the first moves towards the rescue of Thirlestane and Newhailes, then both in chronic disrepair. And on the policy front it formed the Listed Buildings Committee of which Sir Robert and Ronald Cant were the key members. The Committee declined to follow the Holford Committee (as the Maclagan Committee had become) into abolishing Category C (the equivalent of the English Grade III) and ultimately advised making it statutory; and most importantly it recommended a review of the listing of buildings erected between 1914 and 1939 (the Scottish response to Nikolaus Pevsner's initiative on the Holford Committee) and instituted what ultimately, in 1975, became 'the thirty year rule' (i.e. each year buildings which are more than thirty years old become eligible for listing), a guideline which soon spread into English practice.

By 1972 the number of grant offers per annum had begun to average about fifty, in contrast to the single figures of just a few years earlier, and the annual reports were full of heroic rescue operations, perhaps the most memorable being those by Ian Begg, first at the West Bow, Edinburgh, which nearly perished at the hands of Building Control as a result of the owners' failure to take concerted action, and then at Rossend Castle, where he defeated a determined attempt by the Town Council of Burntisland to demolish it and persuaded his own partnership to acquire it and restore it as their offices. Not less importantly the Council began to widen policy on what was 'outstanding' to include industrial archaeology, as at Perth Waterworks and Poldrate Mills in East Lothian in 1971–72, and to the humbler forms of vernacular building with Laidhaye Croft, Caithness and Lochnabo Cottage, Elgin in 1973–74. The only failures with which the Council had become directly involved were the tragic loss of James Adam's Old College residences on Glasgow High Street, where the efforts of the University of Strathclyde to save them were defeated by uncertainty on the line of the Eastern Flank of the ring road, the original mills at Ferguslie, Paisley, where no potential user came forward, and the much less necessary demolition by Renfrew County Council of the Wallace Buildings at Elderslie.

The year 1975 was a very significant one for the Council. In the run-up to local government reorganisation in that year Falkirk Town Council surprised it by undertaking the repair of Callender House, which had long been derelict in its ownership, as also did Motherwell at Dalzell: enthusiasm for conservation had suddenly spread to even the most unlikely places, fuelled by European Architectural Heritage Year, Maurice Lindsay's special rôle in which brought him to the Council. At ministerial level John Smith, who had left the Council because of his duties as Lord Provost of Aberdeen, returned when Lord Kirkhill, as Minister of State, and on the legislative front the representations of the Historic Buildings Council and other bodies brought about what was at first known as Capital Transfer Tax exemption and a raft of further measures in the Finance Act of that year, at last implementing the ideas of the Gowers Committee more than twenty years earlier.

With the appointment of the Earl of Crawford and Balcarres as Chairman of the Council, and the ever-increasing political standing of Betty Harvie Anderson and, in January 1979, the arrival of Dr Brian Lang as Secretary, the Council adopted an ever more powerful rôle. Joint action with the Royal Botanic Garden and the Countryside Commission for Scotland was initiated on historic gardens and landscapes, leading to a pilot study published in 1982. In Edinburgh Lauriston Place was rescued from demolition and a massive programme of repair begun in Leith and in the Edinburgh Old Town, where a more co-ordinated approach was taken from 1981; in Glasgow, St Andrew's Church, the Theatre Royal, Trinity College and many other buildings were retrieved from near-dereliction; in Ayrshire Pilkington's vandalised Trinity Church at Irvine was repaired; in Lanarkshire Chatelherault was acquired and restored, and the conservation of New Lanark put on a sounder footing than it had ever been in the past, bringing its Chairman, Harry Smith, to the Council; in Aberdeenshire the planned auction sale at Fyvie was discouraged pending a solution to the future of that great castle and its contents; and in Banff and Buchan Aden became a country park with its 'round square' restored.

These were but a few highlights in a great programme of policy development and building repair throughout the land. Grants to churches-in-use were a particular feature of the period as congregations grasped the opportunity to catch up on half a century of under-maintenance: had help not come when it did, several of Scotland's few remaining mediaeval churches would certainly have been abandoned. Although it was perhaps too hectic a pace to last, all would have been well had it not been for the change of system from an annual allocation for grant offers to cash limits on grants actually taken up in 1979–80. The Council and its secretariat had to calculate how much commitment they had to have to ensure that their cash-limit was fully used. Careful projections were made from past cases, but the take-up proved to be faster than anyone could have foreseen and the cash-limits were exceeded, resulting in a corresponding reduction in the cash limits for the following years from about £2.8

million to, first, £2.1 million and then £1.5 million, subsequently raised to £1.8 million. Brian Lang having left for the National Heritage Memorial Fund, it fell to his successor, Tom Kelly, appointed in November 1980, to digest the problem. A brief moratorium allowed the 284 applications in the pipeline to be analysed for merit, urgency, financial need and value for money, bringing into being the comparative sifting system which is still the initial stage of the Council's processing of grant applications.

When the Council reviewed the results of this exercise, a particular source of concern was the expenditure on the restoration of derelict or roofless tower houses. Far fewer houses of the fifteenth, sixteenth and early seventeenth centuries had remained in occupation in Scotland than in England and the wave of enthusiasm for them as secure and manageable country residences was increasingly seen as a means of ensuring the future of the more important examples which could not be taken into Ancient Monuments care, resulting in several fairly expensive cases each year. Although in the event expenditure on them was found to have hardly ever risen above ten per cent of the Council's allocation, and had usually been very much less, the Council instructed a first review in 1981, provoked by the costs at Pitfichie and Fawside where rather more masonry had fallen than at the others, and the criteria for merit and feasibility were tightened.

All these events took place against a background of radical administrative change. The Ancient Monuments service had been transferred from the Property Services Agency of the Department of the Environment to the Scottish Office in 1978 and was linked with the Historic Buildings Branch to form the Historic Buildings and Monuments Division under Nigel Sharp. For the first time the Secretary of State had the whole organisation under his direct command. As part of that re-organisation the writer became sole professional assessor rather than joint assessor. But by the end of Tom Kelly's period of office in October 1982, it had become evident that the work of the Council required a secretary wholly devoted to its business without Head of Branch responsibilities, in the persons of Mary Martyn, and subsequently in July 1984 David Christie. Further change took place in November 1984 when the Division became a Directorate, first under Tom Band, and subsequently David Connelly, with the staff for the first time nearly all gathered under one roof in Brandon Street.

In 1983 Lord Crawford gave up the chairmanship to become First

Commissioner of the Crown Estates, in which capacity he initiated a large conservation scheme on Edinburgh's South Side. His successor was the Marquess of Bute, then also the chairman of the National Trust's executive committee. Of all the Council's chairmen, no other experienced such difficulties, or had to devote so much time to its business. The circumstances he chronicled with a characteristically civilised candour in the reports for 1985–88. The events of 1981 and a slower take-up of grants had led to underspends. But inevitably the take-up snowballed, reaching a crunch-point in November 1985 when it became evident that even with a further injection of funds there would have to be a second and much longer moratorium. It lasted sixteen months. Only those applying for buildings of the very highest class or in key locations in conservation areas were advised to re-apply in March 1986 and in April 1987. There were other underlying reasons for the problems which had accumulated, most notably a bulge in high-quality, high-cost applications which could not be refused, and the imposition of VAT on building repair. With a new secretary, Ian Dewar, appointed in April 1986, Lord Bute piloted a working party with great acumen through what he described as the 'dark months' from October 1986 to February 1987: 'dark' because the sensor system which switched the lights on and off at Brandon Street appeared to have been programmed for bats and cats. Nevertheless the long periods of twilight, even darkness, in which the party found itself, seemed peculiarly appropriate.

Painful though they were, the events of 1985–87 ultimately brought about a more realistic appraisal of the resources required. By the time Maurice left the Council in 1987 the cash limit had been raised from £2.5 million in 1982–83 to £6 million. The experience also led to a strict monitoring of expenditure, in which applicants had to be a great deal more disciplined about contract management and the submission of accounts, which has remained in place ever since. And 1985–87 were still years of extraordinary achievement. The chronicle of grants offered included the rescue of the Doune of Rothiemurchus, the one-time home of Elizabeth Grant, 'A Highland Lady'; Boswell's Auchinleck; Fyvie; Barbreck; Formakin, with which Maurice was directly involved as chairman of its trust; Highland Tolbooth St John's, St Paul's and St George's, Pilrig House, Advocates' Close and Tweeddale Court in Edinburgh; St Andrew's by the Green, Thomson's Grecian Buildings on Sauchiehall Street, Wilson's Trinity College, Leiper's Dowanhill and Camphill churches, and David

Hamilton's Aikenhead, all in Glasgow; South Church, which had closed, and the mediaeval church of the Holy Rude in Stirling, which nearly did; Mill No 1, the Institute and the Robert Owen and David Dale houses in New Lanark; and a huge area of central Hawick. All of these would have been lost had not grants been offered. And progress was not to be measured just in terms of big cases, but in more effective systems for the distribution of grant aid. The Churches Working Group was set up in 1982 to liaise with the several denominations: Town Schemes administered by the planning authorities, and the Edinburgh Old Town Committee for Conservation and Renewal in 1984; the Glasgow West End Conservation Advisory Committee and the Friends of Thatched Houses in 1986. Together with the Smaller Grants Scheme introduced in 1988, these created the pattern of grant-aid as we know it today.

The Marquess of Bute's term as Chairman ended in November 1988, but he continued to provide practical help right up to the time of his tragically early death. His successor, Sir Nicholas Fairbairn, brought the same commitment and, like Lord Crawford and Betty Harvie Anderson (Lady Skrimshire) before him, political clout. He was the first Chairman to die in office, on 19 February, 1995. Of his time it is still perhaps too early to write, but it should be said that the same pattern of heroic rescue operations and repair was accompanied by great advances in the science of conservation, particularly in respect of stone, lime mortars, and sash windows.

The Historic Buildings and Monuments Directorate became an Executive Agency in April 1991 under the title of Historic Scotland. In the period since Historic Scotland was established the money available for grants has risen annually to the highest level yet, of around £12 million, although the current Corporate Plan of Historic Scotland shows this falling back a little in 1999–2000.

The Historic Buildings Council and Historic Scotland work closely together and, in contrast to the position which obtained in the 1960s, the Secretary of State has only rejected the Council's advice on a grant case on one occasion since the Agency was established. With the agreement of the Council, Historic Scotland has introduced a pilot scheme whereby grants may be awarded for feasibility studies on historic gardens or designed landscapes. The Architectural Heritage Fund has been allocated resources from which it can offer favourable loans to Building Preservation Trusts both for projects and feasibility studies. Pilot schemes are also being introduced, within the wider ambit of town schemes in selected outstanding conservation areas, whereby enhanced rates of grant are to be offered for the appropriate repair of traditional doors and windows.

Purchase grants have been made to the National Trust for Scotland, in relation to the south side of Charlotte Square in Edinburgh and Balnain House in Inverness, and to the City of Glasgow for the former *Glasgow Herald* building. Historic Scotland, with the support of the Historic Buildings Council, has been pro-active in securing a viable future for important buildings such as Newhailes and Stanley Mills. In both these cases, and in a great many others, success has been achieved through the creation of partnerships through which very substantial additional resources to assist in the conservation of historic buildings have been attracted from other sources such as the Heritage Lottery Fund, local authorities, local enterprise companies, European Union funding schemes and other public and private sources.

The number of cases now being supported (145 in the current year) is vastly greater than in the early years of the Council's work and the range of building types being assisted is far wider: recent years have seen grants going not just to great country houses, tower houses and churches but to mills, bridges, viaducts, theatres, schools, etc. The Council has come a long way from the days when it agonised over Georgian Gothic!

Although there is now a well-established Buildings at Risk register (operated by the Scottish Civic Trust on behalf of Historic Scotland), the Historic Buildings Repair Grants scheme is still predominantly demand-led. In such a scheme it is inevitable that from time to time demand and resources will continue to be out of step. After a period of pressure in the early 1990s the scheme has been in relative equilibrium but such periods of pressure will no doubt arise again. However, there can be no doubting the groundswell of public opinion in favour of conservation, to which the Council has made a very important contribution, and this is surely our best hope for the future.

I have long been convinced that it is useless to teach children Botticelli, Beethoven and Browning if you do not also encourage their awareness of both the natural and man-made heritage which surrounds them. The arts, our buildings and what we do to our environment are the products of our social attitudes, and our heritage is thus indivisible.

(*Thank You for Having Me*, page 180)

CHAPTER NINETEEN

The Edinburgh New Town Conservation Committee

Sir Alan Hume

Parentage

In 1967 the Civic Amenities Act was passed, and the Scottish Civic Trust was founded, with Mr Maurice Lindsay as its Director. These were significant developments in the accelerating growth of the conservation movement.

During the first two decades after the end of the War the efforts of builders and planners, both public and private, had been concentrated upon quickly providing new houses to meet desperate needs. Labour and materials were short, and the devising and implementing of new expedients, from industrial building to the creation of overspill New Towns, absorbed almost all the available energy. In the '60s, however, it began to be realised that the tide of reconstruction was in danger of sweeping away valuable old buildings, neglected for many years; and that whole areas containing many of these buildings were at risk. This realisation gripped the public imagination, and the demand grew for the conservation of outstanding urban areas. Hence the 1967 Act, and the Trust.

The Trust was active from the outset. One of the Trustees was Sir Robert Matthew, the distinguished architect with wide experience in both the private and the public sectors. On his recent return to Scotland he had been deeply perturbed by the deterioration of the Georgian New Town in Edinburgh, and he was convinced that, unless drastic remedies were applied soon, its unique splendour would be lost. Its 318 hectares contained some 11,500 properties, three-quarters of them used for residential purposes, and almost every building was listed for special architectural or historical interest.

However, it was two centuries since construction had started in James Craig's first New Town, and the remaining phases were largely completed in 60 years. Notwithstanding the robust nature of the buildings, time had taken heavy toll of them, not least because of inadequate maintenance by many proprietors down the years. Sit Robert's expert eye detected an immediate danger that the area's integrity would be lost, and so would disintegrate what he regarded as one of the three best townscapes in Europe (the others being Venice and Leningrad). With the support of Mr Lindsay he involved the Civic Trust at once in a strenuous campaign to save the New Town.

First it was necessary to establish the extent of the damage and to estimate the cost of repairing it. For this the Trust turned to the Edinburgh Architectural Association which enthusiastically mobilised a team of over 120 architects, surveyors, engineers and others who surveyed the external fabric of properties in the concentrated centre of the New Town. This operation, which occupied more than a year, confirmed Sir Robert's fears. Erosion and decay were proceeding almost throughout the New Town. Chimney stacks had suffered prominently; the stone on facades was flaking; carved architectural details (cornices, balustrades, architraves, for example) were being lost; roofs, with their gullies, ridges and rhones had become seriously defective; doors and windows had lost characteristic details, including fanlights and astragals. The team concluded that work to deal with these and other deficiencies might take at least 20 years and require the expenditure of £15 million over that period.

This was clearly a major operation which would involve central and local government, the amenity societies, and especially the residents themselves. To mobilise these agencies and groups, the Civic Trust decided to hold a large-scale Conference in Edinburgh, and a Conference Committee was formed, with Sir Robert as Chairman and Mr Lindsay as Secretary. On 6th June 1970 over 1100 participants met in the Assembly Rooms, George Street, to consider 'The Conservation of Georgian Edinburgh'. The Conference, chaired by Lord Muirshiel, was a resounding success. The roll of distinguished speakers included Count Sforza (Council of Europe), Sir John Betjeman, Lord Holford, Professor Colin Buchanan and Professor A. J. Youngson, in addition to Lord Hughes (Minister of State, Scottish Office) and the Lord Provost. Sir Robert Matthew presented the report of the survey, and after discussion the Conference passed almost unanimously a resolution – 'That this Conference re-emphasises the unique importance of Georgian Edinburgh to our national and international architectural heritage, and calls upon the Scottish Civic Trust to start forthwith the setting up of an advisory committee ...

so that necessary steps may be taken, with the practical and financial support of Central Government and the Local Authority, to achieve the conservation of Georgian Edinburgh ...'

Conception

No time was lost by the Trust in initiating the negotiations. These were greatly facilitated by the commitments made at the Conference by the Lord Provost, and by Lord Hughes who said on behalf of the Government that 'the principle of a tripartite cost-sharing arrangement with Edinburgh Corporation and owners of properties in the New Town involving a Government contribution is definitely accepted'.

Careful thought had to be given to the balanced composition of the Committee, to the detailed definition of its functions and to the financing of its work. Harmony prevailed during this process because of the determination of all concerned to fulfil the wishes so cogently expressed at the Conference without loss of the impetus which it had conferred.

The outcome emerged on 22nd December 1970 at a meeting chaired by the Rt Hon. George Younger (later Viscount Younger of Leckie), Parliamentary Under Secretary for Development at the Scottish Office.

(A)   It was agreed that the Edinburgh New Town Conservation Committee should be set up, under the Chairmanship of a former Lord Provost, Sir John Greig Dunbar, with the following membership:

Edinburgh Corporation	6 representatives
Historic Buildings Council for Scotland	4 representatives
Scottish Development Department	1 representative
Scottish Civic Trust	1 representative
Scottish Georgian Society	1 representative
Cockburn Association	1 representative
New Town Residents' Associations	3 representatives

Sir Robert Matthew (as the Secretary of State's Adviser on Conservation Policy).

(B)   The Committee was given the following terms of reference:

1.   To stimulate and co-ordinate action for the conservation of the New Town of Edinburgh.

2.   To advise Central and Local Government from time to time on any major policy issues which arise in this regard, recognising that measures of planning control are matters for the Local Authorities and the Government.

3.   To encourage the production of conservation schemes, and to take such co-ordinating and advisory action as may be required in relation to such schemes.

4.   To advise on the priorities and on the extent to which assistance may be required from such funds as may be available.

5.   To administer, for conservation purposes, such funds as may be raised by public appeal.

6.   To advise, as required, whether particular works of maintenance and repair, although not forming part of a conservation scheme, should qualify for assistance from public funds.

(C)   The Committee's expenditure, including grant payments, should be financed by Central and Local Government in the ratio of two parts by the Scottish Office to one part by Edinburgh Corporation. [This unique ratio had been announced at the Conference.] The owners' contributions to a conservation scheme should reflect their ability to pay, recognising the range of ownership, means and income in the New Town.

It is a remarkable tribute to the foresight of the founders of the Committee that their plans for it have stood the test of 25 years and more.

(A)   The composition of the Committee has remained virtually unchanged. Each of the four elements – central government, local government, amenity societies, and proprietors' associations – has brought a distinctive contribution to the Committee's work. Had there been serious conflicts between these several interests, the Committee would have been in jeopardy. But they have all shared down the years Sir Robert Matthew's aim to 'make the whole New Town good for another two centuries'. This has enabled them to resolve the inevitable differences of approach by calm and reasoned discussion, and consensus has always been reached (with one minor exception!).

(B)   The Committee's terms of reference have also been unaltered.

Unfortunately it has proved impossible to raise funds by public appeal which the Committee could administer, but all the remaining functions have been fully discharged. The main emphasis throughout the Committee's life has been upon encouraging and developing conservation schemes, processing the resultant grant applications, prioritising them in terms of merit, urgency, and commitment, and recommending them in turn to the Secretary of State and the District Council. The other designated functions have certainly not been neglected, however.

(C)   The financial structure has also proved very durable. The ratio of support by Central and Local Government has remained unchanged. For 1972 the Scottish Office provided £50,000, and Edinburgh Corporation £25,000. For 1976 the comparable figures were £700,000 and £350,000. The Report to the 1970 Conference had contemplated the cost of conservation schemes being provided as to 50% by the Exchequer, 25% by the Corporation, and 25% by the proprietors. In the event, the latest statistics reveal that, over the whole period since the Committee's inception, the proportions have been 46%, 23% and 31%.

Activities

Initially the Committee operated from temporary premises with an interim staff. In 1973, however, it acquired the tenancy of a small office in Dundas Street, in the heart of the New Town, which has remained its convenient headquarters. Before then (in April 1972), it had appointed its first Director, Mr Desmond Hodges, an architect with conservation experience who proved to be an inspired choice. He served the Committee with unfailing enthusiasm and great acceptance for 22 years. Throughout this period his supporting staff never exceeded ten in number and, in retrospect, it appears astonishing that they coped with such a massive volume of work. Indeed, this was possible only because the Finance Department at City Chambers acted as the Committee's paymaster, disbursing grants and initially meeting other expenditure.

In charting the way ahead the Committee had first to decide certain important matters of principle:

(a)   Grants were to be administered for external repairs to the fabric of buildings, especially those in domestic occupation, and it was agreed that they could be offered for internal repairs only when this was necessary to preserve the structure. Stonework would be most in need of grant-aid, but repairs to joinery and metalwork should also be assisted. The reinstatement of authentic features such as astragals, railings and balconies should be encouraged, as should the removal of inappropriate additions such as box-dormers and extensions. Repair and rebuilding of garden walls and stone paving could be considered. Normal maintenance work should not be eligible for grant.

(b)   High standards of material and workmanship were to be required in order to restore buildings to their original condition and appearance – so far as this was possible. To assist in ensuring this, no scheme should be approved unless the applicants had received advice from a registered architect. Suitable contracts should be entered into by the proprietors and the engaged firm (and later a model contract was devised and made available).

(c)   In assessing contributions to a scheme from those participating in it, an open, consistent and fair policy should be adopted. The benchmark should be the rateable value of the party's property, and grants should be awarded in inverse proportion to its rateable value. This would secure an equitable division of financial responsibility between the owners of whole properties, and also between the proprietors in a single multi-owned property. At the top end of the market, a wealthy firm in an office might receive no grant; at the bottom end, the resident in a small basement flat might receive 90% of the cost of the scheme in which he or she participated.

With these principles in mind, the Committee embarked on its main activity of promoting, processing, grant-aiding, and seeing through to their completion, schemes of rehabilitation, large and small. The way in which New Town properties were owned and occupied meant that most schemes were complicated, each involving a number of people under a common roof, either in a single house or terrace. The Committee, and especially its staff, had to bring these people together and help them to develop schemes for everything from the rebuilding of a chimney head to the fitting of uniform astragals in windows. None of this could have been done without the co-operation and encouragement of the street associations throughout the New Town.

Progress on the ground was therefore initially slow. In the first three years the Committee paid grants of about £150 (1971–2), £7500 (1972–3) and £80,000 (1973–4). Special attention was given to what Sir Robert Matthew had described as the 'tattered fringes' of the New Town, which were subject to widespread decay and threats of demolition. The most notable achievement in this regard was the comprehensive restoration of the tenement at 23/24 Fettes Row at a cost of £57,500, of which the Committee met £50,000. The work was completed in 1975 – European Architectural Heritage Year – when H.M. Queen Elizabeth the Queen Mother graciously unveiled a plaque on the restored facade.

The appearance of this successful scheme, and of the others, large and small, which were beginning to transform properties in many parts of the Conservation Area, inspired increasing activity by residents with problems to solve. Advice and help from the Committee fostered and hastened the work. The owner (or group of owners) could expect not only architectural and legal assistance, but also directly practical information from the metalwork superintendent who for many years had attended to the New Town balconies, railings, doors and windows, and later from the masonry superintendent who was an expert in the repair of stonework. Under their supervision, a salvage scheme was brought into operation which re-cycled materials recovered mainly from elsewhere in the City, collecting authentic items of stonework, metal and wood and selling them for use in new conservation schemes. This salvage operation continued for many years, until supplies failed.

Experience of problems and solutions with rehabilitation work steadily grew and, after some six years, the Committee decided to codify what had been learned. Under the leadership of the Director, four architectural graduates of high calibre and enthusiasm spent over a year preparing a Maintenance Manual covering every aspect of repairs to buildings in the New Town. After detailed scrutiny by outside specialists, the manual was published early in 1978 as *The Care and Conservation of Georgian Houses*. Intended as a handbook for owners, and a manual for architects, builders and professional advisers, it was received enthusiastically by all three groups. Indeed, it was soon in heavy demand both at home and abroad and further editions had to be printed, the second in 1980, the third in 1986 and the fourth in 1995.

The introduction to the Manual emphasised that 'The owner of a fine old building is more of a Trustee than a proprietor' and continued by drawing attention to the subsidies available for renovation. It was no doubt this combination of altruism and self-interest which led to the steady and substantial increase from 1978 forward in the volume of schemes submitted to the Committee for grant.

Sympathetic as were the Committee's paymasters (the Secretary of State and Edinburgh Corporation/Council), their financial resources were always limited and sufficient money was never available in any year to meet all legitimate demands on the Committee. Prioritisation of applications became a major exercise and deferment became inevitable, however unwelcome. Nevertheless, the work grew apace: in 1973 projects approved cost £180,000, receiving grants of £141,000; in 1983 the figures were £665,000 and £500,000; and in 1990 they had reached £2,126,000 and £1,497,000. Sir Robert Matthew had suggested in 1970 that rehabilitation might cost £15m over 20 years. After the first 20 years of the Committee's life some £20m had already been spent, and it had become clear that much remained to be done. When the Committee was established it was seen as having a finite and limited life, but the experience of quarter of a century has indicated that conservation must be a continuous process which still requires grant-aid from public funds.

It is impossible to summarise the effects of all the Committee's effort and expenditure. A walk around the Conservation Area, however, will be enough to disclose the obvious changes in 25 years. Chimney stacks have been rebuilt, roofs renewed, gutters and rhones replaced, flaking facades repaired and cleaned, new steps provided, balustrades, balconies and railings restored, astragals and fanlights renewed. Passing inspection connot reveal the costly structural work often carried out, below and above ground, to ensure stability. Impressively enough, repair and restoration have been undertaken throughout the whole area. Entire streets, such as Fettes Row, St Stephen Street, Carlton Street and Broughton Street have been transformed; elsewhere severely damaged large tenements have been rescued, preventing unsightly gaps in (for example) Dublin Street, Great King Street and Gayfield Square. The volume of high-quality repairs was greatly enhanced by linking the objectives of the

Committee to the massive programme of common repairs grant-aided by the Housing Committee of Edinburgh Council.

One intangible achievement also deserves mention. The Committee, its constituent members and its staff have stimulated and fostered a real sense of community among those who live and work in the New Town. They now enjoy their surroundings with a feeling of pride, realising how much these are admired near and far.

Recognition

Throughout its life the Committee has appreciated the importance of promoting knowledge of the New Town, locally, nationally and abroad, and thus mobilising widespread sympathy and support for its conservation. Through publications, exhibitions and lectures it has attracted the interest of many in Scotland. Conservation experts from abroad have always been made welcome at Dundas Street. For visitors to the City guided tours were successfully organised, and a helpful booklet describing walks in the New Town has been published.

Although the Committee has not drawn attention in this promotional material to its own successes, its reputation spread widely as the New Town began to regain its early splendour. In 1987, Europa Nostra awarded a Medal of Honour (a high distinction) for 'the magnificent large-scale conservation work in the eighteenth century New Town'.

One year later, in the European Year of the Environment, it received from Europa Nostra a Diploma of Merit for 'an outstanding example of co-ordinated rehabilitation and maintenance management in an area of high architectural value'. Later still, the Committee's work in the New Town contributed to the designation by UNESCO in 1995 of Edinburgh Old and New Towns as a World Heritage Site.

These international tributes recognise that the Committee has gone a long way towards Sir Robert Matthew's target of making the whole New Town good for another two centuries. Its achievements have depended upon the wholehearted participation of its constituent elements – central government, local government, amenity societies and residents' associations; and, in particular, the Scottish Civic Trust must take satisfaction from the leading part it played in creating and sustaining the Committee.

COUNTRY FUNERAL

Under vague humps you lie there, side by side,
who never in life could have endured one another;
wind and rain that once blew against you chide
forever from your tombs, and rough grasses smother

the shape of your each long rest that nobody shares.
Though the country steeple showers its cracked farewells
on mourned and mourners, between your world and ours
is only a different poverty: breath like the sound of the bells.

For you, too, must have felt the thrust of clouds
on your fields, the wrap and unwrap of storms
and as sudden calms; how sometimes a season crowds
itself so much as to make heroic harms.

Forgotten fathers who have done with proving
over again the insane geometries of chance,
encompassed by the easement of your loving
in an as lonely world where different words still glance

and chatter off the same evasions of meaning,
as the afternoon fades into its own dying
and tombs and new-turned earth begin to lose their seeming,
for you and all men dead and now our hearts are crying

wide with compassion who have none to give.
The black snows of darkness gather about the hills;
dust skitters the coffin; the mourners leave to live;
and with its old indifference the abandoned clay refills.

(*Selected Poems 1942–1972*, page 24)

CHAPTER TWENTY

European Architectural Heritage Year
1975

James Stevens Curl

Introduction: Scotland's Architecture – A European Perspective

In 1826 the great German Professor of Architecture and Privy Counsellor for Public Works, Karl Friedrich Schinkel (1781–1841), and the Prussian Privy Counsellor for Finance, Peter Christian Wilhelm Beuth (1781–1853), visited Scotland as part of a tour of France, England, Scotland, and Wales. It was what these days would be called a 'fact-finding mission', on behalf of the Prussian State, undertaken for the purpose of seeing bridges, factories, warehouses, public buildings, and other works recently completed or under construction at the time. Prussia had emerged after the Napoleonic Wars as a major European power, and King Friedrich Wilhelm III (1797–1840), keen to make Berlin worthy of its status as the capital of a great nation, sought to beautify it by urban improvements, the construction of handsome examples of architecture, and the creation of museums and galleries, open to everyone, to house the Royal Collections and thereby educate the populace, thus raising the tone of society. To accomplish these worthy aims he was fortunate in having the services of Schinkel, arguably the greatest architect of his time, and a highly intelligent (and incorruptible) civil servant devoted to his monarch. Great Britain and Prussia had been allies against the French, and joint victors (with Hanoverians and Netherlanders) at Waterloo in 1815, so there was an additional incentive to emulate the wealth of new and advanced achievements of a country acknowledged to be a leader in engineering, industrial developments, and technology. Among the projects Schinkel saw was the British Museum in London (1823–46) then being built to designs by (Sir) Robert Smirke (1780–1867).

Schinkel kept a journal[1] in which he recorded interesting artefacts, mused about the people and architecture, and sketched workshops, machinery, gadgets, landscapes, and much else: it is a unique account of Britain during the reign of King George IV (1820–30), seen through the eyes of a great European intellectual, and one of the few accurate surviving descriptions of the country at the time the Industrial Revolution was already making a huge impact.

On 3 July Schinkel saw Edinburgh 'like an isolated jewel' rising from its plain, and admired the 'splendid new wide streets' of the New Town.[2] He was intrigued to note the similarity between the cupola of St George's Parish Church, Charlotte Square (1811–14), by Robert Reid (1774–1856), and the twin cupolas of the two churches in the Gendarmenmarkt, Berlin (1780–5), designed by Karl von Gontard (1731–91). It is perhaps worth noting that a very similar cupola was erected as part of the Scottish Co-Operative Wholesale Society Ltd's showpiece building in The Gorbals, Glasgow (now just beside the M8 flyover, and a prominent landmark) of 1892–7. Schinkel saw the Tanfield Gas-Works, Canonmills, Edinburgh (1824 – mostly demolished), designed by William Burn (1789–1870), which he pronounced 'excellent', and paid Burn the compliment of committing a drawing of it to the pages of his journal. He was appalled, however, by the unsettling contrast between the New Town's elegance and the wretchedness of conditions in the 'dreadful streets' and alleys that were all too numerous elsewhere in the city.

On 6 July Schinkel and Beuth visited 'Mr Owen's large factory'[3] at New Lanark, where all the girls went 'barefoot', and admired the 'splendid' new streets of Glasgow (where Schinkel thought the domestic architecture 'purer' than that in Edinburgh, but the statue of King William III in the Trongate [now re-sited near the Cathedral] 'dreadful'). Fascinated by the industrial buildings, canals, and everything they saw, the two friends and colleagues travelled on to Loch Lomond, then to Loch Fyne, arriving at Inveraray on the evening of 8 July. An election had just taken place, and everyone in the inn was drunk. Beuth found himself drinking wine with an 'old Scotsman, bragging horribly, and a drunk young man': the Germans found it difficult to get away from 'these two babblers'. That is an encounter I, for one, would love to have witnessed.

The marvellous ensemble of buildings, screen-walls, bridges, and other structures which Robert Mylne (1733–1811) had designed and built for John Campbell, 5th Duke of Argyll (1723–1806), in 1774–89, struck Schinkel as having a 'Picturesque air', although he thought the church was 'awful'. His journal contains a pretty sketch of the Castle (designed by Roger Morris [1695–1749] for Archibald

Campbell, Earl of Ilay and 3rd Duke of Argyll [1682–1761], built 1745–60) in its setting. The drawing shows the building before its towers acquired their conical roofs built to designs by Anthony Salvin (1799–1881) after the fire of 1877. A century and a quarter after the Germans saw Inveraray, both Castle and Town were in a parlous state, and considerable works of conservation were set in hand under the aegis of Ian Douglas Campbell, 11th Duke of Argyll (1903–73), the supervising architect being Ian G. Lindsay. Those works were chronicled by Mr Lindsay and Mary Cosh in their monumental study, *Inveraray and the Dukes of Argyll.* [4]

Schinkel and Beuth visited Tobermory, Staffa, Iona, the Crinan Canal (which had been built in 1801), Greenock (where the handsome Doric Customs-House [1817–18] by William Burn attracted their attention), and returned to Glasgow. Schinkel wrote of 'wonderful, old rough castles', and, as often as he could, made delightful drawings of scenery and buildings. However, to his experienced eye, much needed to be done to improve Scotland's infrastructure, housing, towns, and villages. He was appalled by the poverty, 'desolation', and unkempt appearance of many of the places and inhabitants he saw, and could not avoid noticing the almost immediate improvement in conditions over the Border in England on his way to Carlisle on 15 July. There were few enough Inverarays, Edinburgh New Towns, or handsome new Glaswegian streets. He prophesied that, with the opening up of Scotland by means of public transport (he mentioned on several occasions the steamboats then plying their trade out of Glasgow and Leith), things would change, and that in twenty years or so the country would be transformed.

Schinkel was right. Although Scotland had a legacy of mediaeval buildings, much of that legacy was ruinous thanks to the religious and other upheavals of the sixteenth and seventeenth centuries. Glasgow Cathedral, [5] alone among mainland Scottish cathedrals, survived those vicissitudes almost intact, although its use by three Congregations (one of them Gaelic-speaking) involved its subdivision (which, paradoxically, was probably the main reason why not only the building itself was allowed to remain, but why the superb fifteenth-century *pulpitum* [stone chancel-screen] with early sixteenth-century altar-platforms on the nave side, is still there, because it was the base of the partition separating two of the Congregations [the third was in the crypt]). Furthermore, apart from country houses (many of which were being erected by architects such as Burn when Schinkel visited

Scotland) and the new estate villages associated with them, much of Scotland's architectural heritage had still to be built, for it was the product of wealth accumulated in the later nineteenth and early twentieth centuries, and for that reason it tended to be undervalued in the 1960s and early 1970s.

European Architectural Heritage Year 1975

It was a long time ago when the Council of Europe designated 1975 as European Architectural Heritage Year (EAHY), not just in terms of years, but of perceptions, expectations, and experience. The 1939–45 War, with its devastating destruction on such a huge scale, had ended just over a quarter of a century before, but enormous damage had been done in the intervening period to countless cities, towns, villages, and buildings, for the past was undervalued, and the obliteration of its physical manifestations was very much part of the political agenda as well as of the protagonists of the Athens Charter of 1931 and the Congrès Internationaux d'Architecture Moderne (CIAM) which had adopted wholesale the ideas of the Franco-Swiss architect Le Corbusier (pseudonym of Charles-Édouard Jeanneret-Gris [1887–1965]). Among the dogmas (they were nothing less) accepted and promoted by CIAM were rigid functional zoning of city-plans, a single type of urban housing (high-rise, widely spaced apartment blocks), and the creation of urban motorways, all of which were applied as panaceas to British towns and cities with results that, by the early 1970s, were becoming horrifyingly clear to all but those blinded by their own beliefs.

Post-war reconstruction in countries such as Poland had often involved a painstaking attempt to recover lost fabric (as in Warsaw, deliberately destroyed by the retreating Germans) by scholarly craft-centred rebuilding and restoration: the virtually obliterated former Royal Castle in the Polish capital, for example, has risen again from its rubble, and an extraordinarily fine job has been made of it. Under the inspiring direction of Professor Jan Zachwatowicz (1900–83), a whole generation of architect-conservators was trained during the dangerous years when Poland was occupied, and, as a political entity, virtually ceased to exist. It is no accident that an often-quoted remark in conservation circles to the effect that 'a town without old buildings is like a man without a memory' was by another Pole, Konrad Smigielski. It was essential, to Poles, to give physical reality to their history by rebuilding the shattered fabric of their cities, towns, and buildings to help to re-assert nationhood. In the British Isles, however, nothing like this occurred: in fact it is arguable that more damage was done by local authorities, governments, professionals, and various agencies than the Luftwaffe managed to inflict in five-and-a-half years of war. Whilst the Poles wished to recover their collective historical memory, the British wanted to drink deep of Lethe's waters. Glasgow, as has been so poignantly noted, almost managed to make itself disappear, while the erosion and vulgaris-ation of Edinburgh proceeded. Indeed, Glasgow celebrated the beginning of the EAHY Campaign by demolishing (in the teeth of protests) a fine pair of Neoclassical tenement blocks (1793–5) flanking the entrance to College Street in the High Street, designed by Robert (1728–92) and James (1732–94) Adam, no less, which event, taken with the curious number of inconvenient historic buildings that, rather like an Act of God, 'went on fire' (Alexander 'Greek' Thomson's [1817–75] Caledonia Road Church [1856] was gutted in 1965, for example, and stands a stark ruin there today), lowered the spirits of those few who saw virtues and reasons in conservation.

A prevailing orthodoxy antipathetic to the past, to historic build-ings, and to repair and scholarly conservation, was also in favour of wholesale redevelopment optimistically misnamed 'urban renewal'. This panacea, by which powers would be invoked to enable huge swathes of cities to be bulldozed to provide cleared sites for de-velopers, was an American import, and was really a recipe for greed on an unprecedented scale. By the time it had caught on here, how-ever, the reaction also began to arrive from America when the critic Jane Jacobs (b. 1916), in her devastating critique, *The Death and Life of Great American Cities* (1961), attacked the by then conven-tional wisdom, and argued that zoning, 'urban renewal', and all the nostrums promoted by CIAM-inspired architects, planners, and pol-iticians, were actually killing off not only the cities, but economies as well, and, in the process, doing huge and probably irreversible damage to the fabric of society. On this side of the Atlantic some voices were raised in protest against what was happening. The Civic Trust had been founded in response to a growing awareness of what was being destroyed, and was in the vanguard of promoting legisla-tion put in place that began to give some degree of protection to historic buildings, whole areas (called Conservation Areas), and the like. Attention was drawn to the vanishing country houses after far too many had been lost (not unconnected with fiscal arrangements put in place specifically to destroy inherited wealth). Further problems arose, as churches became redundant, uses changed, and the environment suffered from all sorts of blights, ill-informed tinkering, shortage or surfeit of money (both could be dangerous), short-term requirements of traffic engineers, and all the threats familiar to anyone who has worked in the conservation world.

EAHY in Scotland

EAHY was late in coming, but it would probably not have happened much earlier on such a scale as the climate only began to change in response to the damage being done. Yet everywhere, it seemed, people were awakening to appreciate the orgies of destruction, gradual erosion and other disasters that had been happening all along. When 1975 was designated, the Scottish Civic Trust (SCT) was invited by the Government to provide the Secretariat for the Scottish Campaign, and appropriate finance was provided. Her Majesty Queen Elizabeth the Queen Mother graciously agreed to become President of the Scottish Committee, a widely representative body which met under the Chairmanship of the Viscount Muirshiel, Chairman of the SCT. An Executive Committee was established under the Chairmanship of (Sir) James Dunbar-Nasmith to run the Campaign and provide representation at the monthly meetings of the United Kingdom Council. Maurice Lindsay, Director of the SCT, acted as Secretary to both the Scottish Committee and the Scottish Executive Committee.

Late in 1972 I was appointed the Architectural Adviser for the Scottish Campaign, and took up the post at the beginning of March 1973, having worked for several years with the Historic Buildings Division of the then Greater London Council on *The Survey of London*. Shortly afterwards, Helen Logan was appointed as my Secretary, and served the Campaign with tireless devotion. Like Lord Muirshiel, she, sadly, is no longer with us. During 1973 I visited each of the former counties and other local authorities in Scotland (EAHY had fallen rather inconveniently at a time of major local government re-organisation, which was another problem), endeavouring to stimulate as much civic and private restoration and conservation work as possible, and publicising the Campaign in lectures, broadcasts, regular features in the public prints (*The Scotsman* was an especial ally, and acknowledgement of that help is gratefully reiterated here), and by other means.

I recall lunching with Lord Muirshiel early in 1973 when he told me that, in spite of all the efforts of the SCT, certain local authorities were resistant to the principle of conservation, and indeed it was true that in certain areas no budgets existed for rescuing historic buildings, encouraging repairs, or indeed for anything connected with conservation at all. In fact no Conservation Areas had been designated in those strongholds of reaction where anything old faced destruction if it could be organised. Of course, parts of Scotland were more attuned to the aims of EAHY than others. Edinburgh had established its New Town Conservation Committee in 1970 with the Irish architect Desmond Hodges as its able and effective first Director, and enormous strides had been made, but not before time, as the damage to one of the finest eighteenth- and nineteenth-century urban landscapes in the world was already painfully obvious.

There was also the National Trust for Scotland's Little Houses Improvement Scheme, based on an initial Revolving Fund of the then substantial sum of £100,000, which had been the means by which many houses and flats (notably in the East Neuk of Fife) were restored and adapted for modern living, and it was moving on to consolidate success by rehabilitating many more buildings, sometimes in association with local preservation societies and other bodies. Scotland had its successes, and there were also the many efforts by private individuals that contributed to the national efforts.

Part of my work was to bring into more intense focus projects that were already under way, to encourage others that were having difficulties in getting started, to get new schemes begun that nobody had considered (which involved finding the site, drawing up proposals, and then getting them accepted), and generally to act as an evangelist for the Campaign. Although there was resistance at first, so many organisations and individuals warmed to the idea that we were able to record about 250 projects throughout the country ranging from major rehabilitation schemes (such as the restoration of the Theatre Royal, Glasgow, as a permanent home for Scottish Opera) to modest environmental improvements. Other works included the undergrounding of unsightly overhead power- and telephone-lines in villages of architectural quality; the mounting of many exhibitions; the setting up of competitions; the establishment of new town-trails;

the publication of conservation-area guides by several local authorities; and the restoration of many historic buildings. Thanks to the
co-operation of the editors of journals such as *Country Life*,[6] *Project
Scotland, The Architect*, and other publications, the Campaign was
so effectively promoted that I was invited to meet representatives of
several local authorities that had never taken any active interest in
conservation, and indeed had been hostile to it. As a result, many
new Conservation Areas were designated, and it would be no idle
claim that in certain parts of Scotland the whole climate relating to
the environment and historic buildings was changed for the better
because of the EAHY Campaign.

One of the most remarkable successes of the time was the establishment of the Charles Rennie Mackintosh Society, of which I was
a founder-member. Although hard to believe now, when Mackinto-
shiana is ubiquitous (perhaps over-exposed), several of CRM's
buildings were under threat in 1973, but the Society (which now has
its headquarters in the once-doomed Queen's Cross Church, Gar-
scube Road) has grown from strength to strength under the energetic
and inspiring leadership of Patricia Douglas, and Mackintosh's name
is known throughout Scotland, while his legacy now seems secure.
It is to be hoped that the lively Alexander Thomson Society will be
equally successful, and will be able to rescue what is left of that great
architect's work. In the context of these reminiscences, Thomson
had a set of Schinkel's *Sammlung Architektonischer Entwürfe* (Collection of Architectural Designs)[7] in his own library, and there are
obvious similarities between the buildings of both men. Certainly
Thomson[8] must be recognised as a figure of international architectural importance, although Glasgow celebrated his status by
demolishing another of his buildings in 1997.

Of the 285 United Kingdom Awards for EAHY, 52 came to Scotland, and of the 16 Awards for schemes of exceptional merit,
Scotland obtained four, which reflects well on a country with such
a small population. At one of the three Seminars held as part of the
European Campaign as a whole, the SCT mounted for the Council
of Europe the three-language Seminar in 1974 on The Social and
Economic Implications of Conservation. Delegates were given private hospitality in homes in the New Town, and treated to a specially
organised Burns Supper.

All these successes were achieved against the backdrop of the
three-day week and the economic crisis which beset the United

Kingdom halfway through the Campaign. Maurice Lindsay and I worked closely together through that trying time; wrote the script for the film *Raised from Stone* which Murray Grigor produced, premièred at the Glasgow Film Theatre in September 1975; and attended the EAHY Congresses in Bruges and Amsterdam (both 1975). The latter Congress produced The Declaration of Amsterdam which committed participants to promote the importance of conservation by building on the newly aroused awareness of the value of architectural heritage highlighted during EAHY. Throughout the Campaign it was emphasised that EAHY was only a beginning, not an end, for it was recognised there will never be a time when the survival of the best of our man-made heritage can be left to the vagaries of chance. Any generation is only a custodian, passing on (or not passing on) what it has inherited for the use, enjoyment, and custodianship of those who come after.

I remember Desmond Hodges telling me I would look back on my many journeys throughout Scotland, including, of course, the Islands, as one of the most rewarding times of my life. He was right, and I often think of the many people I met, the extraordinarily generous hospitality and kindnesses I received, the beauties of what I saw, and the many successes and pleasant surprises that helped to make my efforts for EAHY in Scotland all worth while. There were the personal satisfactions of getting Conservation Areas designated by once-hostile local authorities (and seeing the delighted surprise on Jack Muirshiel's face), of firm friendships made, and of receiving heartwarming letters of thanks relating to projects we had encouraged (I remember Charles Stewart's gracious appreciation regarding works at New Abbey with particular affection).

Afterword

And yet it is hard to sum up the experience of EAHY: one sees so many things in memory that the freshness of the images becomes blurred. As I said, it was a long time ago, and I have an uncomfortable feeling that the Campaign, or something like it, needs to start all over again. There are still opinions flying about to the effect that historic buildings and the man-made heritage are somehow irrelevant, for toffs only (and therefore to be opposed); that 'there is too much conservation' getting in the way of 'progress' (a doctrine, as the French have reminded us, of idlers and Belgians); that we must concentrate on the 'spirit of the times' (a dismal notion promoted by Le Corbusier and his cronies that keeps cropping up rather too often); and that everything is disposable because nothing really matters.

Contrary to received opinion, no work of art (or architecture) is 'timeless', for it is subject to decay, alteration, mutilation, destruction, and the fickleness of changing taste. Much in Post-Modernism (despite the occasional nod to Classicising motifs applied with little understanding) questions permanence, harmony, order, and even meaning: it accepts, even welcomes, dysfunction, deformation, fragmentation, discord, destabilisation, and is essentially a violation of all existing conceptions. Confusion, conflict, and relativism, it seems, have encouraged the paradox of a repressive tolerance of the tenth-rate, and, as a corollary, an intolerance of anything with its roots in what was once recognised as Classical paradigmatic culture. The discrimination of the aesthete is no longer wanted, and indeed is virtually forbidden as élitist: anything goes, and the new Pluralism ensures a rather unpleasant dictatorship of the ephemeral, the cheap, and the very nasty. One has a feeling that the Genius of Architecture, in extreme old age, has either entered its second childhood or become too brashly emulative of thoughtless youth for its own good.

In the time leading up to EAHY I often explored, recorded, and wrote about Scotland's architectural and monumental riches, and once took the trouble to retrace Schinkel's route taken in 1826, itself a fascinating exercise. I recall writing of the incomparable Glasgow Necropolis (which I had first seen in 1956, and could scarcely believe was not a mirage, I thought it so wonderful) that it was full of character, a poetic place full of resonances, allusions, and farewells, which had found its place in the landscape for ever to be associated with the towering Gothic mass of St Mungo's Cathedral. Now I am not so sure: vandals have done what they can to wreck the place, and works by the responsible authorities have not been of the most sensitive order. Such frolicsome activities have been no respecters of the dead or of their monuments, but they seem widespread, these latter-day barbarities. Schinkel, of course, asleep beneath his Grecian *stele* in the Berlin Dorotheenfriedhof (blessed spot), never saw the Necropolis, because it was not laid out until six years later, but he commented upon the 'strange monuments' in the Cathedral burial-ground. What he would have made of the visual atrocities perpetrated on the city in the post-war period can only remain in the tenebrous realms of speculation.

Tempora mutantur, et nos mutamur in illis (times change, and we change with them). Without care, effort, scholarship, craftsmanship, beliefs, will, money, and passion, the man-made heritage will not survive. EAHY was a widespread international attempt to raise public awareness, by pilot projects and exemplars to show what could be done, and to give new leases of life to individual buildings and whole areas. Most of all, however, it was about education, creating a sense of purpose, identifying goals, and showing that the built heritage mattered in so many ways as an inseparable part of the landscape and the nation's history. In 1975 we accomplished much. We need to reach new generations if those gains, and much more, are not to be lost. Eternal vigilance, passing expertise on to the young, and making people aware of what they have are essential parts of the mosaic. Once something is lost there is no national will to recreate it: it is gone for ever, and we are left with sad places, veiled in regret.

Notes and references

1. Bindmann, David, and Riemann, Gottfried: *Karl Friedrich Schinkel: 'The English Journey' – Journal of a visit to France and Britain in 1826* (New Haven & London: Yale University Press for the Paul Mellon Centre for Studies in British Art, 1993)
2. Youngson, A. J: *The Making of Classical Edinburgh 1750–1840* (Edinburgh: Edinburgh University Press, 1966)
3. Robert Owen (1771–1858), freethinker, radical, industrialist, and social reformer. See *Dictionary of National Biography* (London: Geoffrey Cumberlege, for Oxford University Press, 1917)
4. Lindsay, Ian G., and Cosh, Mary: *Inveraray and the Dukes of Argyll* (Edinburgh: Edinburgh University Press, 1973)
5. An excellent and succinct account of the building may be found in Williamson, Elizabeth, Riches, Anne, and Higgs, Malcolm: *Glasgow*, in *The Buildings of Scotland* series (Harmondsworth: Penguin Books in association with the National Trust for Scotland, 1990)
6. See especially *Country Life* 8 August 1974, 3 October 1974, 28 November 1974, 13 February 1975, 7 August 1975, 11 December 1975, 4 March 1976, and *The Architect* May 1974, December 1977, January 1978, August 1978, October 1978
7. See Schinkel, Karl Friedrich: *Collection of Architectural Designs* (Guildford: Butterworth, 1989)
8. See McFadzean, Ronald: *The Life and Works of Alexander Thomson* (London, Boston, & Henley: Routledge & Kegan Paul, 1979) and Stamp, Gavin and McKinstry, Sam (eds): *'Greek' Thomson* (Edinburgh: Edinburgh University Press, 1994)

From THE EXILED HEART

And my restless thoughts migrate to a Northern city –
fat pigeons stalking the dirty cobbled quays
where a sluggish river carried the cold self-pity
of those for whom life has never flowed with ease,
from a granite bridge to the green Atlantic seas:

the bristling, rough-haired texture of Scottish manners;
the jostling clatter of crowded shopping streets
where lumbering tramcars squeal as they take sharp corners:
the boosy smell from lounging pubs that cheats
the penniless drunkard's thirst with its stale deceits:

(Selected Poems 1942–1972, page 12)

CHAPTER TWENTY-ONE

The National Heritage in Scotland

Brian Lang

FASHION TRENDS apply to words as much as to clothing. The term 'national heritage' seems to have gone the way of the kipper tie. When the new Labour Government took office in 1997, the former Department of National Heritage was renamed the Department of Culture, Media and Sport. The body allocated hitherto undreamt of sums from the new lottery refers merely to its 'Heritage Lottery Fund'.

The heyday of the national heritage arrived during the 1970s and 1980s. In the first of those decades a whole category of physical attributes of the United Kingdom – landscapes both natural and painted, manuscripts, machines and mansions – was recognised as somehow coming together to represent what we most valued from the past. The value of this 'national heritage' began to dawn as cherished parts of it were 'lost'.

The idea of the 'national heritage' was by no means new. *Country Life* referred to it, and the dangers posed to it, in a leading article in 1930. The National Trust's country houses scheme, designed to prevent the destruction of such houses and the scattering of their contents, was advocated by Lord Lothian in 1937.

However, in the 1970s, letters to the editor, exhibitions in museums and galleries, and lobbying by pressure groups, consolidated the anguish created by the losses and threats into a drive which culminated, in 1980, in the creation of the National Heritage Memorial Fund. The Fund was given the task, in the words of its Act of Parliament, of 'providing financial assistance towards the acquisition, preservation and maintenance of land, buildings, works of art and other objects which, in the opinion of the Trustees, are of outstanding interest and also of importance to the national heritage'.

The irony is that the term 'national heritage' has become *passé* just as massively unprecedented sums of money are being devoted to its salvation.

What were the threats and actual losses in the '70s, and why was it that during this period concern became so great that government action was taken? Since 1918, country houses had been demolished at a rate which, for a period, reached one every fortnight. Paintings by Turner, or by great continental artists which had been gathered by Britons on the Grand Tour, had been trickling to the USA and Japan for decades. Works of art, after all, have always flowed from poorer to richer countries.

In the 1970s, it all just became too much, or so it seemed. A number of influences came together to say 'enough is enough'. In 1974 Marcus Binney, Roy Strong and John Harris mounted the exhibition 'The Destruction of the English Country House' at the V&A. In 1977 *The Times* carried letters to the Editor lamenting the scattering of the library of John Evelyn, the seventeenth-century polymath and man of letters. Nature lovers despaired over the threats posed by modern farming methods to areas such as the Somerset Levels. Great paintings seemed to be crated up and freighted abroad by the week.

In Scotland, Newhailes House was separated from its fine library because of the requirements of the capital tax concession which was intended to protect cherished houses and their contents. Mavisbank House, also just outside Edinburgh, continued to rot, its owner seemingly impervious to the efforts of the planning authorities to force him to carry out repairs. In Glasgow, a fine row of tenement housing by William 'Greek' Thomson was about to be demolished, and the 'Merchant City' looked like losing its best buildings. Exploitation of oil and gas deposits beneath the North Sea meant that coastal areas were threatened by disfiguring construction sites and storage depots.

The last straw was Mentmore, and the story has been frequently told. The Earl of Rosebery decided that he should dispose of his large Victorian pile in Buckinghamshire as it was too expensive to maintain for family use and, after all, he had another house at Dalmeny. Mentmore, its contents (nothing particularly special in its own right but interesting as a collection) and park were offered to the Government for £2m. The Government declined, and the contents were sold by Sotheby's (Lord Rosebery lending a hand with a screwdriver when the auctioneer's sound system failed) in a four-day marquee sale. Many letters of protest were written to the national newspapers, and a well-argued and -constructed campaign was run by Marcus Binney and Save Britain's Heritage. The house was taken over by followers of the Maharishi Mahesh Yogi, for a conference-cum-meditation centre.

The protest was double-edged. First, why should Government allow yet another great country house to lose its beauty and meaning through the dispersal of its contents and conversion to a quite different use? Second, why did Government not deploy the resources of the National Land Fund? This had been established in 1946, with £50m raised from the sale of surplus war material, expressly in order to acquire land and buildings in memory of those who had given their lives during the Second World War. This Fund was controlled by Ministers. The Secretary of State for the Environment, Peter Shore, refused to release the necessary resources. The outcry that accompanied the scattering of Mentmore's contents was so strong that in 1980 a new body, the National Heritage Memorial Fund, controlled by independent Trustees, appointed by the Prime Minister, was created. The 'Memorial' in the title had been inserted by the intervention of Tam Dalyell MP, to give specific reference to the intention of the now defunct National Land Fund, whose assets the NHMF inherited. But only £12.5m went to the new Fund, because it transpired that the Land Fund had been raided for unrelated purposes, by Conservative Treasury Ministers Peter Thorneycroft and Enoch Powell, in an earlier administration.

Scotland was well placed to benefit from the NHMF. The conservation movement in Scotland was, in fact, highly organised and sensibly managed. A plethora of watchdogs and appreciation societies was flourishing. The Scottish Civic Trust, based in a George Square attic in Glasgow, publicised very effectively the threats to Scotland's, and particularly Glasgow's, fine urban buildings. Maurice Lindsay led a team in which John Gerrard and Sadie Douglas were assiduous in their scrutiny of any planning applications which were either unsympathetic to, or threatened directly, good buildings or conservation areas. In Edinburgh, the Cockburn Association, managed by Oliver Barratt, did the same. In Perth, Aberdeen, and in all the major towns, similar bodies took furious pride in their buildings and townscapes.

The Scottish Office came out well. Senior officials were sympathetic. (Having played a major role in getting Haddo House in Aberdeenshire into the safe hands of the National Trust for Scotland, the responsible Under-Secretary at the Scottish Development Department, Ronnie Cramond, was spotted singing in Lady Aberdeen's choir.)

The Minister in charge, for a period, in his first taste of office, was (Sir) Malcolm Rifkind. Government funding for help with repair work and rebuilding came through the Historic Buildings Council for Scotland. During the 1970s, resources were available on a scale that permitted not just repair of buildings of architectural or historical significance, but their virtual rebuilding as well. Ruins, such as Towie Barclay Castle in Aberdeenshire, were rebuilt. Relations between HBCS and the various conservation groups and watchdogs were good, largely because of the sensitive and committed approach taken by HBCS's professional advisers, led by David Walker (who could name the architect and year of completion of any Scottish building pointed out to him) and because those advisers were themselves active in the building conservation movement, through their publishing, speaking and social activities. The Historic Buildings Advisers, who included Anne Riches and Richard Emerson, were formidably knowledgeable. Administrative staff developed good understanding of the needs of property owners applying for assistance. Harry Graham, Wilma Myrtle and Hector Mackenzie, in particular, exemplified the ability to match needs with appropriate help and a sympathetic ear. But they could also separate out the less needy owners and the less deserving properties. While administrative staff came and went in the Civil Service manner, the specialist staff formed a more stable repository of knowledge and conservation expertise.

The appointed members of the Council were similarly disposed towards conservation. Chaired by the Earl of Crawford and Balcarres, owner of the eponymous great house in Fife, and later by Nicholas Fairbairn, who had himself rebuilt Fordell Castle, the Council's other members included Kathleen Dalyell, châtelaine of the Binns, near Linlithgow, and Maurice Lindsay. James Dunbar-Nasmith and Ian Begg were practising conservation architects of high reputation.

The only real problem was lack of money, but grants from HBCS funding could be used to lever help from other sources, such as the Architectural Heritage Fund, and the Scottish Development Agency (SDA). The SDA had already learned the lesson that the restoration of significant historic buildings could encourage refurbishment and other kinds of investment and hence job creation in adjacent areas. The Glasgow Eastern Area Renewal (GEAR) scheme enjoyed substantial financial benefit from SDA in the project to clean up what had become an insalubrious area of the city. St Andrew's Church, a fine eighteenth-century church of national importance, was restored in a substantial works programme.

The HBCS performed marvels, considering the relatively small sums at its disposal, and despite an attempt, on at least one known occasion, to defraud it.

When NHMF was created, its first Chairman was Lord Charteris of Amisfield, whose elder brother, the Earl of Wemyss and March, had a major house at Gosford in East Lothian. Lord Charteris spent his summers in a cottage on the estate, handy for the golf course at Kilspindie. Charteris was Chairman for twelve years, and proved to be wise and shrewd in a relaxed and witty style. Genuinely charming and a raconteur of note, he belied his courtier background. On hot days, he would chair NHMF Trustee meetings in his braces, striped in the colours of Eton College, of which he was Provost. Other Trustees included the Marquess of Anglesey, a military historian who lived atop a National Trust-owned family home overlooking the Menai Straits. John Smith had founded the idiosyncratic Landmark Trust, which restored interesting houses and let them as holiday cottages. Sir Robin Cooke was an acerbic former Conservative MP; Martin Jacomb was appointed partly so he could be 'tried out' for further public appointments; Fred Holliday was persuasive and experienced on countryside issues; Clive Jenkins, who had made trade union membership respectable for the British middle class, saw himself as the representative of the people. Professor Brian Morris spoke authoritatively, wittily and often at length on literary matters, and much else besides. The first Director was the present writer, an Edinburgh Scot who came to NHMF directly from a short spell as Secretary to HBCS. The Act of Parliament which established the Fund also required that one of its Trustees represent Scotland. Maurice Lindsay was appointed, partly on the strength of his good HBCS performance and partly for his wide knowledge of Scotland. For three years he gave NHMF wise Scottish counsel.

He had a hard baptism. Early in 1980, Glasgow University announced that in order to deal with a financial shortfall in building its new Hunterian Gallery, its collection of Whistler portraits would be sold. Outcry followed, not only at the prospect of a public body selling off what was regarded very much as part of the national heritage, but because it was suggested that the University was virtually holding the fledgling NHMF to ransom. The Fund, after all, had not been set up to bail out organisations whose building projects went wrong. But the University stood firm by its declared intention to sell. NHMF decided that priority should be given to fulfilling its mission – to prevent the loss of items of importance to the heritage – and Glasgow University got its money.

NHMF came to the rescue of a long list of paintings and other works of art of importance to Scotland. The National Galleries of Scotland were able to secure some of the pictures from the Duke of Sutherland's collection, which have for many years been on long loan to the gallery. Public collections in other Scottish cities were also given assistance.

A substantial portfolio of great buildings, works of art and areas of countryside was in the safe hands of the National Trust for Scotland (NTS). The safety of these hands was rendered through organisational ability, experience, and staff with a good eye for detail and generally sound judgement of taste. The membership constituted a demonstration of widespread public support for the conservation movement in Scotland, and was growing steadily. NTS also had Sir Jamie Stormonth Darling, who ran NTS benignly but with a hand of steel when necessary. Stormonth Darling was paternal in the best sense, and the organisation reflected his personality. He was succeeded by Lester Borley, who brought with him a lively sense of what could be achieved from the close relationship between tourism and conservation. He also introduced management reforms which made the organisation less dependent on a single personality.

The National Trusts north and south of the Border had a huge advantage over other owners, actual and potential, through the statutorily guaranteed power to declare their properties inalienable. Inalienability meant that properties so designated could be taken out of National Trust ownership only through an Act of Parliament. This was deemed much more secure than, say, local authority ownership, which might be subject to local political whim, or even ownership by a national government body.

The disadvantage of inalienability lay in the need to provide an endowment for the upkeep of the property thus protected.

The National Trusts were determined to secure endowments for newly acquired properties and their memberships, and Government, appreciated the reasons for this. But the sums of money involved were substantial. The National Trust, south of the Border, calculated the endowment fund required by applying a formula established by an accountant, Lord Chorley, a member of their Finance Committee. The Chorley Formula was based on the assumption that the costs of running an inalienable property, mainly wages and building maintenance, rose faster than the combined growth and income from the investments set aside to meet them. An 'uplift' and other factors were therefore applied, with the result that for every £1 shortfall after taking account of visitor and other revenue earned by the property, up to £60 or £70 might be required by way of endowment. Much of the cost was ascribed to 'head office' and organisational overheads.

The NHMF was increasingly asked to provide the National Trusts with endowments. In 1982 Canons Ashby in Northamptonshire required £1m, and later, a grant of £8m was provided to buy and care for Belton House, near Grantham. Kedleston Hall needed £13m to purchase and endow. While the Trusts were regarded as appropriate owners of 'heritage' properties, they were scarcely to be regarded as cheap. The NHMF looked for an alternative which would require less of their resources. There was an additional motive. The NHMF wished quietly to let the National Trusts know that they were not the only bodies capable of providing care in perpetuity, and that other means might be more financially efficient. Provision in legislation existed for the creation of charitable trusts to hold heritage property. Some trusts of this type already existed, but hitherto they had been created where the owner putting property into the hands of such a trust was also able to provide funds or other property to cover their upkeep. The irony was that in such circumstances the property perhaps did not require putting into the safe hands of the charitable trust.

The NHMF looked for an important property which might be appropriate for ownership by a charitable trust, but whose existing owner had not the means to fund it. Thirlestane Castle seemed to suit. Thirlestane is a great confection, on the edge of Lauder in Berwickshire, dating from the sixteenth century. It had long been regarded as a problem by the HBCS, which had been spending substantial sums on repairs and essential maintenance. Its owner, Gerald Maitland-Carew, and his wife, were tenacious in retarding its irreversible deterioration. They wanted desperately to see the ancestral home kept in good order but the resources available to a former junior cavalry officer were not large, following division of what was left of the family assets. A deal was struck such that Maitland-Carew donated the house – save a wing which would remain a family home but would in due course revert to the charity – an area of surrounding land and the contents of the house to a specially created charity. NHMF put in £650,000 to provide for maintaining the house and opening it to the public. Each party nominated Trustees to run the property.

The message to the National Trusts was clear, to the extent that the Director-General of the NT felt constrained to write a letter to the Editor of the *Sunday Telegraph* pointing out that the advantages of NT ownership and endowment should not be overlooked. In the event, it transpired that the original endowment for Thirlestane was inadequate, and in 1988 a further £250,000 was put up by the NHMF. But the sum still did not reach what would have been required by the Chorley Formula.

Scotland had shown the way, and several such charitable trusts, funded by NHMF, were in due course created, for instance for Weston Park in Shropshire, Burton Constable in East Yorkshire and another Scottish house, Paxton, near Berwick. A by-product was the expertise which was developed in finding novel and flexible ways of securing heritage properties, and legal advisers with the relevant experience were in demand. Douglas Connell of Dundas and Wilson exemplified legal astuteness with enormous sensitivity and charm and he was a good match for the heavy guns of NHMF. They were almost invariably advised by Sir Matthew Farrer, who was discreet, highly effective, and thoroughly enjoyed what he was doing.

NHMF continued to support the National Trusts, who retained their reputations for professionalism, financial probity and security. In Scotland, the NTS was regarded as particularly suited to caring for the countryside. 1982 saw the passage into NTS hands of the island of Canna, one of the Inner Hebridean 'small isles', gifted by John and Margaret Lorne Campbell, both noted Gaelic scholars. NHMF provided an endowment and the Campbells continued to live in Canna House.

One of the strengths of the NTS was its ability to bring a wide range of organisations around its board table when circumstances required. When Fyvie Castle, in Aberdeenshire, and its contents were put up for sale on the open market in 1984, such a crisis meeting was immediately called by the Trust. The Chair was taken by Lord Crawford, of HBCS, and attended, as well as by Fyvie's owner Sir Andrew Forbes Leith and his solicitor, by the NHMF (in the person of Maurice Lindsay) and a number of interested individuals including

Marc Ellington of Towie Barclay, a close neighbour to Fyvie. Forbes Leith bowed to pressure and agreed to postpone the sale to give time for the preparation of a 'national' solution. This was in due course achieved, with financial help from NHMF, and Fyvie with its outstanding collection of pictures is now one of the finest houses in the NTS collection. At £3 million for purchase, restoration and endowment, Lord Charteris claimed Fyvie Castle and its contents to have been the best bargain struck by the NHMF.

Some complaints were made that NTS was 'suburbanising' the once desolate areas in its care. A 'Scottish wilderness' movement demanded that signposts, footbridges and 'nature trails' be kept at bay. When the still difficult-to-reach peninsula of Knoydart was put up for sale in 1984, controversy arose over which body was most likely to retain the area's special character. The major fear for Knoydart was that the Ministry of Defence had their eye on it, for armoured vehicle manoeuvres. As one of his first acts when appointed Secretary for Defence, Michael Heseltine demonstrated his sympathy for the countryside by vetoing the purchase of Knoydart. NHMF was willing to help NTS acquire the estate, but the Trust did not feel it could take on this additional, very large, management burden. Knoydart was in due course sold to a private owner and when it came on to the market yet again a few years later, NHMF helped the John Muir Trust to buy a significant part of it.

Throughout this period, money for conservation of the national heritage in Scotland was still in relatively short supply. The birth of the National Lottery in 1995 changed all that. The step change in the resources available meant that when John Kluge, an American businessman, put his Scottish estate, Mar Lodge, on the market, the issue was not so much whether a conservation solution could be afforded, as whether it might be regarded as ideologically acceptable. The Conservative Government had frequently expressed doubts about the use of public funds to intervene in and distort, as they saw it, the market for real property. Such doubts were generally dispelled, but nonetheless such attitudes had to be borne in mind by those disbursing financial help for the heritage. Mar Lodge was assured appropriate protection in NTS hands, by the allocation of £10.3m from the Lottery. In previous years, such a sum would have been difficult to find.

The Lottery has been a massive boon for the cause of conservation. Maurice Lindsay and his fellow Trustees in the early days of the NHMF would have found the sums involved difficult to conceive, let alone spend. Yet it speaks for the quality of the pioneering decisions they made in the early 1980s and the confidence that they inspired in government, applicants for help, and the heritage conservation movement as a whole, that in due course NHMF was entrusted with the Lottery proceeds intended for the purpose they had championed. The expression 'the national heritage' may now sound dated, but in providing an easily understood label for a broad and complex subject, it served a first-class purpose very effectively.

From THIS BUSINESS OF LIVING

Midges fasten their mist-cloud over the river,
zizzing and zazzing, stitching intricacy,
an uncolliding shimmer, a pattern
that satisfies some midge necessity.

(*Selected Poems 1942–1972*, page 34)

CHAPTER TWENTY-TWO

Europa Nostra

Tim O'Driscoll

EUROPE has a magnificent heritage of cities, historic towns and charming villages, much of which has evolved over two or three thousand years. Within these settlements and also throughout the surrounding countryside are monuments of infinite variety – monoliths, tombs, temples, cathedrals, churches, forts and castles, historic houses and gardens, homesteads, mills and features as humble as street signs or milestones. These things embody our history; they are the product of Europe's collective inspiration; they represent our collective memory; they deserve our reverence and care.

In the early 1960s the Council of Europe became very aware of the environmental imperatives of the second half of the twentieth century and was feeling its way towards the forms of action most appropriate for such a body. It felt the lack of any organised contact with Non-Governmental Organisations in the environmental field and therefore in 1963 encouraged Europa Nostra into existence.

Europa Nostra was created as an extension of Italia Nostra's activities onto a Europe-wide platform. The first President was Umberto Zanotti-Bianco. The actual participants in the official founding ceremony were representatives of La Ligue Urbaine, Les Vieilles Maisons Françaises, The National Trust, The National Trust for Scotland, The Civic Trust, The Irish Georgian Society, Italia Nostra, Associazone (SP) dei Centri Storichi, Bond Heemschut, and Schweizer Heimatschutz. Senior officials of the Council of Europe were also present at its beginning.

Since 1963, there has been a great shift in public opinion. Many factors have contributed to this increasing public awareness. Not least, to quote Europa Nostra, has been the tireless work of thousands of unofficial conservation associations throughout Europe. Their roots go back a hundred years or more, and today they express themselves internationally through Europa Nostra, the Federation for the Protection of Europe's Culture and Natural Heritage.

In 1969, Lord Duncan-Sandys took over as President and provided a new impetus for the activity of the Federation. At a Conference in London in 1972 in the presence of Her Majesty Queen Elizabeth the Queen Mother, I expressed the view that the greatest asset Europa Nostra had was Lord Duncan-Sandys himself. He said that 'the main asset of Europa Nostra is the dedication of its officers, its member organisations and its tiny staff'. An early recognition of its work was provided by the selection of Europa Nostra for the 'Olympia Prize of 1982'. Europa Nostra was highly pleased at this prestigious award and regarded it as a great sign of encouragement for a continuation of its activities, as they say themselves, at the 'grass roots level'.

Europa Nostra has been very fortunate in its officers. Duncan Sandys was succeeded by Hans De Koster of the Netherlands, who sadly died while still in office, and then the present leaders, HRH Prins Henrik, the Prince Consort of Denmark, and the Jongkheer Daniel Cardon de Lichtbuer of Brussels, and by the succession of Honorary Secretary Generals including Maurice Lindsay and Lester Borley, both from Scotland, now both Honorary Life Members. Shortly after Hans de Koster took over the Presidency, the Secretariat was moved from London to accommodation in The Hague generously provided by the President.

Europa Nostra states that its aims are to encourage

i)   the protection and enhancement of the European architectural and natural heritage;

ii) high standards of architecture and of town and country planning;

and

iii) the improvement of the European environment in general.

In order to achieve these aims, the Federation seeks to influence public opinion and the work of international, national and local bodies and authorities. It does this through conferences, seminars, workshops, exhibitions, publications, study tours and scientific studies. It is well known for its annual awards scheme to recognise architectural conservation and sympathetic development, affecting both the architectural and natural heritage. It also recognises the achievements of individuals through the award of Medals of Honour and uses its Restoration Fund to support small restoration schemes.

Its members in General Assembly and Council draw attention to areas of concern about European heritage by passing Declarations and Resolutions which are addressed to competent authorities and opinion makers. The Europa Nostra network has a collective membership of more than 200 organisations concerned with heritage conservation and more than 100 local government and other authorities in 32 European countries as allied members. It also has an important network of individual members throughout Europe and other parts of the world.

Europa Nostra maintains close contact with the Council of Europe and the institutions of the European Union. Europa Nostra is financed by support from these bodies, by subscriptions from its members, and by donations from commercial and non-commercial organisations and individuals.

Much has been done in arousing interest in, and indeed in rewarding, the restoration of heritage buildings and their conversion to new uses by the Europa Nostra Award Scheme. Since 1978, each year recognition is given to exemplary restoration, rehabilitation, adaptation and new projects which are sensitive to their environment. These awards attract extensive publicity throughout Europe and have proved to be enormously successful in focusing public attention on the most imaginative work being done in this field. Major support for the awards scheme has been provided by the two big sponsors, Franklin Mint and American Express. In recent times, the European Commission has become a sponsor of the awards scheme. Each year there have been up to 200 entries, all backed by sufficient technical detail. Europa Nostra awards medals to outstanding entries, roughly six each year, and diplomas to impressive entries, above 25 in number.

It is relevant perhaps to list the award winners in Scotland over the whole period: it is really unnecessary to state that this successful record has nothing whatsoever to do with the strong Scottish representation among the officers of the Organisation!

Europa Nostra Awards in Scotland

MEDALS

1984	Glasgow Vennel, Irvine
1986	Fort George, Ardersier, Inverness
1987	Georgian New Town, Edinburgh
	Village Square, New Lanark
1988	Merchant Quay, Glasgow
1991	Inveraray Jail, Argyll
1993	Fyvie Castle, Turriff, Aberdeenshire

DIPLOMAS

1978	Home Farm, Culzean Country Park
1979	Hotel, Isle of Barra
	Town Centre, Fraserburgh
1980	Nineteenth-Century Buildings, Edinburgh
1981	Ballachulish Village
1982	Highland Craft Point, Beauly
1983	Lister Site, Edinburgh
1985	Fife Folk Museum, Ceres
1986	Aiket Castle, Dunlop
1987	Clan Donald Centre, Armadale Castle, Isle of Skye
	Chatelherault, Lanarkshire
1989	House of Dun, Angus
1991	Cromarty Courthouse
	Ca' d'Oro Building, Glasgow
	Glasgow Cathedral Precinct
	Italian Centre, Glasgow
	Scotland Street School Museum
	Spiers Wharf, Port Dundas, Glasgow
	Robert Smail's Printing Works, Innerleithen
1992	Gas Court Complex, Culzean Country Park
	8 Queen Street, Edinburgh
	Barony Hall, University of Strathclyde, Glasgow
1993	Aikwood Tower, by Selkirk, Selkirkshire
1995	St Teresa's Church, Glasgow

The market research of the European Travel Commission, an organisation of 27 national tourist boards, shows that the greatest single attraction for overseas tourists to Europe is its heritage. Activity to protect and enhance this heritage is a vital underpinning of the Commission's marketing programme. At a very early stage the realisation of this encouraged the Commission to join and support Europa Nostra.

I was the first Executive Director of the Commission from 1971 to 1986 and developed a very close relationship with the officers of Europa Nostra. This relationship has been continued by my successors.

A major co-operative effort was the Copenhagen Conference in November 1973. It was convened in support of the 1975 campaign for European Architectural Heritage Year and had two purposes: one, to emphasise the common interest which exists between, on the one hand, the national tourist boards and tourism industries and, on the other hand, the organisations concerned with conservation; two, to lay the foundations for future collaborations between these two groups and between them and the governments and other relevant organisations of Europe. The very comprehensive Report of that Conference was made the subject of a special publication by the *Architects Journal of Great Britain* and was widely circulated to governments, local authorities and other organisations throughout Europe.

One of the delegates to the Conference was Maurice Lindsay, then the Director of the Scottish Civic Trust. In illustrating the statement that 'tourists should be assisted to understand the places that they visit', a photograph was reproduced in the Report of the Visitor Centre at Ben Lawers, Perthshire, created by the National Trust for Scotland. Another illustration was of the houses restored in Pittenweem, Fife, under the Little Houses Improvement Fund of the National Trust for Scotland.

The Report recommended that there should be established a joint committee with the aim of realising the objectives defined by the Conference and developing effective collaboration in the fields of tourism and conservation. At a later stage this committee was replaced by an elected member of the Europa Nostra Council – myself – in 1984 as a full member under the new statutes which were ratified at the Annual General Meeting of Europa Nostra in Scotland. The overall title of the Copenhagen Conference, incidentally, used for the first time anywhere, I think, was 'Tourism and Conservation – Working Together'.

The 1973 Conference was opened by HRH Prins Henrik, the Prince Consort of Denmark, who is currently President of Europa Nostra. The speaker from American Express was so impressed with its objectives that at a later conference in Asia he proposed and secured the establishment of 'Pacifica Nostra'.

Later at the European Architectural Heritage Conference held in Brussels in March 1980, organised under the auspices of the Council of Europe and Europa Nostra, the European Travel Commission arranged a special session entitled 'Tourism and Conservation'. The European Travel Commission and its members have through the years been a substantial subscriber to Europa Nostra.

Europa Nostra has always recognised that a crucial problem of our time is unemployment. Tourism provides about 35 million jobs in Europe at present and the forecast growth in tourism will provide millions more. That growth will materialise only if the heritage which provides the basic appeal for so many tourists is preserved and presented in an imaginative way. At the Cultural Ministerial meeting of the Council of Europe in Helsinki in 1996, the first principle agreed was that: 'Tourism makes a significant contribution to wider public access to the cultural heritage and the revenue derived from tourism can provide substantial resources for the upkeep and preservation of the cultural heritage'.

In the various measures, political and other, required to achieve the preservation and improvement of the heritage, Europa Nostra accepted the axiom that 'Unity is Strength' and took the initiative in combining the efforts of the numerous other Non-Governmental Organisations interested in preserving the heritage. In November 1994 the leading European-level Non-Governmental Organisations involved in safeguarding and enhancing our cultural heritage decided to work together within the European Heritage Group. Europa Nostra provided the initiative for this collaboration and its secretariat provides the co-ordination.

The present list of member organisations is:

The European Environmental Bureau (EEB)

The European Confederation of Conservator Restorers Organisation (ECCO)

The European Council for the Village and Small Town (ECOVAST)

The International Council of Museums Regional Organisation (ICOM Europe)

The International Council of Monuments and Sites Liaison Committee with the European Union (ICOMOS Europe)

The Pegasus Foundation

The King Baudouin Foundation (European Heritage Days Coordination)

European Forum of Heritage Associations

Network of European Museum Organisations

The Conservation Foundation (European Conservation Awards)

The National Trust European Exchange Programme

Union of European Historic Houses Associations

European Office of the World Monuments Fund

A Statement prepared by the group on the initiative of Europa Nostra states that the main aim of the group is to promote the cultural heritage as a factor in sustainable development and as a tool in European integration and in the establishment of European citizenship. An action programme has been drawn up which Europa Nostra believes is sufficiently practical to produce results.

A continuing concern of Europa Nostra is to secure the recognition that, in Europe, 90% of the substance of the cultural heritage is in private ownership and so deserving of particular State action. The point about private ownership was made forcefully by Lester Borley, the then Secretary General of Europa Nostra, to the Fourth European Conference of European Ministers responsible for the cultural heritage in Helsinki in May 1996. Combining with the Union of European Historic Houses Associations, a 'Declaration' on this aspect is being given wide publicity by both organisations.

In 1996, the Council of Ministers of the European Union arrived at a unanimous agreement on its action programme regarding cultural heritage. The principal objective is to support and complement the activities of the member states in the context of heritage of European importance. An interesting definition by the Council of 'cultural heritage of European importance', which in essence agrees with the Europa Nostra policy, was that 'by cultural heritage is meant':

real estate and movables: museums and collections: libraries

archives, including photographic, cinema and sound archives:

archaeological and marine heritage:

architectural heritage and cultural collections:

sites and landscapes (cultural and natural collections).

A noteworthy development in Europa Nostra activity in recent years has been the development of connections with the countries of Central and Eastern Europe. This, of course, is very much related to Europe as a whole and has certainly produced happy results in Hungary, Poland and elsewhere. A major involvement is in encouraging participation in Europa Nostra activities. This was assisted by the Hans de Koster Fund set up to mark the devoted and distinguished service to Europa Nostra of its late Executive President. The Fund plays an important rôle in enabling representatives of heritage organisations in Central and Eastern Europe as well as young professionals and leaders of environmental groups from the same regions to participate effectively in Europa Nostra meetings and forum discussions. Another form of practical contact consists of seminars and conferences at which the experience of member organisations of Europa Nostra could encourage emerging Non-Governmental Organisations. It was encouraging to see many younger professionals from Central Europe participating in those activities. Extension of the Award Scheme to the East provided opportunities for expanding interest in the heritage. Co-operation with the Council of Europe, the European Union and UNESCO opened up many avenues.

In the wider European context, the successful organisation of Forums on topical subjects is a recent progressive activity. Examples are the Forum on the cultural landscape of the river valleys in Europe (Strasbourg 1994), Restoring and Adapting Historic Buildings (Berlin 1994), the Threat to Wooden Architecture (Krakow 1995), Conserving Industrial Heritage (Manchester 1995), Jugendstil (Vienna 1996), Nature and Education (Madrid 1997), and the Preservation of Archaeology (Thessaloniki 1997).

On 14th September 1991 at the conclusion of a joint meeting in Dublin of the General Meeting of Europa Nostra and of the General Assembly of the International Castles Institute, a Resolution was unanimously adopted merging the two organisations. This was on the understanding that both organisations were merged under the name 'Europa Nostra United with the International Castles Institute'.

It is not difficult to justify the activity of Europa Nostra and its kindred organisations, but it is nevertheless worth quoting the opening wording in a comprehensive statement by the European Union in 1995 on the heritage, which said 'We are engaged in a race against time'.

The current Secretary General of Europa Nostra, Antonio Marchini-Camia, summed up the situation after the most recent Forum when he wrote: 'Europa Nostra, as a pan-European non-governmental organisation with an important representational role must work to bring attention to the current major problems which fall within its field of activity, namely protecting and giving prominence to Europe's cultural heritage, in particular through the instrument of the forums which it organises. In this manner, Europa Nostra can help to draw attention to Europe's common cultural heritage, a role assigned to the European Union by Article 128 of the EEC Maastricht Treaty, as well as raise awareness of Europe's cultural identity, one of the principal objectives of the Council of Europe. The problem of education about, through and by Nature, which Europa Nostra emphasised at its 1997 forum, involves three major issues of European society: nature conservation, education and employment'.

As the Executive President has said in his 1996 Annual Report: 'Whilst we shall develop further our co-operation with similar European organisations, our effectiveness will depend on attracting more sponsorship for our work from foundations, institutions and corporations which share our aims of developing a well-informed civil society'.

Europa Nostra has always been fortunate in the people it has attracted to its cause. Knowledge of the needs of conservation, and the never-ending work of raising public awareness, have always attracted people with the gift of communication. Maurice Lindsay has been pre-eminent in his field, and in the years which have passed since we first met in Copenhagen, I have always valued his ability to understand the public mood, and to observe the way in which people react to their surroundings. He is of course a poet, first and last, and I should like to end my contribution by sharing with you a poem composed by him in 1991 at the Dublin Meeting when he ended his eight successful years as Secretary General of Europa Nostra.

Thank you, Maurice, for having us.

Impromptu VIII: In Dublin

As I walked out through Grafton Street
I saw a sight you wouldn't meet
in Scotland if a month of Sundays
stretched to a century of Mondays;
a young man with, around his neck,
a placard telling you, on spec,
he was prepared by rote to say
as many pomes as you might pay
him for. He listed Yeats – by far the greatest of his greats –
Kavanagh, Muldoon, Seamus Heaney.
The Irish Garda, not being many,
strolled by to show that no one bothers
what harmlessly may turn on others
when people choose thus to rehearse
the pleasures of well-spoken verse
here, in a land where poetry's
a stuff to share with you and me.
I wondered what would happen if
a youth stood up and, to the good
and great of Edinburgh's High
Street said – not that The End is Nigh
(such pious rubbish is accepted
when said in place; indeed, protected;
Free Speech, they call it) – not for free
but for a very modest fee,
he'd speak MacDiarmid's lyric rhymes
in Scots; or, out of later times,
MacCaig, Smith, Lindsay or George Bruce;
or concrete Eddie Morgan, spruce
in fashion's avant-guardest suit.
Some boot upon another foot
would lash out insults like 'elitist'
(which really means the best and neatest
way that a thing can be achieved;
but teaching's now so misconceived
the best's thought stuffier than the worst,
the latest easy least put first).
Police would appear to urge him on.
Advertisements should rest upon
an A-board which must have two flaps,
a front and rear with shoulder straps,

and must keep moving through the streets,
like constables upon their beats.
They'd threaten the Fair Trading Act
since what he offered wasn't fact
that could be measured out and weighed,
tested for density, assayed:
then all else failing, run him in
for making a malicious din,
breaking the peace.
        There's no condition
in Scotland so invites perdition
as showing off in public places.
We move about with narrow faces
like all true Calvinistic races,
rarely, if ever kicking traces
the Irish shattered in their stride,
breaking a rule that meant divide;
and worry, after years of Union
with England's rollering dominion,
about our self-identity -
are we a nationed entity,
or just a folksy region losing
distinctiveness by our own choosing?
Well, here in Dublin I'm past caring
while for a coin or two I'm sharing
enjoyably the sound and sight
dead poets fashioned from delight.
Whoever makes or breaks the laws,
affirming life's the poet's cause.

                    Maurice Lindsay

A Bibliography of Maurice Lindsay

As I Remember: Ten Scottish Authors Recall how Writing Began for Them. Edited Maurice Lindsay. 1979

At the Wood's Edge (Verse). 1950

A Book of Scottish Verse, by Robert L Mackie. Revised Maurice Lindsay. 1967

The Buildings of Edinburgh. Anthony F. Kersting and Maurice Lindsay. 1981

The Burns Encyclopedia. 1959

The Burns Quotation Book. Ed. Joyce and Maurice Lindsay. 1994

By Yon Bonnie Banks. A gallimaufry. 1961

The Castles of Scotland. 1986

Clyde Waters. Variations and diversions on a theme of pleasure, etc. 1958

Collected Poems. 1979

The Comic Poems of William Tennant. Ed. Maurice Lindsay and Alexander Scott. n.d.

Comings and Goings. Poems. 1971

The Conservation of Georgian Edinburgh. The proceedings and outcome of a conference organised by the Scottish Civic Trust in association with the Edinburgh Architectural Association and in conjunction with the Civic Trust. Ed. Sir Robert Matthew, John Reid and Maurice Lindsay.

Count all men mortal: a history of Scottish Provident 1837–1987. 1987

John Davidson: a Selection of His Poems... Edited with an Introduction by Maurice Lindsay.

(Die Entscheidung) The Decision. An opera in three acts derived from a television play by Ken Taylor, based on a true incident. Libretto by Maurice Lindsay, music by Thea Musgrave. 1967

The Discovery of Scotland. Based on accounts of foreign travellers from the thirteenth to the eighteenth centuries. 1964

Dunoon on the Firth of Clyde. Official Guide. (n.d.)

Edinburgh Past and Present. 1990

Enemies of Love. Poems, 1941–1945. 1946

The Exiled Heart. Poems, 1941–1956. 1957

The Eye is Delighted: Some Romantic Travellers in Scotland. 1971

Francis George Scott and the Scottish Renaissance. 1980

The French Mosquitoes' Woman and Other Diversions and Poems. 1985

The Good Scottish Gardens Guide. Joyce and Maurice Lindsay. 1995

History of Scottish Literature. 1977

Hurlygush. Poems in Scots. 1948

An Illustrated Guide to Glasgow, 1837. 1989

John Davidson: A Selection of His Poems ... Ed. Maurice Lindsay. 1961
Killochan Castle, Ayrshire ... History and Description of Contents. Ed. M.L.&
    D. Somervell. 1961
Lindsay of the Mount. Poems. Selected and edited by Maurice Lindsay. 1948
Lowland Scottish Villages. 1980
Lowlands of Scotland. Glasgow and the North ... 1953
Lowlands of Scotland: Edinburgh and the South, etc. 1956
Modern Scottish Poetry. An anthology of the Scottish Renaissance, 1920–1945.
    Ed. M.L. 1966
The Music Quotation Book: a Literary Fanfare. Ed. Joyce and Maurice Lind-
    say. 1992
A Net to Catch the Winds, and other poems. 1981
News of the World: Last Poems. 1995
No Crown for Laughter. Poems. 1943
No Scottish Twilight. New Scottish Short Stories. Ed. M.L. and Frank Ur-
    quhart.
Ode for St Andrew's Night, and Other Poems. 1951
On the Face of it: Collected Poems. 1993
One Later Day and Other Poems. 1964
Perhaps To-morrow (Verse). 1941
A Pleasure of Gardens. Ed. Joyce and Maurice Lindsay. 1991
A Pocket Guide to Scottish Culture. 1947
Poetry Scotland. Ed. Maurice Lindsay. 1943
Predicament ... Poems. 1942
Requiem for a Sexual Athlete, and Other Poems. 1988
Robert Burns: The Man, His Work, the Legend. 1954
Robin Philipson. 1976
Sailing To-morrow's Seas. An Anthology of New Poems ... Ed. Maurice
    Lindsay etc. 1944
Saltire Modern Poets. Ed. D. Young and Maurice Lindsay. 1947
Scotland: An Anthology. Comp. Maurice Lindsay. 1974
Scottish Comic Verse: an anthology. Comp. Maurice Lindsay. 1981
Scottish Gardens. Joyce and Maurice Lindsay. 1994
Scottish Poetry. Ed. Maurice Lindsay. 1966
The Scottish Quotation Book: a Literary Companion. Ed. Joyce and Maurice
    Lindsay. 1991
The Scottish Renaissance (Lecture ... delivered before the Royal Philosophical
    Society of Glasgow on 18th February 1948. A ... critical examination of the
    achievements in Scots and Gaelic poetry). 1948
Selected Poems of Alexander Gray. Ed. Maurice Lindsay. 1948
Selected Poems of Marion Angus. Ed. Maurice Lindsay. 1950
Selected Poems, 1942–1972. 1973
Selected Poems. 1947
Snow Warning and Other Poems. 1962
Speaking Likenesses: a Postscript. 1997

Thank You For Having Me: a Personal Memoir. 1983

The Run from Life: More Poems, 1942–1972. 1975

The Scottish Dog. Ed. Joyce and Maurice Lindsay. 1989

The Theatre and Opera-Lover's Quotation Book: a Literary Bouquet. Ed. Joyce and Maurice Lindsay. 1993

This Business of Living. 1969

Unknown Scotland in Colour. 1984

Victorian and Edwardian Glasgow from Old Photographs. 1987

Walking Without an Overcoat: Poems, 1972–6. 1977

The Youth and Manhood of Cyril Thornton, by Thomas Hamilton. Ed. Maurice Lindsay. 1990

Contributors

LESTER BORLEY CBE D.Litt FRSGS. A geographer with extensive international experience of marketing cultural tourism and sustaining the cultural heritage of nations. Was Chief Executive of Scottish and English Tourist Boards, Director of the National Trust for Scotland and Secretary General of Europa Nostra. Now spends time advising other bodies, especially in Central and Eastern Europe.

GEORGE BRUCE OBE MA D.Litt. BBC Producer 1946–1970, 1971–1973 first Fellow in Creative Writing, Glasgow University, 1974–1986, appointments USA colleges and universities. 1982 Scottish-Australian Writing Fellow. Publications include *Seat Talk* (1944), *Collected Poems* (1970), *Perspectives – Poems 1970–1986*. Pending, *Pursuit Poems 1986–1998*. Since 1944 George Bruce has collaborated in many literary and broadcasting projects with Maurice Lindsay.

DR CAIRNS CRAIG. Head of the Department of English Literature at the University of Edinburgh. He is the author of *Yeats, Eliot, Pound and the Politics of Poetry* (1981) and *Out of History: Narrative Paradigms in Scottish and English Culture* (1986). He was the General Editor of *The History of Scottish Literature* (1987–9) and is also General Editor of the *Determinations* series published by Edinburgh University Press.

PROFESSOR JAMES STEVENS CURL FSA. A well-known architectural historian with many publications to his credit. An architect with a Doctorate in History, he has practised in the private and public sectors, was Architectural Editor of *The Survey of London* (1970–3), and Architectural Adviser to the Scottish Committee for European Architectural Heritage Year (1973–5). He holds the Chair of Architectural History, De Montfort University, Leicester.

PROFESSOR SIR JAMES DUNBAR-NASMITH CBE BA RIBA PPRIAS FRSA FRSE. Founded an architectural practice with Graham Law in 1957. Professor and Head of Department of Architecture at Heriot-Watt University/ Edinburgh College of Art 1978–88. Chairman of Scottish Civic Trust and Vice President of Europa Nostra. Past

President of the Royal Incorporation of Architects in Scotland and at various times served on the Ancient Monuments Board, the Historic Buildings Council for Scotland and the Royal Commission on the Ancient and Historical Monuments of Scotland, among many other public appointments in the field of conservation.

PROFESSOR ALEXANDER FENTON CBE DLitt FRSE. Professor Emeritus of Scottish Ethnology, former Director of the School of Scottish Studies in the University of Edinburgh, and of the National Museum of Antiquities of Scotland. Has written extensively on the ethnology of Scotland and other European countries. Currently Director, European Ethnological Research Centre.

JOHN FOSTER CBE. Chartered surveyor, architect and planner specialising since the early 1950s in countryside planning and environmental issues, first as Director of the Peak District National Park and subsequently as Director of the Countryside Commission for Scotland until retiring in 1985; since then involved in Scotland and abroad in private consultancy and voluntary activities related to the same themes.

SIR WILLIAM KERR FRASER GCB. Born 1929 and educated in Glasgow, joined the Scottish Office in 1955 and was Permanent Under Secretary of State from 1978 to 1988. Then for seven years was Principal and Vice Chancellor of the University of Glasgow. Now, among other things, is Chairman of the Royal Commission on the Ancient and Historical Monuments of Scotland.

JOHN GERRARD MBE FRIAS DA MA(Cantab). Educated Corpus Christi College, Cambridge and Edinburgh College of Art. Assistant Architect, Sheffield Corporation and Planning Department, Oxford City Council, before becoming Assistant Director, Scottish Civic Trust (1968–1984). Succeeded Maurice Lindsay as Technical Director, Scottish Civic Trust (jointly with Administrative Director). Trustee of numerous building conservation and similar charitable trusts concerned with Scotland's built heritage. Compiled *New Uses for Older Buildings in Scotland* (HMSO 1980).

SIR ALAN HUME KCB. Entered the Scottish Office in 1936, and retired in 1973 as Secretary of the Scottish Development Department, whose responsibilities included planning and caring for the environment. Served as Chairman of the Ancient Monuments Board for Scotland from 1973 to 1981, and of the Edinburgh New Town Conservation Committee from 1975 to 1990.

BRIAN LAMBIE MBE FSA Scot. Director of Biggar Museum Trust since 1983, following 37 years in business locally as an ironmonger. In 1976 he was awarded a Churchill Travelling Fellowship to study museums in the United States, a country which has drawn him back on many occasions since.

DR BRIAN LANG. Dr Lang was born in Edinburgh and read social anthropology at Edinburgh University, spending a period conducting research in Kenya. After four years lecturing at Aarhus University in Denmark and a period with the Social Science Research Council, he joined the Scottish Office in 1979 as Head of the Historic Buildings Branch. From 1980 he was Secretary of the National Heritage Memorial Fund and in 1987 joined the National Trust as Director of Public Affairs. He was appointed Chief Executive and Deputy Chairman of the British Library in 1991.

ROBERT N. S. LOGAN. Son of the manse and Edinburgh graduate, lived in Glasgow and was a Scottish Television executive. As councillor for Kelvinside, he chaired the city committee which launched the Burrell building. He chaired Glasgow Print Studio and Westbourne Music, and local and national bodies representing friends of museums.

MARY MARQUIS MBE FRSAMD. Her extensive career as a broadcaster, which began with Border Television, has covered news, current affairs and the arts on BBC television and radio in London and Scotland. She is a Fellow of the Royal Scottish Academy of Music and Drama, a Director of Scottish Opera/Theatre Royal, and a Governor of the Pitlochry Festival Theatre.

MICHAEL MIDDLETON CBE Hon FRIBA. Art critic, *The Spectator* 1946–56; sometime editor *Picture Post, Lilliput, House & Garden,* 1948–57. Director Civic Trust, 1969–87. Director-General UK Campaign for European Architectural Year 1975. Has written and lectured extensively on art, design and the environment. Books include *Group Practice in Design, Man Made the Town, Cities in Transition.* Pro Merito medal Council of Europe 1976.

DR TIM O'DRISCOLL. An honorary LL.D. of Trinity College Dublin, he was Irish Ambassador to the Netherlands, first Director-General of the Irish Tourist Board, and the first Executive Director of the European Travel Commission. He was President and Chairman of An Taisce, the Irish National Trust, and represented it and the European Travel Commission on the Council of Europa Nostra for 25 years.

CORDELIA McINTYRE OLIVER. Born Glasgow 1923. Educated Hutchesons' Grammar School and Glasgow School of Art. Married fellow student George Oliver; has lived in London, Edinburgh and Glasgow since 1950. Has been art teacher, painter, art and theatre critic (mainly for *The Guardian*), lecturer and exhibition organiser. Books include biographies of Joan Eardley and James Cowie, as well as a history of Scottish Opera.

KENNETH ROY. Editor of *The Scottish Review* and publisher of *The Journalist's Handbook*. He was a BBC Scotland anchorman for 10 years. His newspaper work has included regular columns in *The Observer*, *The Herald* and *The Scotsman*. Among his books are *Travels in a Small Country* and *The Closing Headlines*.

PAUL H. SCOTT CMG. Born and educated in Edinburgh; a former diplomat and former Rector of Dundee University; President of the Saltire Society. He has written many books on Scottish subjects, including *Walter Scott and Scotland* and *Andrew Fletcher and the Treaty of Union*. His most recent publication (1997) is *Scotland: An Unwon Cause*.

DR KENNETH SIMPSON. Director of the Centre for Scottish Cultural Studies, University of Strathclyde, and organiser of the Burns Conferences held annually since 1990. A specialist in Scottish literature and the literature of the eighteenth century, he is author of *The Protean Scot* (1988) and *Robert Burns* (1994), and editor of *Burns Now* (1994) and *Love and Liberty: Robert Burns: A Bicentenary Celebration* (1997).

HARRY SMITH MBE JP. Chairman of New Lanark Conservation Trust since 1972. Member of Lanark Town Council, 1946–1971, and first Labour Provost of Lanark, 1971–75, and on Strathclyde Regional Council until 1982. Has served as Member of Historic Buildings Council for Scotland, the Ancient Monuments Board, the Mental Welfare Commission and Lanarkshire Health Board. A long-time friend and colleague of Maurice Lindsay.

WILLIAM LEGGAT SMITH CBE MC JP DL LLD. Son of the Scottish manse, educated at the Glasgow Academy and the Universities of Glasgow and Oxford. After war service 1939–1946 in UK, Europe and USA, was solicitor in Glasgow, 1948–1987. Chairman of the Glasgow Academy and the Glasgow School of Art, Dean of the Royal Faculty of Procurators in Glasgow and a member of the Reviewing Committee on the Export of Works of Art from the UK.

MICHAEL T. R. B. TURNBULL. Born in Istanbul in 1941, he was educated at the Universities of Cambridge and London and the Edinburgh College of Art. A former member of the Scottish Opera Chorus, he is the author of *Joseph Hislop: gran tenore* and *Mary Garden*, both published by Scolar Press.

PROFESSOR DAVID WALKER OBE LLD FRSE. He joined the staff of the Scottish Office's Historic Buildings Branch in 1961, working under the supervision of Ian Lindsay. He advised the Historic Buildings Council for Scotland from 1966 and, on promotion to Principal Inspector of Historic Buildings in 1978, became its assessor. He retired as Chief Inspector at the end of 1993, to become Professor of Art History at St Andrews University.

Index